THE RISE AND DECLINE OF
THE AMERICAN "EMPIRE"

The Rise and Decline of the American "Empire"

Power and its Limits in Comparative Perspective

GEIR LUNDESTAD
Norwegian Nobel Institute

OXFORD
UNIVERSITY PRESS

OXFORD
UNIVERSITY PRESS

Great Clarendon Street, Oxford OX2 6DP

Oxford University Press is a department of the University of Oxford.
It furthers the University's objective of excellence in research, scholarship,
and education by publishing worldwide in

Oxford New York

Auckland Cape Town Dar es Salaam Hong Kong Karachi
Kuala Lumpur Madrid Melbourne Mexico City Nairobi
New Delhi Shanghai Taipei Toronto

With offices in

Argentina Austria Brazil Chile Czech Republic France Greece
Guatemala Hungary Italy Japan Poland Portugal Singapore
South Korea Switzerland Thailand Turkey Ukraine Vietnam

Oxford is a registered trade mark of Oxford University Press
in the UK and in certain other countries

Published in the United States
by Oxford University Press Inc., New York

British Library Cataloguing in Publication Data
Data available

Library of Congress Cataloging in Publication Data
Data available

Typeset by SPI Publisher Services, Pondichery, India
Printed in Great Britain
on acid-free paper by
MPG Books Group, Bodmin and King's Lynn

ISBN 978-0-19-964610-4

1 3 5 7 9 10 8 6 4 2

Preface

In most of my academic writings I have focused on various aspects of the role of the United States in the world after 1945. While it is difficult to compete with the many American historians who write about US foreign policy, based on a lifetime of study and living in the country, perhaps we foreign historians may make an advantage of our inevitable shortcomings. Foreign policy is, by definition, policy toward some outside party; we are this outside party. We foreigners may be particularly sensitive to the "receiving end"—those other countries that the United States is dealing with.

Americans have a tendency to assume that the United States is unique. America is built on this belief. John F. Kennedy referred to "our right to the moral leadership of this planet." Ronald Reagan affirmed that "The American dream lives—not only in the hearts and minds of our countrymen, but in the hearts and minds of millions of the world's people in both free and oppressed societies who look to us for leadership. As long as that dream lives, as long as we continue to defend it, America has a future, and all mankind has reason to hope." In his inaugural address, Barack Obama spoke to the entire world "from the grandest capitals, to the small village where my father was born: know that America is a friend of each nation and every man, woman, and child who seeks a future of peace and dignity, and we are ready to lead once more."

Foreigners have a natural skepticism of such claims to specialness. None expressed this better than that close friend of the United States, Winston Churchill, when in 1945 he was faced with yet another American lecture about the evils of power politics: "Is having a Navy twice as strong as any other power 'power politics'? Is having an overwhelming Air Force, with bases all over the world, 'power politics'? Is having all the gold in the world buried in a cavern 'power politics'? If not, what is 'power politics'?"[1] Every country is of course unique in certain ways; it also resembles other countries in many ways. Detailed study, not faith, can tell us how special a country really is.

Three comparative questions have long fascinated me. The first is the relative strength of the United States. How strong has the United States really been in the years after the Second World War, and how strong is it today? Strength is a relative term, and the basis of comparison will be both other countries and earlier periods in the recent history of the United States.

---

[1] Quoted from Christopher Thorne, *Allies of a Kind: The United States, Britain, and the War against Japan, 1941–1945* (Oxford: Oxford University Press, 1978), 515.

My conclusion is that the United States has clearly been the most important power since 1945. Predictions that the Soviet Union, Japan, and the European Union would come to surpass the US have not proved correct. Now China is definitely the main challenger. It may well happen that the size of China's economy will surpass that of the United States in the course of surprisingly few years. The United States is undoubtedly in relative decline. China and several other leading countries are growing much faster than the US; America's debt is piling up; the effects of its still vast military lead are smaller than Washington had hoped, as we have seen in Afghanistan and Iraq. Nevertheless, on a per capita economic basis, in military strength, and in the importance of its allies, China will continue to lag far behind the United States.

The second question is the expansion of the United States. Militarily, politically, economically, and culturally the United States expanded even more than Britain had done in its imperial heyday. What distinguishes America's expansion from the expansion of other Great Powers? I have long argued that the American version of "empire" was an empire by invitation, particularly in crucial Western Europe. This is a further effort to explore the nature of the expansion of the United States. My conclusion on this point is that while invitations are still being issued to the US (related to the first point), an American "empire" by invitation hardly exists any longer. If it does, it is primarily in East Asia, and in much more modified form than in America's strongest decades—after 1945 in Western Europe, and again, in the 1990s, in Central and Eastern Europe. However, despite its decline, the United States is still the only truly global superpower. Others, like China, are becoming increasingly global economically, but in most other respects they are still primarily regional. Nevertheless, in every part of the world, the US role is limited by at least one major regional power.

The third question is the paradoxical nature of power in international relations. What could the United States actually achieve? It is easy to demonstrate both the power and the defeats of a Great Power, even a superpower. The United States had been an "empire"; it still dominated the international structure; at the same time it suffered significant setbacks. How do these aspects fit together? Throughout history, empires have risen and fallen. Changes could be very dramatic. One day the Soviet Union was the world's second leading power; the next it was gone. The conclusion here is that while no power has ever been omnipotent or more successful than the United States, a whole array of local factors has come to take on ever greater importance. Globalization is accompanied by fragmentation in a very complex mixture, and even very small groups can now offer serious resistance against the mighty United States. The present account is a tentative discussion of these complex questions.

Acknowledgments

This book represents the summing up of my thinking on themes and topics I have worked on as an historian since I started my career in 1970. I have written and edited several books on the origins of the Cold War, on American–European relations, and on more general developments in international politics, in all cases primarily dealing with the years after the Second World War.

I am grateful to the University of Tromsø, where I had some good years from 1974 to 1989, and to the Norwegian Nobel Institute, where I have been working with great inspiration since 1990. Without the Institute's superb library my work would have been much more difficult. I learned an awful lot from my time at Harvard University (1978–79, 1983) and at the Woodrow Wilson Center in Washington, DC (1988–89). Through the research program at the Nobel Institute we were able to bring more than 100 top historians and political scientists from all over the world to Oslo. What a treat this has been! I have learned from each and every one of them.

Virtually all of my books have been published by Oxford University Press (OUP), and I am highly appreciative of their good work. English is not my mother tongue. After Arthur M. Schlesinger, Jr. wrote about my first book that it was written in "clear, but occasionally awkward English," I told OUP's copy-editors I did not want to see that phrase again. Anthony Mercer has been the copy-editor for the present volume; we shall see what the reviewers write this time. I have very much enjoyed working with him. I am particularly grateful to senior editor Dominic Byatt for the interest he has shown in my work.

I would like to thank the four readers at OUP who commented on the present manuscript in some detail, and participants at seminars in the United States and Norway who offered suggestions for improvement.

Last, but certainly not least, I want to thank my wife Aase. She once said it was small compensation for my many mental and physical absences to be thanked in the acknowledgments. Yet, when I stopped doing so, she made her displeasure known. So, here we go again. Thanks also to our grandchildren Jørgen, Oscar, Alfred, and Helmer for the inspiration they continually provide.

G.L.

September, 2011

Contents

Tables

Abbreviations

ABM	Anti-Ballistic Missile
ANZUS	Australia, New Zealand, United States Security Treaty
ASEAN	Association of Southeast Asian Nations
BASIC	Brazil, South Africa, India, and China
BRIC	Brazil, Russia, India and China
BRICI	BRIC + Indonesia
BRICS	BRIC + South Africa
BRICSAM	BRIC + South Africa and Mexico
CDE	Conference on Disarmament in Europe
CDU	Christian Democratic Union
CENTO	Central Treaty Organization
CESDP	Common European Security and Defence Policy
CFE	Conventional Forces in Europe
CoCom	Coordinating Committee for Multilateral Export Controls
ECA	Economic Cooperation Administration
ECB	European Central Bank
EDC	European Defense Community
EFSF	European Financial Stability Facility
Euratom	European Atomic Energy Community
FDI	foreign direct investment
GATT	General Agreement on Tariffs and Trade
GDP	gross domestic product
GL	Geir Lundestad
GNP	gross national product
ICBM	intercontinental ballistic missile
IMEMO	Institute of World Economy and International Relations
IMF	International Monetary Fund
INF	intermediate-range nuclear missiles
MFN	most favored nation
MITI	Ministry of International Trade and Industry
OECD	Organisation for Economic Co-operation and Development
OEEC	Organisation for European Economic Co-operation

OPEC	Organization of Petroleum Exporting Countries
PLA	People's Liberation Army
PLO	Palestine Liberation Organization
PPP	purchasing power parity
SALT	Strategic Arms Limitation Treaty
SDI	Strategic Defense Initiative
SDP	Social Democratic Party
SEATO	Southeast Asia Treaty Organization
START	Strategic Arms Reduction Treaty
WEU	Western European Union
WTO	World Trade Organization

Introduction

The Rise and Fall of Great Powers

Whether we call them superpowers, Great Powers, empires, or hegemons, one thing seems certain: they come and go, they rise and fall. No state has managed to remain permanently Number One; although few, if any, historical laws exist, it is most unlikely that any state will in the future be able to remain permanently on top. As we learned from our Eurocentric history books, the Roman Empire rose and fell; so did the Carolingian Empire (732–814), the Hapsburg Empire, and, allegedly, three German Reichs; so did the British and the French colonial empires; and by 1991 the Soviet empire had not only collapsed, but the Soviet Union itself was dissolved into its 15 constituent parts.

In a wider geographical context, after the fall of the Roman Empire the vast Muslim expansion started with Mohammed in the 620s, and ended with the fall of Baghdad to the Mongols in 1258. The conquered territory stretched from the initial base in Saudi Arabia, to Spain in the west, and Uzbekistan in the east. The Mongols under Genghis Khan (1162–1227) and Tamerlane (1336–1405) established one of the biggest empires ever, combining ruthlessness with surprising ethnic and religious tolerance. As John Darwin has argued, Tamerlane's "empire was the last attempt to challenge the partition of Eurasia between the states of the Far West, Islamic Middle Eurasia and Confucian East Asia."[1] Yet that vast empire was soon divided into several different parts. Empires in Byzantium (395–1453), and various versions in different centuries in Iran, rose and fell. In the sixteenth and seventeenth centuries the Ottoman Empire (1299–1922) threatened even Vienna, until it started its protracted decline that ended with modern Turkey.

The Mogul Empire in India flourished for a few centuries until even its last formal remnants were abolished in 1857. China remained dominant much longer. Centuries earlier its position had been quite similar to that of the Roman Empire. The two empires were broadly comparable in terms of size

---

[1] John Darwin, *After Tamerlane: The Rise and Fall of Global Empires, 1400–2000* (Penguin Books, 2008) is the most recent, inspiring, and comprehensive treatment of these huge historical processes. The quotation is on 5–6.

Table 1. Relative shares of world manufacturing output (1750–1900)

	1750	1800	1830	1860	1880	1900
(Europe as a whole)	23.2	28.1	34.2	53.2	61.3	62.0
United Kingdom	1.9	4.3	9.5	19.9	22.9	18.5
Habsburg Empire	2.9	3.2	3.2	4.2	4.4	4.7
France	4.0	4.2	5.2	7.9	7.8	6.8
German States/Germany	2.9	3.5	3.5	4.9	8.5	13.2
Italian States/Italy	2.4	2.5	2.3	2.5	2.5	2.5
Russia	5.0	5.6	5.6	7.0	7.6	8.8
United States	0.1	0.8	2.4	7.2	14.7	23.6
Japan	3.8	3.5	2.8	2.6	2.4	2.4
Third World	73.0	67.7	60.5	36.6	20.9	11.0
China	32.8	33.3	29.8	19.7	12.5	6.2
India/Pakistan	24.5	19.7	17.6	8.6	2.8	1.7

Source: Paul Kennedy, *The Rise and Fall of the Great Powers: Economic Change and Military Conflict from 1500 to 2000* (New York: Random House, 1987), 149.

and population, and for a certain period even somewhat alike in chronological terms, although the Chinese empire lasted well beyond the fall of Rome in 395.

It has been estimated that as late as 1800 China's share of world manufacturing output was still 33.3 percent, and India's 19.7, while Europe as a whole produced 28.1 percent. Even at this late stage, production was still primarily a reflection of population. The greater the population, the greater was generally the production. As a matter of course China viewed itself as the leader of the world, as could be witnessed in Emperor Qianlong's reply to Lord Macartney in 1793 when the latter, on behalf of King George III, asked for the establishment of trade and diplomatic relations between Britain and China: "We have never valued ingenious articles, nor do we have the slightest need for your country's manufactures. Therefore, O king, as regards your request to send someone to remain at the capital, while it is not in harmony with the regulations of the Celestial Empire we also feel very much that it is of no advantage to your country."[2]

With the financial and industrial revolutions throughout the nineteenth century, this situation changed rapidly, so that in 1900 China's and India's percentages had been reduced to 6.2 and 1.7 percent respectively, while Britain's share alone was 18.5 and that of the United States 23.6. (See Table 1.)

Thus the Eastern expansion was replaced by a huge Western wave that, to simplify matters vastly, could be said to have started in 1492 when Columbus discovered America and the *Reconquista* in Spain was completed with the fall of Grenada, reversing the wave of Muslim expansion. First Spain and

[2] Jonathan D. Spence, *The Search for Modern China* (New York: Norton, 1990), 122–3.

Portugal, then Britain and France, and even smaller European countries, established their vast colonial empires. From its small base, Britain came to control about 20–25 percent of the world's territory and population. North and South America, Australia, much of Asia, and even more of Africa, came under European control. Colonial control appeared to last forever, but of course it did not. The United States was the first colony to establish its independence. To almost everybody's surprise, after India's independence following the Second World War, the colonial empires quickly ended.

The rise of the United States (and Russia) had been talked about since the 1830s. They had the territory and would have the resources and the population to become the world's leading powers. Very soon after the Civil War the United States had the world's largest gross national product (GNP).[3] Its military force was, with a partial exception for the US Navy, still quite limited; its strategic focus was on the Western hemisphere and the Pacific. In Europe it intervened in the First World War, but then withdrew, more convinced than ever of the merits of "isolationism."

Since the Second World War the United States has clearly been the single most important power in the world. Apparently no country had dominated the world to the extent that the US did in 1945. And in the 1990s, after a couple of difficult decades, it even enjoyed its "unipolar moment"; with the collapse of the Soviet Union the US had no military competitor, and its vast economy blossomed.

Still, America's fall was frequently predicted, with glee or with fear. Some referred to the general laws of history; no country could dominate forever. Soviet leaders predicted the inevitable global triumph of communism. Doubts were frequently expressed even inside America. "God's own country" was allegedly in constant danger of falling behind, particularly militarily, be it, in the 1950s, the "bomber" or the even more dangerous "missile" gap and the shock of Sputnik, and, in the 1970s to early 1980s, the alleged gap in intercontinental ballistic missiles (ICBMs). There were always some who had an interest in warning about the decline of the United States. There were Vietnam, Nixon's "five great power centers" (the US, Western Europe, Japan, Russia and China), and Carter's diagnosis of national "malaise."

Yet, most Americans probably believed that America's predominance would last forever. Ronald Reagan proclaimed "morning in America" and celebrated its uniqueness and exemption from the laws of history. Few leading American politicians disagreed. You do not become popular in the United States by predicting the fall of "God's own country." On the other hand, many

---

[3] The statistics in this book, taken from other accounts, are sometimes based on gross national product (GNP), but more often on gross domestic product (GDP). GDP is a nation's total output of goods and services in a given period, usually one year. GNP is GDP + total gains from overseas investment—income earned by foreign nationals domestically.

leading American political economists had been suggesting that, in various ways, the relative position of the United States was slipping. Robert Gilpin, David Calleo, and Robert Keohane were among the most prominent ones.[4] Yet, at the end of Reagan's presidency Professor Paul Kennedy at Yale did more than anyone else to revive the modern study of the rise and fall of the Great Powers. He clearly saw the United States as declining.[5] Many, also outside the Soviet leadership, had earlier agreed that the Soviet Union would come to overtake the United States. In the 1980s Japan clearly emerged as the leading challenger. Kennedy himself came to think that the twenty-first century would ultimately belong to Japan. Despite its problems, which after all were smaller than the problems of any other Great Power, "Japan appears to have constructed a machine that can go by itself."[6] This future was not to be. In 1991 the Soviet Union collapsed because of its many "internal contradictions." A few years later Japan went into a political and economic crisis that still has not been resolved almost twenty years later.

In between bouts of Euro-pessimism there were those who thought that the European Union would, or should, overtake the US. After the end of the Cold War and the apparent economic unification of Europe, a series of books were written about the superiority of European values and attitudes. European lifestyles were celebrated, but the question remained of how powerful this new Europe would be in international politics. T. R. Reid argued that "That's the key point: the leaders and the people of the EU are determined to change a world that had been dominated by the Americans. Indeed, that goal has become a powerful motivator for the New Europe—to create a United States of Europe that is not the United States of America."[7] This was not to be either. While increasing its geographical membership dramatically, in foreign and security policies, and in some respects even in economic policies, such as taxation and budget decisions, the EU was unable to move much beyond the confines of the nation state.

Today all the talk is about the glorious future of China. The market is flooded by books and articles about its rapid rise. With the Chinese economy booming, and the American one in trouble, the projections for when China's gross domestic product will surpass that of the United States with, presumably,

---

[4] Robert Gilpin, *War and Change in World Politics* (Cambridge: Cambridge University Press, 1981); David P. Calleo, *The Imperious Economy* (Cambridge: Harvard University Press, 1982); Robert O. Keohane, *After Hegemony: Cooperation and Discord in the World Political Economy* (Princeton: Princeton University Press, 1984).

[5] Paul Kennedy, *The Rise and Fall of the Great Powers: Economic Change and Military Conflict from 1500 to 2000* (New York: Random House, 1987).

[6] Paul Kennedy, *Preparing for the Twenty-First Century* (London: Harper Collins, 1993), 161.

[7] T. R. Reid, *The United States of Europe: The New Superpower and the End of American Supremacy* (Penguin, 2004), 6.

China becoming the world's leading power, are constantly being moved forward in time.

The many books and articles about the decline and even the fall of the United States continued to meet with almost universal opposition from US politicians. Most leading academics, particularly in the United States, also criticized Paul Kennedy's predictions, from the early opposition of Joseph S. Nye and Samuel Huntington,[8] to the recent one of Josef Joffe, and Stephen G. Brooks and William C. Wohlforth. Joffe argued that "Addicted to constant reinvention, it (the United States, GL) should not fall prey to the rigor mortis that overwhelmed the Ottoman, Austrian, Russian and Soviet empires."[9] Brooks and Wohlforth categorically state that "The main feature of the distribution of capabilities today is thus unprecedented American primacy."[10] No country presumably ever had such a lead militarily, economically, and technologically as the United States still does. G. John Ikenberry recently presented the liberal version of American optimism. He thought that the United States might be able to incorporate China in the liberal world order it had created. As he stated, "I argue that the future is actually quite bright for a one-world system organized around open and loosely rule-based principles and institutions—and in which the United States remains centrally positioned."[11]

At one stage, even Paul Kennedy himself argued that the "forecasters of doom missed a number of important points": the weakness of the Soviet Union, the remarkable capacity of the United States to "re-tool" itself, the new technologies. He was of course himself the prime example of those "forecasters."[12] In recent years Kennedy has again become more pessimistic about the future of the United States, and even he stresses the rise of China, although he has his doubts about China becoming "the new global hegemon." He has in fact argued that the United States should be pursuing an element of

---

[8] Joseph S. Nye Jr., "Understating U.S. Strength," *Foreign Policy*, 72 (Fall 1988), 105–29; Nye, *Bound to Lead: The Changing Nature of American Power* (New York, 1990); Samuel P. Huntington, "The US—Decline or Renewal?," *Foreign Affairs* (Winter 1988/89), 76–96.

[9] Josef Joffe, *Überpower: The Imperial Temptation of America* (New York: Norton, 2006); Joffe, "The Default Power," *Foreign Affairs*, 88:5 (2009), 35.

[10] Stephen G. Brooks and William C. Wohlforth, *World Out of Balance: International Relations and the Challenge of American Primacy* (Princeton: Princeton University Press, 2009). The quotation is from 35.

[11] G. John Ikenberry, *Liberal Leviathan: The Origins, Crisis, and Transformation of the American World Order* (Princeton: Princeton University Press, 2011), 336.

[12] For this article, see Paul Kennedy, "The Next American Century?," *World Policy Journal*, 16:1 (Spring 1999), 52–8.
In 2002, Kennedy even wrote that: "It seems to me that there is no point in the Europeans and Chinese wringing their hands about US predominance, and wishing it would go away. It is as if, among the various inhabitants of the apes and monkeys cage at the London Zoo, one creature has grown bigger and bigger—and bigger—until it became a 500 lb gorilla." "The Eagle Has Landed: The New U.S. Global Military Position," *Financial Times*, February 1, 2002.

appeasement in its foreign policy, though the word itself should be avoided: "we shall make a concession here, a concession there, though hopefully it will be disguised in the form of policies such as 'power sharing' and 'mutual compromise' and the dreadful 'A' word will not appear."[13]

Naturally middle positions developed. The most striking one was found in Fareed Zakaria's *The Post-American World*. In the opening sentence of the book he states that "This is a book not about the decline of America but rather about the rise of everyone else." In many ways Zakaria remained optimistic about the United States. "Unipolarity continues to be the defining reality of the international system for now ... "; the United States has the opportunity to "remain the pivotal player in a richer, more dynamic, more exciting world." Still, if the rest of the world, particularly China and India, did rise, this would inevitably lead to at least the *relative* decline of the US, and power is almost always relative.[14] In absolute terms very few powers actually decline; almost all of them are richer and more powerful today than they ever were before. Joseph Nye placed himself in the dead center of the debate: "The United States is not in absolute decline, and in relative terms, there is a reasonable probability that it will remain more powerful than any single state in the coming decades,"[15] a fairly modest statement in view of what the American position had been. In analyzing power at the international level, Nye tried to combine realism and liberalism, hard power and soft power, into a liberal realist smart power analysis, whatever that might be.[16]

No one can of course be certain what the future holds. The record of academics in making projections about the future is not particularly encouraging. Reality is just too complex to be captured by simple formulas. History does not really repeat itself. The general causations of social scientists are often based on an incomplete use of the historical record. Still, the present account is skeptical to analyses that foresee a dramatic decline, even a collapse, for the United States, at least in a short-term perspective. Particularly militarily, the United States, despite the undisputed general decline since the 1990s, is still in a league of its own. On the other hand, those who insist most strongly on the continued US lead tend to underplay the dramatic changes that have taken place since the turn of the millennium, particularly on the economic side. The deficits in the federal budget and in current accounts represent huge

---

[13] Paul Kennedy, "A Time to Appease," *The National Interest* (July/August 2010), 7–17, quotations on 14, 15. See also his "Rise and Fall," *The World Today* (August/September 2010), 6–9; "Marching to Different Tunes," *International Herald Tribune* (November 27–28, 2010), 8; and "Back to Normalcy," *The New Republic*, 241:20 (2010).

[14] Fareed Zakaria, *The Post-American World* (London: Allen Lane, 2008), 218–19.

[15] Joseph S. Nye, Jr., "The Future of American Power: Dominance and Decline in Perspective," *Foreign Affairs* (November/December 2010), 2–12. The quotation is from 11–12. For Nye's longer study, see his *The Future of Power* (New York: Public Affairs, 2011).

[16] Nye, *The Future of Power*, 231.

challenges to the United States. By focusing so much on a few limited long-term data sets, these academics tend to miss the flux and dynamism of the current situation.

So, while it would seem obvious that sooner or later the United States will be replaced as Number One, most Americans, despite their recurrent periods of doubt, continue to believe that the US is largely immune to "the laws of history." America's mission in history will continue. Foreigners are skeptical about the mission and America's exemption from the laws of history, but who would actually overtake the US? The challengers came . . . and went.[17]

Only the future can tell what will happen; historians certainly cannot. We make "predictions" about the past, not the future. Yet, sometimes it is just too tempting to speculate about the future. But speculation it is.

[17] For a leading European academic who is skeptical about the view of American decline, see Michael Cox, "Power Shift? Not Yet," *The World Today* (October 2010), 20–2.

Part I

Power

1

America's Position

AMERICA'S VAST STRENGTH

In 1945, at the end of the Second World War, the position of the United States was frequently compared with that of Great Britain in 1815 at the end of the Napoleonic Wars. British Foreign Secretary Ernest Bevin thus argued in 1947 that "... the US was in the position today where Britain was at the end of the Napoleonic wars." British professor and politician Harold Laski was definitely closer to the truth when he stated that "America bestrides the world like a colossus; neither Rome at the height of its power nor Great Britain in the period of its economic supremacy enjoyed an influence so direct, so profound, or so pervasive..."[1]

In his famous article in *Life* in 1941, Henry R. Luce had announced the "American Century" with great optimism in his own curious blend of nationalism and internationalism: "Most important of all, we have that indefinable, unmistakable sign of leadership: prestige. And unlike the prestige of Rome or Genghis Khan or 19th century England, American prestige throughout the world is faith in the good intentions as well as the ultimate intelligence and ultimate strength of the whole of the American people."[2] It was a little odd to announce America's century when four decades had already passed without Washington assuming the mantle of leadership—and Luce certainly underestimated the importance of both economic and military power—but in predicting the future he was still basically correct.

In 1945 the United States was really in a league of its own compared to any of its predecessors. In the nineteenth century Britain probably had the world's largest gross national product (GNP), but only for a short period around 1860. In 1870 the United States and Russia each had higher production. Throughout much of the century Britain was the industrial leader and remained the

---

[1] Much of what follows in the next few pages is based on my *The American "Empire" and Other Studies of U.S. Foreign Policy in a Comparative Perspective* (Oxford–Oslo: Oxford University Press, 1990), particularly 39–46. More complete documentation will be found there.

[2] Henry Luce, "The American Century," *Life Magazine* (February 17, 1941).

mercantile leader, but at no time did it produce more than roughly one-third of the world's total manufactures. In 1945 the United States alone produced almost as much as the rest of the world put together, a situation presumably never seen before in history and unlikely ever to happen again. The US lead tended to be greater the more advanced the technology. In the decade 1940–50 the United States was behind 82 percent of major inventions, discoveries and innovations. The highest corresponding percentage for Britain had been 47 percent in 1750–75.[3]

With 6 percent of the world's population the United States had 46 percent of the world's electrical power, and held 49.8 percent of the world's monetary gold, reserve currencies, and International Monetary Fund (IMF) reserves. Just like Britain's overall lead in the nineteenth century had been based on its huge coal supplies, the US lead in the twentieth, particularly after 1945, was based on its oil resources. For the first three-quarters of the century the United States was the world's leading oil producer; in addition, American companies controlled additional resources in many parts of the world. Only in the 1970s did production in the Soviet Union and in Saudi Arabia surpass that in the US. Then, too, the balance of power definitely shifted away from American distributors to local producers.[4] Overall Soviet GNP figures are not known, but a very rough guess is that total Soviet production in 1945 was perhaps a quarter of that in the US. Quite likely it was even smaller than that.

The strong economy provided the basis for America's military strength. Until 1949 it had a monopoly on nuclear weapons. After the Soviet Union exploded its bomb, the US still had a strong lead at least until the early 1970s. It had by far the strongest air force in the world. Before the Second World War the Royal Navy had still been somewhat larger than the US Navy, but in December 1947 Admiral Chester Nimitz could argue that the US Navy now had a "control of the sea more absolute than ever possessed by the British." True, after demobilization the United States had a smaller army than that of the Soviet Union, but the Second World War had illustrated how quickly the US could mobilize even a full-scale army.

In various ways the United States frequently intervened with armed force of one sort or another. In the period 1946 to 1965, at least 168 such instances were recorded, with by far the highest frequency occurring in the years 1956 to 1965. Most of these interventions were in Third World countries. By comparison, Moscow intervened only around ten times in Third World countries in the same period. Most of America's interventions were

---

[3] Lundestad, *The American "Empire,"* 40.

[4] David S. Painter, "Coal, Oil, and the Sinews of Imperial Power in the 19th and 20th Centuries," preliminary manuscript, September 2010. For an account of the new multipolar world that pays considerable attention to oil and energy, see Dilip Hiro, *After Empire: The Birth of a Multipolar World* (New York: Nation Books, 2010).

rather small scale; many received support both locally and internationally. Interventions could also be invited. The American response to the various crises over Berlin provided the best example of this.[5]

The atomic bomb and the dollar were the supreme signs of America's power. The bomb was an American invention, although British scientists certainly played a role in the early phase of its development. The United States consistently maintained a qualitative lead in the nuclear arms race with the Soviet Union. The bomb was not used again after August 1945. Despite the constant search by strategists and military for new "windows of vulnerability," which only new types of nuclear weapons would then be able to close, it was very difficult to foresee any scenario where the new weapon would actually be directly employed. In this sense President Charles de Gaulle may have been right when he argued that it was unlikely that the United States would risk the obliteration of New York or Washington, DC for Hamburg or Paris. Yet, as early as August 1945, Truman had told de Gaulle that "the bomb should give pause to countries which might be tempted to commit aggressions."[6]

It was not easy for Washington both to deter the Russians and to reassure the Europeans. The second part was actually more difficult than the first. Or, as British defense minister Denis Healey formulated it: "it takes only five per cent credibility of American retaliation to deter the Russians, but ninety-five per cent credibility to reassure the Europeans."[7] The Soviet Union could never be entirely certain that the United States would not retaliate by using nuclear weapons. This was the nature of deterrence. America's allies pressed for a nuclear guarantee; they had their persistent doubts about its effectiveness, but they generally assumed it would remain effective. So the bomb was seen to protect not only the United States, which was after all not so directly threatened, but also many of its allies around the world, particularly its most important ones. Ultimately the bomb was at the heart of America's commitment to crucial NATO allies, and to additional key allies such as Japan, South Korea, and Taiwan, although several wars in Asia and Africa showed the limitations of America's guarantee. Even today, with the end of the Soviet Union, most of the NATO allies still want the United States to maintain a nuclear land presence in Europe, and not simply a more general or sea-based deterrence.[8]

[5] Barry M. Blechman and Stephen S. Kaplan, *Force Without War: U.S. Armed Forces as a Political Instrument* (Washington, DC: Brookings, 1978), 14, 23–8, 547–53; Stephen S. Kaplan, *Diplomacy of Power: Soviet Armed Forces as a Political Instrument* (Washington, DC: Brookings, 1981), 42.

[6] *Foreign Relations of the United States* (hereafter *FRUS*), 1945, IV, Memorandum of Conversation Truman–de Gaulle, August 22, 1945, 710.

[7] Denis Healey, *The Time of My Life* (London: Penguin Books, 1990), 243.

[8] David S. Yost, "Assurance and US Extended Deterrence in NATO," *International Affairs*, 85:4 (2009), 755–80. The NATO meeting in Lisbon in November 2010 confirmed that most

After 1945 the United States was able to set up a "liberal internationalist" order of surprising force and duration. The UN and, even more important in this context, the Bretton Woods institutions, the International Monetary Fund (IMF), and the World Bank, were set up immediately after the Second World War. The General Agreement on Tariffs and Trade (GATT) followed in 1948, as did the Atlantic-oriented Organisation for European Economic Co-operation (OEEC), from 1960 renamed the more global Organisation for Economic Co-operation and Development (OECD). Through these economic organizations Washington provided a set of global institutions and rules of considerable importance. G. John Ikenberry has argued that "The United States has presided over this ensemble of governance institutions, but it has tended to do so through the exercise of liberal hegemony rather than imperial control."[9]

The dollar was the symbol of America's economic supremacy. In Valéry Giscard d'Estaing's phrase, the dollar was the "exorbitant privilege" of the United States. The United States had access to a "gold mine of paper" which gave it advantages not fully available even to Britain in its heyday. While it cost the Bureau of Engraving a few cents to produce a 100 dollar bill, other countries had to pay the full 100 dollars to obtain one. The dollar's reserve status in the world gave the United States great advantages compared to all other countries. The US could run up deficits which no other country could.[10]

Through the IMF, where the US was by far the single most important member, and its bilateral diplomacy, the United States helped maintain the international structure of exchange rates. The dollar was long tied to gold, and all the other international currencies were tied to the dollar, in a way similar to what had been the case under the classical gold standard (1870–1914) under British leadership. Yet the role of the dollar was significantly stronger than that of the pound under the gold standard. Due to the imbalance in trade between the United States and Western Europe, full convertibility in trade between the two sides of the Atlantic was introduced only in 1958, but the basic structure of the Bretton Woods system lasted from 1945, and certainly until 1971–73 when the dollar was taken off the gold standard and exchange rates were permitted to float freely. In fact, the central role of the dollar continues to this very day, despite the many ideas, especially from, first, the French, and

European NATO allies still preferred an American nuclear land presence in Europe, however limited.

[9] G. John Ikenberry, "A Crisis of Global Governance?," *Current History*, 109 (November 2010), 315–21. For fuller accounts, see his *After Victory: Institutions, Strategic Restraint, and the Rebuilding of Order After Major Wars* (Princeton: Princeton University Press, 2001) and, most recently, *Liberal Leviathan: The Origins, Crisis, and Transformation of the American World Order* (Princeton: Princeton University Press, 2011).

[10] For a good account of these privileges, see Barry Eichengreen, *Exorbitant Privilege: The Rise and Fall of the Dollar* (Oxford: Oxford University Press, 2011), particularly 2–6.

now, more hesitantly, even the Chinese, for a broader, more international standard.

After 1945 the United States long maintained a flow of capital to borrowers in the same way as the British had done in the nineteenth century. Even more than in the British case, virtually every country in the world received some form of economic support, and in most cases the United States was the most important source of such support. In addition, the United States dominated the World Bank, as it did the IMF, through economically weighted voting arrangements and in other ways. In financial crises the United States served as the lender of last resort. The Marshall Plan was the best example of this role; the clearest sign of its success was perhaps the call for new Marshall Plans in ever new parts of the world. Under the Marshall Plan, as Theodore H. White wrote from France, the American expert "has become... as much a stock character as was the British traveler of the nineteenth century, as 2,000 years ago the Roman centurion must have been in conquering Greece."[11] Only later did it emerge that the Marshall Plan was probably far less important for the economic reconstruction of Western Europe than was perceived at the time. Yet, perceptions exert their own force politically, culturally, and even economically.

The United States provided a market for distress goods from political friends, and supplied such goods itself. The unilateral concessions provided to the struggling Japanese in the 1950s were the most striking example here. The United States competed with West Germany to be the world's leading exporter; recently it has been surpassed by both China and Germany. It remained by far the world's largest importer. The resulting deficit may definitely have had its disadvantages, but there were also advantages. It resulted in a higher standard of living for Americans; it also brought in new investment; it could even give Washington leverage vis-à-vis other countries. With the huge amounts in question, the advantage was not always with the exporter.[12]

Washington was the leader in coordinating international macroeconomic policies, particularly trade policies. Under America's leadership world trade moved steadily in a more liberal direction. The GATT system, based on the most favored nation (MFN) principle, was the key in this context. To a large extent the United States even dominated the international property regime. In the nineteenth century, Britain had established a regime strongly biased in favor of the British investor. Expropriations of foreign investments were strongly discouraged. Challenges to this system were generally defeated through a combination of bondholder sanctions and use of the Royal Navy.

[11] Theodore H. White, *Fire in the Ashes* (New York: Harper & Row, 1953), 359. See also White, *In Search of History: A Personal Adventure* (New York: Harper & Row, 1978), 273–318.
[12] For a recent treatment of these questions, see Carla Norrlof, *America's Global Advantage: US Hegemony and International Cooperation* (Cambridge: Cambridge University Press, 2010).

After 1945 the United States was able to establish a similarly strong property regime in the non-communist world biased in favor of (American) multinationals. Sometimes challenges to this property regime were defeated through covert means (Iran, 1953; Guatemala, 1954). In addition to its military and economic power, the United States long possessed some crucial additional strengths. Isolationism had ended; the US was prepared to play an active role almost all over the world. For several decades presidential leadership and bipartisanship between Democrats and Republicans to a large extent characterized the American political system. The Republican right occasionally objected to the Truman administration's initiatives, but almost without exception it lost out, in part because key Republicans supported the administration. Only in the 1970s did this basic system begin to crumble.

Internationally the United States represented values that were seen as attractive by millions around the world. It stood for democracy and self-determination, for international cooperation and freer trade. These values were never fully practiced, even in the US itself. The Truman administration, and Secretary of State Dean Acheson in particular, in Dean Rusk's phrase, generally "overlooked the brown, black, and yellow peoples of the world." The Eisenhower administration did little to end racial segregation, particularly in the South. Southerners, from James Byrnes to William Fulbright, had to support the racism of their region if they wanted to maintain their political base. This tension in values lasted well into the 1960s. Protectionist elements have always been part of US foreign economic policies—also after 1945, when the United States pushed for a more liberal order from a position of overwhelming strength. There were always some sectors, even in the US, which allegedly would benefit from "temporary" protection.

Yet these fundamental values still served to support the overall US role and buttress its tremendous power. The support for these ideals did not necessarily require their full implementation in practice, although naturally that helped. Implementation was almost always relative, compared to others, and particularly compared to the Soviet Union. It certainly helped that America was also the richest country in the world, with broad-based material benefits that citizens of most other countries could only dream of. America's popular culture quickly spread to the most distant corners of the world. This process was well under way in the interwar years, but the pace picked up considerably after the Second World War.

The United States had its problems and suffered its defeats. The Soviet Union gained control in Eastern Europe; the communists won the civil war in China. Yet no previous Great Power had seen the entire world as its staging ground. Even Hitler's Germany and Stalin's Soviet Union had had clearly defined geographical priorities, despite Hitler's *Weltanschauung* and the Soviet Union's universalist aspirations. Soon the United States expected to play a leading role in virtually all important parts of the worlds. This was ambition on a grander scale than any other empire. Almost all previous versions had been basically regional. The biggest of all the recent ones, the vast British Empire, was geographically very comprehensive, but in the very center of international politics, on the European continent, Britain's influence was quite limited.

QUESTIONS AND DOUBTS

America had its pessimistic moments. America has always been challenged; it always will be. As Charles Dickens observed in 1844, "If its individual citizens, to a man, are to be believed, (America) always is depressed, and always is stagnated, and always in an alarming crisis, and never was otherwise."[13] Thus, during the Cold War the Soviets often felt "ten feet tall." Yet the basic mood was optimistic. In the long run the United States was bound to win. It had unrivalled power; it fought the good fight. Even George F. Kennan, that strong critic of the moralistic–legalistic tradition in American foreign policy, wrote that the American people should be grateful to Providence for the Kremlin's implacable challenge since it "has made their entire security as a nation dependent on their pulling themselves together and accepting the responsibilities of moral and political leadership that history plainly intended them to bear."[14] In his inaugural address, John F. Kennedy optimistically stated that America "shall pay any price, bear any burden, meet any hardship, support any friend, oppose any foe to assure the survival and success of liberty." As Arthur Schlesinger, Jr. wrote, with special reference to these early days of the Kennedy administration, but really with much wider relevance: "Euphoria reigned; we thought for a moment that the world was plastic and the future unlimited."[15]

By the 1970s both the statistics and the mood had changed. While in 1945 the United States had produced almost as much as the rest of the world put together, this slipped to approximately 40 percent in 1950, 30 percent in 1960, and 25 percent in 1975. By 1960 the French, West German, Italian, and Japanese economies had constituted respectively 17, 26, 10, and 15 percent

---

[13] Charles Dickens, *Martin Chuzzlewit*, quoted in Joseph Nye, *The Future of Power* (Public Affairs, 2011), 156.

[14] George F. Kennan, "The Sources of Soviet Conduct," *Foreign Affairs*, 29 (Summer 1947), 581–2.

[15] Thomas G. Paterson, *Kennedy's Quest for Victory: American Foreign Policy, 1961–1963* (Oxford: Oxford University Press, 1989), 15.

of the American economy; in 1975 these percentages stood at 22, 28, 13, and 33 percent. They all grew faster than the United States.[16]

In October 1957, Sputnik, the world's first artificial earth satellite, underlined Soviet progress. Khrushchev spoke about the goal of the Soviet Union being "to catch up with and overtake the West," actually surpassing the United States in several crucial economic fields, including milk, meat, and butter—even about "burying" the capitalist system in the long run. At the huge party congress in 1957 celebrating the October Revolution, Khrushchev stated that "Comrades, the calculations of our planners show that, within the next fifteen years, the Soviet Union will be able not only to catch up with but also to surpass the present volume of output of important products in the USA." Mao Tse-Tung immediately announced that China would outstrip Great Britain within 15 years: "Comrade Khrushchev tells us that the Soviet Union will overtake the United States in fifteen years. I can tell you that in fifteen years we may well catch up with or overtake Britain." This was the beginning of China's Great Leap Forward.[17]

Economic progress appeared much faster in the Soviet Union than in the West. Thus, in a paradoxical example, in the summer of 1960 some leading Norwegian politicians were afraid that in 10–15 years the rapid economic expansion on the Kola Peninsula could lead to political loyalty conflicts on the Norwegian side of the border where economic development was apparently much slower.[18] Norwegians would want to move to the Soviet Union. A few decades later there were indeed huge differences, but in Norway's favor.

Yet it gradually became clear that where the Soviets did presumably take the lead, the fields were no longer so crucial. Who needed all that steel and cement when the future belonged to much more advanced technologies? After having visited the United States in 1959, Khrushchev was clearly impressed: "They are really rich. Rich indeed."[19] On the civilian side, most definitely including agriculture, the Soviet Union was far behind. Only in some military fields could the Soviet Union actually rival the US. This equality was the basis of the Strategic Arms Limitation Treaties (SALT) of the 1970s.

While Korea had been a draw, the Vietnam war was widely perceived as a major defeat for the US. In turn, it led to a reaction against the "imperial" presidency, and to internal bitterness and division. The war also seemed to make a mockery of America's ideals of democracy and international

---

[16] U.S. Department of Commerce, *Statistical Abstracts, 1981* (Washington, DC: Government Printing Office, 1982), 880.

[17] The most recent account of these matters is Frank Dikötter, *Mao's Great Famine: The History of China's Most Devastating Catastrophe, 1958–62* (London: Bloomsbury, 2010), 13–14.

[18] William Taubman, *Khrushchev: The Man and his Era* (New York: Norton, 2003), 508–13; Knut Einar Eriksen and Helge Øystein Pharo, *Kald krig og internasjonalisering 1949–1963* [Cold War and Internationalization 1949–1963] (Oslo: Universitetsforlaget, 1997), 227.

[19] Taubman, *Khrushchev*, 393.

cooperation. The Nixon economic shocks of the early 1970s led to the end of the dollar's convertibility into gold, to devaluation, and to strengthened protectionism.

In the 1970s there was a lot of talk, even in high circles, about the decline of the United States. In 1971, Richard Nixon referred to the good old days of 1947, when the United States had been the undisputed leader, both militarily and economically. Now, however, and looking five to ten years ahead, he stated: "First, instead of just America being number one in the world from an economic standpoint, the pre-eminent world power, and instead of there being just two superpowers, when we think in economic terms and economic potentialities, there are five great power centers in the world today." He referred to the US, the Soviet Union, Western Europe, Japan, and China. Nixon even compared the United States to past empires: "I think of what happened to Greece and Rome; what is left—only the pillars."[20] The 1970s was clearly the decade when the references to the decline of the United States were the strongest. In various ways the Nixon administration tried to build up regional powers that could take some of the load off America's shoulders.[21]

Ronald Reagan changed the rhetoric dramatically. For eight full years America was celebrated in terms even more extravagant than those used by Kennedy twenty years earlier. True, there had been the setbacks in the 1970s. "How did all this happen?" Reagan rhetorically asked. He gave the answer himself: "America had simply ceased to be a leader in the world." In 1988 he celebrated his own achievements: "... a complete turnaround, a revolution. Some years ago, America was weak and freedom everywhere was under siege; today, America is strong and democracy is everywhere on the move..."[22]

Academic observers argued that Reagan had certainly changed the rhetoric, but perhaps not really reality. In his *The Rise and Fall of the Great Powers* (1987), Paul Kennedy argued to critical and popular acclaim that the United States was in decline and was bound to go the way of earlier Great Powers. His advice to Reagan was that the president manage America's decline gracefully, so that "the *relative* erosion of the United States' position takes place slowly and smoothly, and is not accelerated by policies which bring merely short-term advantage but longer-term disadvantage."[23] What was more implicit in *Rise and Fall* was then explicitly presented in Kennedy's *Preparing for the*

---

[20] *The Public Papers of the Presidents of the United States. Richard M. Nixon, 1971* (Washington, DC: 1972), 804, 812.
[21] For a fine study of this process, see Robert S. Litwak, *Detente and the Nixon Doctrine: American Foreign Policy and the Pursuit of Stability, 1969–1976* (Cambridge: Cambridge University Press, 1984).
[22] *The Public Papers of the Presidents of the United States. Ronald Reagan, 1982* (Washington, DC: 1983), 78; and *1983* (Washington, DC: 1984), 265, 271.
[23] Paul Kennedy, *The Rise and Fall of the Great Powers: Economic Change and Military Conflict from 1500 to 2000* (New York: Random House, 1987), 534.

Twenty-First Century six years later: Japan was clearly America's successor among the superpowers.

In the barrage of statistics in Kennedy's two books the most important set was clearly the share of world production held by the United States. Kennedy more or less assumed that America's decline—from almost 50 percent in 1945, down to 25 percent in 1975—would continue. Japan's curve, on the other hand, would be extended upwards; sooner or later a Japan on the way up was bound to surpass the United States on the way down.

Kennedy was clearly wrong. The US share of world production remained at around 25 percent. There was no significant further slippage. No sooner was *Rise and Fall* out than the Soviet Union collapsed, a phenomenon not exactly foreseen in the book. And, no sooner was *Preparing for the Twenty-First Century* out than Japan entered into a long period of economic decline and political sclerosis. So much for predictions about the future, even from the most eminent of historians.

AMERICA'S "UNIPOLAR MOMENT"

In fact, the 1990s were to be America's unipolar moment. Charles Krauthammer's original article "The Unipolar Moment" was published in *Foreign Affairs* in 1990/91.[24] In it, he argued that the new order would last for at least a generation or for "decades." Both Bill Clinton and Madeleine Albright proclaimed that the United States was indeed "the indispensable nation"; it allegedly "stands taller and sees further into the future" than other actors. In fact, in his State of the Union Address in January 2000, Clinton stated that "the state of the union is the strongest it has ever been."

True, America's relative economic position had been much stronger in 1945 than it was at the end of the Cold War. Yet, in the early years American military strength had always been balanced by Soviet power. In fact, in the years after 1945 the Soviet expansion was to a very large extent based on the strength of the Red Army. Now there was no Soviet Union and no Red Army. The US had no significant other military rival either. Washington had dreamed of one world in 1945, but ended up with two antagonistic camps, East and West. Now, for the first time, the United States had the possibility to dominate the entire globe. The Cold War East quickly disintegrated, slowly to be replaced by the traditional East of East Asia.

---

[24] Charles Krauthammer, "The Unipolar Moment," *Foreign Affairs, 70/1 America and the World 1990/91* (Council on Foreign Relations, 1991), 23–33.

The Soviet Union's problems and eventual disappearance, and Russia's weakness, facilitated a string of US-led military invasions which started in the traditional Latin American backyard, in Panama in 1989, continued with the Gulf War in 1991, the interventions in Somalia in 1992–93, in Haiti in 1994, in Bosnia in 1994–95, in Kosovo in 1999, in Afghanistan after September 11, 2001, and climaxed with the Iraq War of 2003. The Somalia experience was seen as a failure and became a crucial factor in the decision not to intervene in the Rwandan genocide in 1994. The rest were generally considered successes, at least in a short-term perspective. The Gulf and Iraq wars were huge military operations, with the United States transferring up to 500,000 soldiers to the other side of the globe. No other military power could even dream of performing such operations. Some of these operations were done with the approval of the world community. Others, particularly Kosovo and Iraq, were done without such approval. It did not matter much. No one was going to challenge the United States anyway.

Political science realists argued that no alliance had survived the disappearance of the threat against which the alliance had been directed. Yet NATO not only survived the end of the Soviet Union; it seemed to become increasingly popular with the addition of many new members. Kenneth Waltz, the father of neo-realism, blamed Bill Clinton for thus reversing the alleged laws of history by undertaking various actions to keep NATO alive.[25] So much for political science laws. Realists had also argued that when one power became predominant, other states would inevitably balance against it. In the 1990s there was very little balancing against the United States. Relations with Yeltsin's Russia were improving, in part because the two presidents got along so well; and with Jiang Zemin's China they were satisfactory, despite the consequences of the harsh measures taken by the Chinese leaders against the demonstrators on Tiananmen Square in June 1989.

America's leading allies in Europe and Asia definitely wanted to continue the alliance structure, even in the new post-Cold War world. In 1999, Poland, Hungary, and the Czech Republic became members of NATO; many others were to follow a few years later. In connection with the war in Afghanistan the US established bases in several countries in Central Asia (formerly part of the Soviet Union). It was difficult to imagine a more complete demonstration of US power at the expense of Russia, the troubled inheritor of the Soviet legacy, and China, allegedly the rising power. Despite initial cuts in defense spending in Clinton's first years, such spending soon rose a great deal. America's lead over any possible combination of enemies was huge. Also, for that reason, any

---

[25] Kenneth Waltz, "Structural Realism After the Cold War," *International Security*, 25:1 (2000), 5–41. See also G. John Ikenberry, *American Unrivaled: The Future of the Balance of Power* (Ithaca: Cornell University Press, 2002).

effort to balance the United States appeared futile. Not even a combination of all the possible challengers to the US would fully measure up, and most of the challengers had a better relationship with Washington than with most of their potential allies.

The American economy blossomed in the 1990s. Growth was high; employment increased rapidly. More than 22 million jobs were created in the Clinton years, a high number compared both to earlier periods in American history, and to other parts of the world in the 1990s. For the first time in decades the federal budget was balanced, due to a combination of higher taxes, reductions in some expenditures, and higher growth. America and much of the world marveled particularly at the growth in productivity. The United States had seemingly found the key to ever-renewed success; the new information technology apparently provided a great deal of the answer. Many books and articles were written celebrating various aspects of the American political–economic model—books and articles that continued well past the turn of the millennium. History had come to an end in that no real alternative existed to the American political–economic model; peace, democracy, and free markets had all proved their superiority.[26] With the collapse of the Soviet Union, and Japan's growing economic problems, there appeared to be no true economic competitor to the US. The American economic model was spreading to ever new corners of the world. Even in Scandinavia, home of the alleged alternative between communism and capitalism, deregulation and the free market took control.

Democracy was experiencing a "third wave" across much of the world; Eastern and Central Europe, even the new Russia, almost all countries in Latin America, many in Asia, and even some in Africa, became more or less democratic. America's "soft power" was spreading rapidly. The proliferation of television channels and new media presented golden opportunities for America's mass culture. Bill Clinton had his problems, with a definite lack of political and personal discipline, and he was never able to find that elusive new term that was to characterize his overall foreign policy in the way "containment" had done during the Cold War (the Kennan "sweepstakes"). Yet he remained popular in the United States and in much of the rest of the world as well. He had a unique ability to convince almost anyone that he was

---

[26] For some examples, see Francis Fukuyama, *The End of History and the Last Man* (New York: Free Press, 1992); Michael Mandelbaum, *The Ideas that Conquered the World: Peace, Democracy, and Free Markets in the Twenty-First Century* (Oxford: Public Affairs, 2002); Mandelbaum, *The Case for Goliath* (New York: Public Affairs, 2005); Walter Russell Mead, *Power, Terror, Peace, and War: America's Grand Strategy in a World at Risk* (New York: Knopf, 2004); Mead, *God and Gold: Britain, America and the Making of the Modern World* (New York: Knopf, 2007).

actually on their side, whether he was talking to Third Way Europeans, troubled Russians, or the increasingly important Chinese.[27]

Some of the rising neo-conservatives had difficulties with the wave of American interventions, at least initially. They despised Bill Clinton and virtually anything he stood for. "Nation building" was a term they disliked. They also felt that many of Clinton's interventions had a humanitarian objective which they did not share. Interventions were meant to take care of Great Power interests, little else. Military power was not be used for such additional purposes. There would also be rising costs in terms of human lives and money. This attitude was clearly noticeable even in the first months after George W. Bush took over as president in January 2001. Yet, more and more, the following question was asked: When America was so strong, and its intentions were so good, and many Americans were really taking both for granted, why should it not use its unipolar moment to reorganize the world? Soon this question was asked both by the growing number of (neo-)conservatives and by liberals. Shocked into action by the events of September 11, 2001, the Bush administration went on the offensive. Al Qaeda and the Taliban, which the administration had not really focused much on before September 11, were to be swept out of Afghanistan. First Iraq, and then, hopefully, Iran and North Korea, were to experience regime change. Reagan had allegedly liberated Eastern Europe and the Soviet Union. Bush would now set the Middle East free. The United States did not really need permanent allies. In Donald Rumsfeld's words: "The mission determined the coalition; the coalition did not determine the mission." If the US just took the lead and showed the way, much of the world would follow. In June 2002, President Bush declared that "America has, and intends to keep, military strength beyond challenge, thereby making destabilizing arms races pointless and limiting rivalries to trade and other pursuits."[28]

AMERICA'S DECLINE

The world looks much different today. Charles Krauthammer, who had proclaimed the unipolar moment in 1990, declared in 2002 that if America

---

[27] The best book on the 1990s is Derek Chollet and James Goldgeier, *America Between the Wars: From 11/9 to 9/11—the Misunderstood Years between the Fall of the Berlin Wall and the Start of the War on Terror* (New York: Public Affairs, 2008).

[28] For an interesting account of this period, see Peter Beinart, *The Icarus Syndrome: A History of American Hubris* (London: HarperCollins, 2010).

did not wreck its economy, unipolarity would last 40 years.[29] In the sense that the United States could do almost anything it liked, unipolarity lasted only a few more years. While the operations in Afghanistan went surprisingly well, with small US forces overthrowing the Taliban with local support, after the initial victory the United States was soon to face much larger problems in Iraq than it had ever dreamed of; George W. Bush was to prove a rather unpopular president in much of the world outside the United States; and, most importantly, the United States was to face financial problems of such a magnitude that they could potentially threaten its overall position as the world's leading power.

True, the United States is still clearly the pre-eminent military power in the world. It spends almost as much on defense as all the other Great Powers added together. US military supremacy is still at the core of the many alliances, bilateral treaties, and bases involving the United States. America is definitely still the leading guarantor of the security of other countries. Thus, when so many Eastern and Central European states were eager to join NATO, it was primarily to get the much sought-after military guarantee from Washington. When China rises, many of its neighbors either renew their alliances with the US—such as Japan and South Korea—or they seek stronger ties for the first time, like India. When so many countries are willing to participate in the American-led war in Afghanistan against the Taliban, this is to a large extent because they feel that a satisfactory long-term relationship with the United States requires that they do so. A refusal to do so would also have a negative impact on NATO.

Yet the events in Iraq and Afghanistan have dramatically illustrated the limitations of US military power. The expectation of the Bush administration had been for a short war with early withdrawal of the American forces, the establishing of a popular Iraqi government which would lead to the transformation of politics in the entire Arab world, and the financing of all this through rapidly increasing Iraqi oil production.[30]

None of this happened. The march to Baghdad was quick, but then the problems started. With the fall of Saddam Hussein's government, the dissolution of the Iraqi army, and the purge of Baathist officials, chaos followed. Elections were held and, slowly, more popular structures emerged; but the new governments did not pursue the policies the United States had favored. Any

---

[29] Stephen Szabo, "The Washington Bubble: Why US Foreign Policy is Oversized," *Current History*, 108 (2009), 369. In more traditional political science realist terms, it could be argued that unipolarity lasted much longer.

[30] For the conduct of the war from the American side, see Michael R. Gordon and General Bernard E. Trainor, *Cobra II: The Inside Story of the Invasion and Occupation of Iraq* (New York: Pantheon, 2006); Thomas E. Ricks, *Fiasco: The American Military Adventure in Iraq* (Penguin, 2006); and *The Gamble: General David Petraeus and the American Military Adventure in Iraq, 2006–2008* (Penguin, 2009).

popular government was unable either to establish peace with Israel, or pursue a containment policy vis-à-vis Iran. With so much chaos, oil production remained stagnant, and the costs of the war for the US increased rapidly.

No one wants to fight a conventional war against the United States. So opponents of the US fight asymmetrical wars in the way we saw first in Iraq and then in Afghanistan. They are not able to defeat the US; but neither is the US able to defeat them entirely. Then the inevitable question arises of who is able to keep at it the longest.

George W. Bush's policies were unpopular in most parts of the world, particularly in Western Europe and in the Muslim world. The standing of the United States fell considerably. The Bush administration was criticized strongly and frequently, but many points of criticism went well beyond the administration. The use of force, lack of concern about the environment, the death penalty and America's social problems, and the rise of the religious right were some of the points raised. America and some of its allies, particularly in Europe, were drifting apart. As we shall see, Obama made the United States more popular again in many circles.

Economically the United States still has by far the biggest gross domestic product (GDP) in the world. China's economy overtook that of Japan in the second quarter of 2010 and thus became the second largest in the world. Today, it is still only about 40 percent of that of the United States. While the US share of world GDP had declined—from almost 50 percent in 1945, to around 25 percent in the mid-1970s—there was no really significant further decline, so that in 2010–11 it still remained at around 22–23 percent. The majority of the most advanced companies in the world are still American. American science and universities still lead the world, as can be seen in the number of Nobel Prizes received, and in the many rankings of universities in the world. American productivity and even the growth in productivity are still high, although not necessarily the highest in the world in every respect.

Most importantly, the United States was running up huge new deficits in its federal budget. The projected deficit for the 2011 fiscal year was 1.3 trillion dollars—or almost 11 percent of America's entire economic output: among the highest in the world. Total government debt came to almost exactly 100 percent of GDP, and was expected to become even higher before it started to go down. America was becoming "an empire of debt." Only Japan, among the major powers, and some smaller countries, both in Europe and elsewhere, were worse off in this respect. (See Table 2.)

There were two major reasons for the huge US deficits. First, the policies of the Bush administration had a very negative effect. At the end of his administration, Bill Clinton had actually been able to balance the federal budget, but tax cuts in 2001 and 2003 reduced income substantially, by roughly two trillion dollars over ten years. And the tax cuts were not accompanied by cuts in expenditure; on the contrary, the increase in expenditure was

Table 2. Debt statistics

Diverging paths, 2011 projections

The emerging countries of the G-20 are increasingly seen as the main engine of global economic growth since the downturn that began in 2007, while many advanced G-20 members will be saddled with large debt burdens in coming years.

	change in G.D.P	Gov't budget balance as a share of G.D.P	Government debt as a share of G.D.P
Advanced G-20	2.4 %	− 7.9%	108.5%
South Korea	4.5	+ 2.5	28.8
Australia	3.0	− 2.5	24.1
Canada	2.8	− 4.6	84.2
United States	2.8	−10.8	99.5
Germany	2.5	− 2.3	80.1
European Union	1.8	− 4.8	80.0 (2010)
Britain	1.7	− 8.6	83.0
France	1.6	− 5.8	85.0
Japan	1.4	−10.0	229.1
Italy	1.1	− 4.3	120.3
Emerging G-20	7.5	− 2.0	33.6
China	9.6	− 1.6	17.1
India	8.2	− 8.3	70.8
Saudi Arabia	7.5	+12.8	8.3
Indonesia	6.2	− 1.5	25.4
Russia	4.8	− 1.6	8.5
Argentina	4.7	− 6.0	40.7
Turkey	4.6	− 1.8	39.4
Mexico	4.6	− 1.7	42.3
Brazil	4.5	− 2.4	65.7
South Africa	3.5	− 5.7	40.5

Sources: International Monetary Fund, Eurostat

Source: International Herald Tribune (May 26, 2011), 6

very large. The new prescription-drug benefit to Medicare was very expensive; so were the wars in Afghanistan and Iraq.

Second, the financial and economic crisis of 2007–09 had much greater effects than even the Bush policies, although the two were of course related. Thus, the huge debts—federal, state, and private—were probably an important cause of the crisis. Economists and business people had not really learned to manage their affairs so as to produce a constantly growing economy, as they had so proudly believed they would. The recession that started in the housing industry in the US in 2007 spread to the banks and industrial giants of America, and to much of the rest of the world. Huge crisis packages had to be passed under both Bush and Obama to save the financial system and to stimulate the economy. Naturally, in this situation, tax income also fell, so the deficit exploded. This was clearly the most dramatic economic setback since 1945.

Although the first signs of recovery could be seen in the middle of 2009, the United States was badly hit. The prospects for the future were also quite troublesome. Particularly after 2020, the rapid increase in the number of elderly people will have dramatic consequences for social security and health expenses. Then, interest on the rising debt will increase exponentially. Rising debt will most likely also hold down economic growth.[31]

It was less important that, during the recession, the (traditionally) even more serious deficit in US current accounts now actually fell somewhat, because imports declined even more than exports. The US had long been the world's biggest debtor. Now its debts had become so huge that basic questions were being asked about America's economic future. It was running up big deficits in most categories:

- fifteen out of thirty-two major categories of capital goods, and all but three of twenty-five categories of consumer goods
- the traditional huge exporter of agricultural products had turned into a net importer of food, feed, and beverages
- there was a considerable deficit even in the trade of advanced technology products
- the country's international investment position had turned negative in 1986, and in the following decades this deficit exploded.[32]

The US had lectured the rest of the world about the importance of balancing its books; otherwise collapse would follow. Washington had, however, made one huge exception for itself. Now reality might finally be catching up with it.

Power normally shifts immeasurably almost every day, but now the shifts could be measured virtually every day. While the US had a dramatic recession and a very slow recovery, China's setback came in the form of (only) 6 percent growth and a quick recovery. There was a tendency in some circles to assume that the debt problem would just go away. After all, the US debt had been much higher after the Second World War than it was now. Rapid growth after 1945 had taken care of most of that problem. Now, however, the debt problem was long term, and the prospects for growth much more limited.

No one could be certain of the consequences of the problem. The optimists pointed out that the federal government was having little trouble raising the money required, and at interest rates that were very low by historical

---

[31] In explaining these developments I have found Roger C. Altman and Richard N. Haass, "American Profligacy and American Power: The Consequences of Fiscal Irresponsibility," *Foreign Affairs*, 89:6 (November/December 2010), 25–34 most useful. See also Michael Mandelbaum, *The Frugal Superpower: America's Global Leadership in a Cash-Strapped Era* (New York: Public Affairs, 2010).

[32] For a most interesting treatment of these issues, see Vaclav Smil, *Why America is Not a New Rome* (Cambridge, MA and London: MIT Press, 2010), 67–9.

standards.[33] Unlike the euro countries, the United States had its own central bank and its own currency. This made it easier for the US to handle its debts than was the case for euro debtors. The default risk was seen as much smaller.

Pessimists emphasized that although the United States was still a superpower with the world's leading currency, and was generally able to handle its growing debt, market forces could ultimately descend on it in the way they descended on various European countries with only marginally larger debts than those of the US.[34] Then the government might have to impose draconian measures almost overnight. Endless discussions about how to reduce the budget deficit, between President Obama and the Republican House of Representatives, resulted only in short-term solutions. And had not the decline and fall of Great Britain after the Second World War been accompanied by a series of more or less failed measures to adjust to new economic circumstances? As we shall see, there was also the question of how long the Chinese would continue to finance America's deficits. A foreign policy crisis could well lead to dramatic action, as when Washington had forced London to stop the Suez invasion in 1956 when Britain needed additional financial support from the US. The deepest question was the one Larry H. Summers, Obama's first chief economic adviser, used to ask before he re-entered government, "How long can the world's biggest borrower remain the world's biggest power?"[35] This was a key question—maybe *the* key question—for the future role of the United States.

The soaring deficits were bound to limit America's freedom of action severely. New large-scale military interventions would be very difficult to undertake. This was clearly one of several factors in the Obama administration's reluctance to carry out military action against Iran, and to provide only late and limited action against Muammar Gaddafi's Libya in March 2011. Existing interventions ought to be ended or at least reduced as quickly as possible; Obama thus insisted on withdrawing according to schedule from Iraq and Afghanistan, although the schedule was more flexible in the latter case. All forms of aid and assistance had to be dispensed much more carefully than before. So after the revolutions in North Africa in 2011, Washington offered rather limited economic assistance to the new governments. Even the defense budget would be negatively affected, although the political elite in both parties favored higher defense spending than did the public. While political leaders had their own priorities, the public clearly wanted Washington to focus much more on the domestic situation, and less on the needs of various foreigners. All this was bound to result in a lower profile for the United States.

---

[33] Paul Krugman, "Dumbing Deficits Down," *International Herald Tribune* (March 12–13, 2011), 7.

[34] See, for instance, Graham Bowley, "Debt Could Cost U.S. its Triple-A Status, Rating Agencies Warn," *International Herald Tribune* (January 15–16, 2011), 12.

[35] David E. Sanger, "Behind Deficit, Fear of Eclipse," *International Herald Tribune* (February 3, 2010), 14.

If Washington was able to cooperate with other capitals, the transition to a somewhat lower profile would be easier. There was therefore a definite need for the United States to work closely with other leading countries in the new "multi-partner" world. However, there was no guarantee that this multi-partner world, in the administration's language, would not develop into a multi-polar world, with the uncertainties that would then follow.[36] The United States was quite simply overextended, and it badly needed help in shouldering its global burdens. Rising powers such as China, India, Brazil, South Africa, and Nigeria, in addition to the EU and Japan, had to be integrated into a world where the US would be carrying a smaller load than in the past.

BARACK OBAMA'S FOREIGN POLICY: WHAT CAN THE US DO AND NOT DO?

Individuals may make a difference, but their significance is increased when they act in harmony with larger historical forces. Or, as Karl Marx put it in the opening paragraphs of *The Eighteenth Brumaire of Louis Napoleon*: "Men make their own History, but they do not make it as they please; they do not make it under self-selected circumstances, but under circumstances existing already, given and transmitted from the past."

As Joseph Nye has stressed, resources do not automatically produce certain outcomes. The United States may have the greatest resources in today's world, but these have to be converted into policies and, ultimately, outcomes, through leadership, strategy, organization, etc. Thus, the power-conversion strategies of the various powers are crucial.[37]

The shift from George W. Bush to Barack Obama is a case in point. The nationalistic policies of the Bush administration were putting the United States at odds with many governments and, even more so, with public opinion around much of the world. This undoubtedly had a negative effect on the general position of the United States. It was also becoming increasingly difficult to distinguish clearly between the policies of the Bush administration and the role of the United States itself. Bush was becoming America.

The change to Obama saw a sharp rise in America's popularity, particularly in Western Europe, but also in most of the rest of Europe, Latin America, and Africa. This rise in popularity was less pronounced in the Arab world, and with the governments and publics of the Asian giants, Japan, India, and China, (where it was difficult to speak about public opinion). In June 2010, after about

---

[36] For a stimulating discussion of this question, see Stewart Patrick, "Global Governance Reform," *Contemporary International Relations* (July/August 2010), 33–70, particularly 37–9.

[37] Nye, *The Future of Power*, 9–10.

18 months in power, Obama was still seen as likely to do the right thing in world affairs by 90 percent of Germans, 87 percent of the French, and 84 percent of Britons, compared to 65 percent of Americans. His popularity was also on the rise in Russia and China; as expected, he had the greatest difficulties in the Muslim world. Later on, there was a clear downward slide in the United States, where fewer than half said they approved of Obama's policies, while elsewhere his popularity held up surprisingly well, particularly in Western Europe.[38]

There was bound to be disappointment about Obama; he could not possibly live up to all his promises. And despite the big shift from Bush to Obama, America was still, to a large extent, the same country. The United States was not as reform-oriented as many observers thought; in fact, Obama himself was not so reform-oriented as many on the political left had hoped. Change was limited, except that the US had done what had been thought impossible—elected a black president in a country still overwhelmingly white. The United States was right in the middle of the most serious recession since the 1930s, and Obama's first urgent task was to avoid a total financial collapse in the US and elsewhere. His freedom of action was further limited by America's political system in general, and its deep polarization in particular.

Yet individuals can indeed make a difference. No one dreamed about celebrating China's aloof leaders in the way the world did the new American president. This is undoubtedly one important aspect of superpower status as well. It does not contradict the fact that there were definite limits to what Obama could achieve through his foreign policy. Still, the fact that the United States had elected a black, progressive president—Obama avoided the term "liberal"—who spoke to the world in the most inspiring of terms, apparently made all the many generalizations about the United States being an increasingly conservative and nationalist country obsolete.

Barack Obama's presidency provides an illustration of what the United States can and cannot do. Without doubt, the American president is the most powerful individual in the world. America holds more power than any other country. Despite America's system of checks and balances, the president generally dominates the scene, particularly the foreign policy arena. In some form or other most American presidents develop ambitious agendas which they want to carry out during their term(s) in office. This definitely applies to Barack Obama.[39]

---

[38] Nicholas Kulish, "Obama Still Very Popular Abroad, Says Global Survey," *International Herald Tribune* (June 18, 2010), 3; Judy Dempsey, "Europe Still Likes Obama Despite Foreign Policy Doubts," *International Herald Tribune* (September 16, 2010), 2.

[39] The best early account of the Obama administration is found in Jonathan Alter, *The Promise: President Obama, Year One* (New York: Simon & Schuster, 2010).

Obama wanted to promote international cooperation and multilateral diplomacy. He had an ambitious agenda for nuclear arms control, and even established a nuclear-free world as his ultimate objective—though he added that this nuclear-free world might not happen in his own lifetime. In part, as a result of his ambitious nuclear agenda, he wanted to press the reset button in relations with Russia. And he favored cooperation with the new emerging China. Dialogue and negotiation were to be preferred in his diplomacy in the Middle East, and even in relations with the most challenging countries, such as Iran and North Korea. The United States was to ratify several international treaties that it had earlier opposed, or at least not ratified. The use of torture was to be ended; Guantanamo was to be closed. Obama wanted to pursue an international agreement to stop global warming.

In theory, in trying to achieve all these and many other objectives, the United States had a huge arsenal at its disposal—from nuclear and conventional weapons, to all kinds of economic instruments and political appeals. Obama's popularity was impressive. In fact, as we have seen, it quickly became evident that his popularity was considerably greater in many foreign countries than in the United States itself. At home, though Obama was soon to run into a wall of opposition from Republicans on the domestic side, he had more support from many of them on the foreign policy side; they liked Obama's tough side, in the form of the wars in Iraq and Afghanistan, far better than his various initiatives to strengthen multilateralist principles.

In reality, however, America's instruments were more circumscribed than this description seemed to indicate. Even before the atomic bombs were dropped in August 1945 over Hiroshima and Nagasaki, American politicians had wondered how they could exploit the supreme new weapon diplomatically. The answer was generally that this could not be done explicitly; the atomic bomb was just too dramatic an instrument to be used as a direct threat. It was also assumed that the world would respond negatively to any American effort to act as some sort of "nuclear bully." Washington just had to hope that its enemies would be sufficiently impressed to make the necessary concessions anyway.

The bomb primarily served as a effective deterrent vis-à-vis Great Power attacks on the United States and its major allies; the great number of smaller wars the United States was involved in demonstrated that deterrence went only so far. During the Cold War there may well have been a Long Peace in Europe, but other factors worked alongside nuclear weapons to produce this striking result: the dramatic consequences of even a conventional war, as demonstrated during the Second World War, and the stability provided by the bloc structure and the overall roles of the United States and the Soviet Union. Yet, outside Europe, the military conflicts were many. Some of them were also quite significant in scope, particularly the Korean and Vietnam wars.

In diplomatic negotiations there are few definitive examples of the power of nuclear weapons.

By the time Obama came to power the use of conventional weapons was also severely circumscribed. He had promised to withdraw American troops from Iraq, although he left some room for a non-combat presence even after 2011. He did step up the US military role in Afghanistan significantly, and in Pakistan in a more limited, but still dramatic, way. These campaigns strained America's resources, particularly its military manpower. Iraq also demonstrated how wrong things could go. The invasion in March 2003 had been quite successful in a narrow military sense; the real problems started when victory was declared on May 1. If the intervention in Iraq had gone as planned, and the Bush administration had done any meaningful planning for the post-war phase, it would have put tremendous pressure on Iran and North Korea. At the time, Iran showed a willingness to bargain; but with its emphasis on regime change, the Bush administration showed little interest.

Now, with Obama in power, the military option was not taken entirely off the table vis-à-vis these two countries. In fact, this option was stated time and again, but its credibility was limited by past experience. This was particularly the case with North Korea when it produced an atomic bomb. America's partners in the Six-Party Talks clearly favored negotiations; Seoul lay within easy range of North Korean artillery. The rulers in Teheran and Pyongyang must have rated the chances of a US military response as fairly low. The consequences of a military strike would just be too dramatic. Washington was left to work with an escalating series of sanctions whose effects were less than hoped for, although they had more bite with Iran than with the more isolated North Korea.

So although Obama might have the best of intentions, diplomatic breakthroughs could only be guaranteed if they were in the interest not only of the United States but of the other side involved. Russia favored new agreements limiting strategic nuclear weapons. Such agreements could enhance its status as the nuclear equal of the United States, but at a somewhat reduced economic cost, which would be quite attractive for a hard-pressed Russia. The Strategic Arms Reduction Treaty (START) agreement of April 2010 provided hope for further bilateral and international agreements. Obama's vision of a nuclear-free world had stimulated optimism, though there was absolutely no sign of any of the other nuclear powers being willing to abandon their nuclear weapons. Israel, India, Pakistan, North Korea, and even Iran had all demonstrated the advantages that many still perceived these weapons to have. Once you had nuclear weapons, the danger of an attack—in this case from the United States—declined substantially.

Obama did stretch out his hand to Iran and North Korea, but they were simply not willing to abandon their nuclear programs. Obama agreed to work directly with the existing governments, thus ending all talk of regime change, even when the government in Teheran was directly challenged in elections and demonstrations. This disappointed some of Obama's supporters. And it did not help either country much.

Obama's freedom to act was also curtailed by a whole set of domestic factors. He had not even promised to end "rendition" and military tribunals. He did end torture by US personnel, but Guantanamo could not be closed within the promised one year since many prisoners could not be transferred elsewhere. Opposition, not only from Republicans, but also from Democrats (particularly in coal-and oil-producing states), limited the president's freedom of action as far as global warming was concerned. There had been little or no support for the Kyoto treaty, even under Bill Clinton. The limited result Obama achieved in Copenhagen in December 2010 was perhaps the most he could get through the American Congress. It may in fact have gone too far, particularly after the Republican victory in the 2010 Congressional elections. Copenhagen illustrated the president's role; he probably did more than anyone else to secure an agreement, but the agreement did little to solve the problems at hand.

While Obama had ultimately been able to get his economic crisis package through Congress in 2009–10, after the Republican victory in the Congressional elections in 2010 the situation changed. The initiative was now with the more fiscally fundamentalist Tea Party movement of the party. Endless negotiations were carried out. Obama had to sacrifice tax increases for the rich; cuts in discretionary spending were to be deep. Growth faltered; a double-dip recession threatened. It was obvious that when Obama's economic leadership was so limited at home, he could not really lead the world either in these challenging times. The world stood without an effective international leader.

In the Middle East Obama acted under severe international and national constraints. Israel had its most conservative–nationalist government ever; and the Palestinians were more divided than ever before—though in the spring of 2011 there were new efforts to bring about reconciliation between the Palestine Liberation Organization (PLO) and Hamas. As has been said, Israel might ostensibly be interested in the peace process itself, to keep the Palestinians calm, but not so much in the result, as this would inevitably involve substantial concessions and internal division. The Palestinians, on the other hand, might be interested in the agreement itself, but not in the process, as it would be a tortuous one for them. It was not easy to see how an agreement could be reached when this was the situation for the two main parties involved.

There was broad agreement that only the United States, if anyone, could force the parties to the conference table, and, later, into an agreement. Since Israel, the strongest party, with possession of almost all of the disputed territory, had to make most of the difficult concessions, leverage over the Israelis was what counted. But also, for domestic American reasons, it would be extraordinarily difficult for the Obama administration to force such decisions on the Israelis. In fact, in the past, several US administrations had applied considerable pressure on Israel, particularly those of Dwight D. Eisenhower and George H. W. Bush. And virtually all administrations had had more limited disagreements with Israel. The US did, after all, have significant interests in the Arab world; the oil companies had consistently pushed for the US to pursue an "American," not an "Israeli," policy in the Middle East.

Yet it remained hard to imagine the United States forcing Israel to make the necessary concessions. Limited pressure was one thing; being willing to withhold economic and military aid was entirely different. The Israelis had come to expect occasional tough talk from Washington, but Tel Aviv pretty much excluded the possibility of the United States going to extreme lengths to force Israel's hand. The Jewish lobby in America was extremely well organized; the Christian right was a fervent believer in Israel; and, most importantly, there was a basic sympathy throughout most of the US toward the Israelis. There was hardly any domestic political risk in supporting Israel; but there was a great deal of risk in supporting the Palestinians, particularly for Obama, since support for Israel was traditionally even stronger among Democrats than Republicans. Thus, more than 70 percent of American Jews still favored the Democrats. As George H. W. Bush had clearly understood, the Jews would not vote for him regardless.[40] There were signs of change: many Jews in America were moving toward the center, even toward the left as far as Israel's position was concerned; US identification with Israel was having negative effects, crucially in Iraq and Afghanistan. However, these signs did not change the larger picture of solid US support for Israel. At least not yet.[41]

AN AMERICAN DOMESTIC BALANCE SHEET

As we have seen with all the predictions about the rise and fall of the various Great Powers, it is impossible to make accurate predictions about the future. And, at best, the predictions about the fall of the United States have so far proved premature. Though America's problems need to be addressed, the US still has a strong basis for economic growth in its considerable resources, the largest and deepest financial markets in the world, and, even more, its highly educated and generationally balanced population.

---

[40] For a somewhat overstated account of the influence of the Jewish lobby, see John J. Mearsheimer and Stephen M. Walt, *The Israel Lobby and U.S. Foreign Policy* (New York: Farrar, Straus & Giroux, 2007). The pro-Israeli attitude goes far beyond the traditional Jewish lobby, important as it is.
[41] Peter Beinart, "The Failure of the American Jewish Establishment," *New York Review of Books* (June 10, 2010), 16–20.

The higher up the age scale, the greater the US lead in research and education, despite rising problems financing its higher (particularly public) education, and barriers to admitting foreign students after September 11. US spending on research is still considerably higher than in EU countries. In fact, the United States spends more on research and development than the next seven largest spenders put together; on a per capita basis among the developed countries, only Sweden and Finland spend more. Scientists throughout the world find American scientists the most popular working partners; and the results, whether judged in Nobel Prizes or in business innovation, are impressive.[42] In addition, there are the many foreign leaders who have been educated in the United States. It has been estimated that 46 current—and 165 former—foreign heads of government were educated in the United States.[43]

With the exception of the young population of India, the United States probably also has the economically most desirable age structure among the Great Powers. The American population is still rapidly growing, and is expected to grow further in the future, possibly reaching 500 million by 2050, and one billion by 2100. In fact, America boasts the highest fertility rate; 50 percent higher than Russia, Germany, and Japan, and well above that of China. In addition, one has to add the impact of continued large-scale immigration. Twenty years ago the Soviet Union had a population considerably larger than that of the United States. But Russia's low birth and extremely high mortality rates have reduced that country's population to about 140 million. By 2050, Russia's population may be only one-third that of the United States, though Moscow plans otherwise.[44] China's one-child policy will lead to the rapid aging of its population, with the problems that inevitably follow. In relative terms the United States will maintain a youthful and dynamic population.

In the developed world immigration will become an even more crucial issue than today. The United States attracts highly skilled immigrants from all over the world, even Europe. It is estimated that in the future more than half the people moving to developing countries may go to the United States, and it is likely to remain the favorite destination for educated and skilled migrants. Concern has been expressed about the continued ability of the US to handle the large rise in its Hispanic population, from about 16 percent of the population today, to roughly 30 percent in 2050. The US has recently seen a significant political backlash against illegal immigration. But there is still a reason to be optimistic about the assimilation process when compared to

[42] Adam Segal, *Advantage: How American Innovation Can Overcome the Asian Challenge* (New York: Norton, 2011), 236–7, 247; OECD statistics, 2008.
[43] Nye, *The Future of Power*, 96, 106.
[44] Nicholas Eberstadt, "The Enigma of Russian Mortality," *Current History*, 109 (2010), 288–94.

Europe's increasing problems with its Muslim population. China and Japan are culturally resistant to diversity and are unlikely to welcome immigrants, a distinct disadvantage in our increasingly globalized world. As David Brooks argues, ". . . the United States is a universal nation . . . A nation of immigrants is more permeable than say, Chinese society."[45] The combination of large-scale immigration, excellent universities, and a huge unrestricted national market, is likely to give the United States an edge in the future.

However, in the new millennium, the United States also faces many problems—some old; some new. The educational system is struggling, particularly at the lower levels, and many international studies indicate that the US is lagging far behind the leaders. It is another matter that, at this level, America had not really done well for many decades.[46] The US legal system is carrying justice to extreme lengths, and is also extremely costly. Its health care was the most expensive in the world, delivering wonderful care to many, but poor results for large parts of the population. In some fields, such as infant mortality, the US is at the very bottom of international comparisons of industrialized countries. Even life expectancy is relatively low in the United States. Obama's health reform promises better results for most of the many uninsured, but it is very controversial and the costs uncertain. And despite the fall in serious crime over several decades, the murder rate in the US is still the highest in the developed world.[47]

Inequality has grown greatly in the United States. The share of total income going to the top 1 percent has increased from roughly 8 percent in the 1960s, to more than 20 percent today.[48] The lack of real growth in most people's income has undoubtedly contributed to increased hostility in American politics; such inequalities are even greater in China, but the two countries cannot really be compared on this point. They are just too different for that.

The polarization of the two main political parties was becoming a serious matter. Most Americans were extremely proud of their constitutional system,

---

[45] David Brooks, "The Crossroads Nation," *International Herald Tribune* (November 10, 2010), 9; Joel Kotkin, *The Next Hundred Million: America in 2050* (Penguin Press, 2010), 1–29; Amy Chua, *Day of Empire: How Hyperpowers Rise to Global Dominance—And Why They Fall* (New York: Doubleday, 2007) pays particular attention to the skills of the population, and in this context the importance of immigration for the position of the Great Powers.

[46] Ben Wildavsky, "Relax, America. Chinese Math Whizzes and Indian Engineers Aren't Stealing Your Kids' Future," *Foreign Policy* (March/April 2011), 49–52.

[47] For a discussion of some of these factors, see Fareed Zakaria, "Yes, America Is in Decline," *Time* (March 14, 2011) and David Von Drehle, "No, America Is Still No. 1," *Time* (March 14, 2011), 28–35; Nye, *The Future of Power*, 187–202. Many of the relevant statistics are found in U.S. Bureau of the Census, *Statistical Abstract of the United States: 2011* (Washington DC, 2010), Chapter 30: International Statistics.

[48] Robert C. Lieberman, "Why the Rich are Getting Richer," *Foreign Affairs* (January/February 2011), 154. 80 percent of the total increase in income from 1980 to 2005 went to the top 1 percent of the population. For this, see Chrystia Freeland, "The Super-Rich Pull Even Further Ahead," *International Herald Tribune* (January 26, 2011), 1.

but the many checks and balances could often block necessary action. Certain structural developments had made the situation worse. The shift of the South into the Republican column had unified the Democrats, who had lost most of their conservative wing. The conservative nationalist Southern input and the Republican losses in the Northeast made the Republicans too much more of a unified conservative force. The gerrymandering of the Congressional districts made for limited competition between the two parties and more competition within parties, often resulting in a weakening of moderate candidates. The gradual disappearance of national independent media, in the form of television companies and newspapers with broad support, was also important. More and more Americans could choose their own media—cable television, political radio, social media—without facing anything that contradicted their prejudices. This was not a good climate for dialogue and debate. The increased polarization under Obama could also have been influenced by the race issue; a majority of the white population voted against him for president, particularly in the South, where there were strong expressions of antagonism toward him.

Even the 1990s had been highly polarized, however, with the Republicans working for the impeachment of Bill Clinton. The highly contentious election of George W. Bush strengthened this trend. With the weakest of popular mandates he ruled, particularly in his first four years, rather firmly. The triumph of Barack Obama was then seen as a strong swing to the left—so strong in fact, that some conservatives feared for America's democratic future. This did not bode well for America. On the other hand, the picture should not be seen as too bleak. On the foreign policy side there was more domestic cooperation, as could be witnessed over Iraq and Afghanistan. When America faced its huge financial crisis in 2008–09, Congress was ultimately able to respond somewhat more concertedly. And Barack Obama was finally able to get his health reform through Congress, although that happened without Republican votes. Yet, in 2011, the Republicans were becoming increasingly skeptical of "Obama's wars"; they cost too much and gave the president too much power. The Republicans, who for so long had been tough on the Soviet Union, were now turning away from foreign interventions. Ever new budget disputes arose. With the rising debt the situation was serious indeed.

It was not impossible to see a solution to America's economic problems. As various commissions suggested, the federal budget could be balanced through a combination of drastic cuts in expenditures and new taxes. If the Americans were willing to pay for their gas at anything like a European price, this would bring substantial new income and also reduce the current account deficit and US dependence on imported oil. But the United States is not Europe. Republicans have made opposition to taxes a "theological" issue; Democrats strongly dislike cuts in the social programs they have worked so hard for. This is a recipe for gridlock, as we have already seen in California and several other states. Yet the many gridlocks of the past have ultimately been broken.

Again the question arises of how long the United States can remain Number One. Doubts about US supremacy had initially been expressed by believers in the Soviet experiment, then by academics who argued the case for Japan, and later by some who saw even the EU rising to the top. In much of the world, however, the leadership role of the United States had been taken for granted, for good or bad. Now a rapidly increasing number of observers all over the world were looking into the future and concluding that America's century—it was actually only a good half-century after 1945—might be over. And, according to recent polls, about 60 percent of Americans also believe that their country is both heading in the wrong direction and in long-term decline.[49]

No country could forever remain Number One. But the fact that America's fall has been predicted so many times before ought to stimulate further reflection. There are few, if any, laws in history. One possible such law, however, may be that no country can remain the leading country in the world forever. Sooner or later the United States will be overtaken by some other power, although previous challengers have come and gone. Whether the new leader will be China, and the transition will take place in the first half of the twenty-first century, still remains to be seen.

[49] For an optimistic interpretation of the meaning of these facts, see David Brooks, "Relax. America's Future is Exceedingly Bright," *International Herald Tribune* (April 4, 2010), 6.

2

America's Challengers

As of today, the United States is still the world's only true superpower. Militarily, politically, and culturally it is the only country with a really significant role in virtually every region of the world. All the other Great Powers are, with the exception of trade and possibly even investment, primarily regional in their approach, particularly militarily, although this regional role may of course become more global over time. And, although the United States is the only country to have such a global role, its position has increasingly become limited by the growing roles of these various regional powers. In every region of the world there is a regional power that will increasingly challenge the United States for the leading role. To mention just one example, in the diplomacy surrounding the situation in Zimbabwe, no country has more influence than South Africa. But what is perhaps most striking about Zimbabwe is how limited the influence of all outside powers is. If a country insists on going its own separate way, it has considerable freedom to do so.

In 2001 Jim O'Neill of Goldman Sachs coined the term BRIC countries for Brazil, Russia, India, and China. He wanted to focus attention on the fact that these four countries contained 25 percent of the world's landmass and 40 percent of the world's population. By 2050 their economies could eclipse the combined economies of the current richest countries in the world. He did not argue that BRIC would become a new political unit, although in 2009 the countries actually started meeting for consultations. In fact, they are all characterized by an insistence on their own national sovereignty, a fact which gives them a common perspective, but also limits the extent of their cooperation.[1] O'Neill's analysis was primarily a prognosis about the shift in world economic power in the future. Other terms have also been used: BRICS includes South Africa, BRICI Indonesia, BRICSAM both South Africa and Mexico, and BASIC encompasses Brazil, South Africa, India, and China.

---

[1] Jorge G. Castañeda, "Not Ready for Prime Time: Why Including Emerging Powers at the Helm Would Hurt Global Governance," *Foreign Affairs*, 89:5 (2010), 109–22; Stewart Patrick, "Irresponsible Stakeholders? The Difficulty of Integrating Rising Powers," *Foreign Affairs*, 89:6 (November/December 2010), 44–53.

Among the BRIC countries, Brazil is often seen as having the weakest claim to Great Power status, although it has a population that is considerably larger than that of Russia (193 million as opposed to 142), a territory that is larger than that of the United States (if you exclude Alaska), and a gross domestic product slightly greater than that of both Russia and India. Brazil has more arable land than any other country in the world, is already the world's leading producer of several different farm products, and among the leaders in minerals, water, energy, and airplanes. Its federal budget has gone from serious deficits to big reserves.

Yet, despite the considerable economic progress Brazil has made, it still has major social and economic problems to deal with. Poverty and illiteracy have been reduced, as has inequality, but much remains to be done. This certainly includes the inferior position of the black population. Violence remains high. The gap between the prosperous south and the poor north and northeast is widening. Its informal economy is still much too large. The quality of its educational system, the degree of the country's innovation, and its basic infrastructure still lag behind. Brazil's separate geographical position reduces its role in international politics; partly for this reason it plays a smaller military role than other BRIC countries. This is to some degree compensated by its rapidly increasing role in international peacekeeping, from Haiti to Lebanon. Its political influence is also primarily focused on the Western hemisphere. Even here both Mexico and Argentina are ambivalent about recognizing Brazil's regional supremacy (with the United States), as seen in the discussions about permanent membership on the UN Security Council. Brazil's efforts to play an important role even outside the Western hemisphere have met with setbacks, as could recently be seen in its joint diplomacy with Turkey over Iran.[2]

India's challenge is the most long term. In the 1990s India finally ended its decades of what was often derisively called "the Hindu rate of growth," where growth rates just barely exceeded the increase in population. Economic growth was now substantial—around 7–9 percent—far higher than in the West, although slower than in China. India had many highly educated English-speaking men and women who could participate in the global economy on the ever-growing service side, even including new medical services. The entrepreneurial spirit was considerable and innovation was growing. Its democracy was bound to be a factor of strength over time. India's population would soon overtake China's as the largest in the world. Its population was

---

[2] For a recent article discussing some of these factors, see Julia E. Sweig, "A New Global Player: Brazil's Far-Flung Agenda," *Foreign Affairs*, 89:6 (November/December 2010), 173–84. For the most recent histories of modern Brazil, see Riordan Roett, *The New Brazil* (Washington, DC: Brookings, 2010) and Larry Rother, *Brazil on the Rise: The Story of a Country Transformed* (Houndmills: Palgrave Macmillan, 2011).

young and vibrant. Culturally Bollywood was surpassing Hollywood, in volume in 1980, and somewhat later even in income. In large parts of Asia and Africa Indian films had tremendous appeal.[3]

With its growing economic base India was also investing more in defense. It had the third largest military force in the world, after China and the United States, and was upgrading this force technologically. With two aircraft carriers under construction, India was developing significant capabilities for power projection.[4] It even had a space program. Its diplomatic offensive covered both most parts of Asia and certain parts of Africa. After decades of lecturing the world about morals from a weak position of power, it now pursued a more normal diplomacy. After decades of relying on the Soviet Union, particularly for weapons and energy, after the end of the Cold War New Delhi slowly developed a closer relationship with Washington. This was capped by the 2005 agreement between the two countries about civilian nuclear cooperation, based on the indirect recognition by Washington of India's status as a nuclear military power. Indian scientists, particularly within computer science, moved freely between the United States (particularly California) and India, stimulating important scientific and economic developments in both countries. Yet there was still a considerable traditional anti-American sentiment in India.

At the same time, India's minuses were obvious. With the exception of certain pockets, it was still a poor country. Life had not really changed that much in most of India's thousands of villages. Pessimism was deep in the countryside, as the appalling number of suicides indicated. India had huge domestic needs to take care of. Its gross domestic product was less than one-third of China's. Its infrastructure—its ports, roads, and railroads—was also very inferior to China's, as any visitor to the country could quickly testify to. The differences in the successful handling of the 2008 Olympics in China and the somewhat chaotic 2010 Commonwealth Games in India proved the point. However, in the long run, some argued that the Indian model would outperform the Chinese. The two were different in that India relied more on domestic consumption compared to China's export-led growth, on services more than manufacturing, on private enterprise rather than state-led companies, and on democracy rather than one-party rule.

While India was now finally working harder to end illiteracy, the lack of effort in previous generations meant that the female literacy rate was still only

---

[3] For an interesting discussion of some of these factors, see Dilip Hiro, *After Empire: The Birth of a Multipolar World* (New York: Nation Books, 2010), 247–9. A most recent treatment of India in general is Patrick French, *India: A Portrait: An Intimate Biography of 1.2 Billion People* (London: Allen Lane, 2011).

[4] Walter C. Ladwig III, "India and Military Power Projection: Will the Land of Gandhi Become a Conventional Great Power?," *Asian Survey*, 50:6 (2010), 1162–83.

65 percent, compared to China's more than 90 percent. In many parts of the country girls were still lagging far behind in education. Women were often treated badly. The traditional problems with castes and tribes remained, despite some progress. Life expectancy was still low at 63 years for men and 64 for women, compared to 70 and 74 in China. India's main concerns related to its more traditional enemies, Pakistan and China; it had unsolved border issues with both of them, and its diplomacy focused first and foremost on these two countries. Its military forces were not really up to Great Power standards. The Indian Ocean had never really been, and certainly was not now, an "Indian" ocean; many different navies, including those of the United States and increasingly also China, operated in these waters. Although India had not collapsed, as some had long predicted, domestically it was now plagued by serious separatism in the Northeast, and Naxalite groups in central India. These problems only seemed to be getting worse.[5]

The Soviet Union had been one of two superpowers during the Cold War. After the end of the Cold War, Russia still had the world's second largest nuclear arsenal. It even tried to maintain some sort of nuclear parity with the United States, although declining resources made this equality somewhat fictitious. Its military forces had been reduced from 3.4 million to one million personnel. This was still quite substantial, though the forces lacked modern equipment and were also plagued by morale problems, as could be seen in the various military actions undertaken in the Caucasus region and in Georgia in 2008. In an effort to update its forces Russia was buying four Mistral-class amphibious assault ships from France. This would be Russia's most significant acquisition of foreign weapons since the Second World War, and thus a sign of the new times. Russia's own arms sales soon fell. Even here Russia was not fully competitive in the international market.

The Russian economy had more or less collapsed in the 1990s. The reforms undertaken by Mikhail Gorbachev had only made the situation worse. The drop in production was of a size most often seen during wars. There were reports of local starvation. Russian life expectancy fell to Third World levels, actually below 60 years for men. The population declined. This indicated a deep social crisis, with alcoholism, widespread accidents, and declining hospital standards. In 2009 life expectancy had increased to 74 years for women

---

[5] For a discussion of some of these dimensions, see Bill Emmott, *Rivals: How the Power Struggle between China, India and Japan will Shape our Next Decade* (London: Allen Lane, 2008). More general is Martin Sieff, *Shifting Superpowers: The New and Emerging Relationship between the United States, China, and India* (Washington, DC: Cato Institute, 2009). For particularly useful articles, see Akash Kapur, "Lighting the Path to Development," *International Herald Tribune* (November 5, 2010), 2; "A Bumpier but Freer Road," *The Economist* (October 2, 2010), 67–9. For a stimulating, recent account of developments in India, see Patrick French, *India: A Portrait*.

and 62 for men. Despite alcoholism undoubtedly being more prevalent among men, this huge discrepancy was still something of a mystery.[6]

The total collapse in the ruble in 1998 actually helped the economy. With a weak ruble the Russians could now gain new markets. Statistically Russia now had a GDP larger than that of Sweden, but smaller than that of the Netherlands. In the new millennium the increasing price of oil changed this situation dramatically. Exports grew considerably, but were largely limited to oil and gas, certain other raw materials and, still, weapons. In 2010–11 its GNP was slightly smaller than that of Canada and India. Many countries in Eastern, but also some in Western Europe, were quite dependent on Russian energy, but this also made Russia dependent on hard-cash earnings from the Europeans. While oil and gas had long been abundant, based on the exploitation of the sources most easily available, Moscow now had to move further out and deeper down to reach new sources. This made it more dependent on foreign technology.

The state of the Russian economy definitely resembled "Dutch disease," when an increase in income from natural resources (in this case oil and gas) pushed up the country's currency, making exports more expensive and imports cheaper. The economic crisis of 2007–09 demonstrated how vulnerable even the stronger Russian economy was. Debt was piling up. With the low price of oil, budgets had to be cut severely. It became evident that, with disappointingly few exceptions, little real transformation had taken place in the Russian economy. It had a considerable resource base and the educational system had been relatively good, although it faced many problems. But the individual attitudes that could, in the long run, transform Russia were largely missing. The state still played a dominant role; political interference was rampant; conditions for foreign investors were uncertain. Corruption remained endemic; Russia actually ranked among the most corrupt countries in the entire world.

The nationalist–authoritarian style of the Putin government may have had its political advantages at home, but limited both the Russian economy and Russia's appeal abroad, certainly in the West. Putin had proclaimed the collapse of the Soviet Union "the greatest geopolitical catastrophe of the last century." Some of the old Soviet republics still followed Russia's leadership, but others had taken up much less cooperative positions. Russia's efforts to work with China to limit the US role brought some striking rhetoric, but rather limited concrete results, with the exception of increased arms sales. China in particular was more interested in cooperating with the United States than with Russia.

---

[6] Nicholas Eberstadt, "The Enigma of Russian Mortality," *Current History*, 109 (October 2010), 288–94.

Under President Medvedev—but with Prime Minister Putin still being the dominant figure—Russia was determined to regain as much of the former Soviet position as possible. Putin might have called the collapse of the Soviet Union the greatest tragedy in the twentieth century, but the past could not be resurrected. The liberated countries in Central and Eastern Europe were determined to chart their own course. In 2010–11 there were actually signs that Moscow was trying to establish a basis of cooperation with these countries, particularly with Poland, moving away from the traditional spheres-of-influence notions that had antagonized the Europeans. The lingering problems in Chechnya and other parts of the Caucasus continued, although somewhat reduced. Apparent progress could suddenly be interrupted by spectacular terrorist actions in Moscow itself. And the war with Georgia in 2008 strained relations with that country.

Japan's future had long looked bright, as evidenced in book titles from the 1970s to the 1990s.[7] Starting with the Korean War Japanese growth rates had been very impressive indeed, year after year, decade after decade. The world had allegedly seen nothing quite like this before. Many observers thought Japan was destined to overtake the United States economically. Japan was becoming the leader in many of the most advanced sectors, such as semiconductors and computers. The Ministry of International Trade and Industry (MITI), "the pilot agency," appeared to be guiding Japan to a glorious future. Traditional capitalism was apparently losing out to a new planned economy. As US Vice President Walter Mondale asked a group of American electrical workers, "What are our kids supposed to do? Sweep up around the Japanese computers?" In the 1980s the Reagan administration tried, in various ways, to contain the Japanese threat. In a preview of the present situation with regard to China, Tokyo was encouraged to let the yen appreciate, pressure was applied to open the Japanese market, Japan was more or less forced to accept voluntary export restraints on cars, machine tools, and other goods. Nothing seemed to really work, although the United States did rebound technologically. In the 1970s Japan actually surpassed the United States in per capita income, something which is impossible for China in the foreseeable future.[8]

---

[7] The best known ones were Herman Kahn, *The Emerging Japanese Superstate: Challenge and Response* (New York: Prentice Hall, 1971); Ezra F. Vogel, *Japan as Number One: Lessons for America* (New York: Harper & Row, 1980); Chalmers Johnson, *MITI and the Japanese Miracle* (Stanford: Stanford University Press, 1982); T. R. Zengage and C. T. Ratcliffe, *The Japanese Century* (Hong Kong: Longman Group, 1988); Clyde V. Prestowitz Jr., *Trading Places: How We Allowed Japan to Take the Lead* (New York: Basic Books, 1988); Karel van Wolferen, *The Enigma of Japanese Power* (New York: Knopf, 1989); Paul Kennedy, *Preparing for the Twenty-First Century* (New York: Random House, 1993); James Fallows, *Looking at the Sun: The Rise of the New East Asian Economic and Political System* (New York: Vintage, 1994).

[8] This is the story told in Prestowitz, *Trading Places*. The Mondale quote is from Steve Lohr, "Challenge from China puts U.S. on familiar path," *International Herald Tribune* (January 24, 2011), 16.

Then, in the early 1990s, when its future appeared particularly bright to so many, Japan suffered serious setbacks. The predictions about Japan becoming Number One and overtaking the United States were silenced. MITI was doing nothing right. It turned out that the Japanese economy was not so planned after all. In 2003 the country finally seemed to be on the way out of its economic problems. This did not last long, however. The economic crisis after 2007 hit Japan more severely than almost any other major power. It had long had the second largest economy in the world, but in 2010 it was surpassed by China; and although their economies were only one-third the size of the US economy, Japan was now clearly behind the US on a per capita basis as well. The bad years had taken their toll: Japan's debt was more than twice the size of its GDP, in part the legacy of huge public works projects that had long fueled the politics of Japanese governments. No Great Power had such enormous debts as Japan. Such a large debt was only possible because it was owed almost exclusively to Japanese savers still willing to make the necessary investment, not to the outside world. Deflation made the debt even more troublesome and was also a great problem in itself.

Among Japan's more structural problems the rapidly aging population stood out. No Great Power has as old a population as Japan, and the imbalance would grow dramatically in the next decades. The country's population is expected to fall from 127 million now to 90 million in 2055. About 40 percent of the population will be over 65. The labor force will shrink greatly. This combination of rapid aging and a smaller labor force threatened the country's public finances dramatically. Old people are expensive. Japanese education was impressive in many ways, and spending on education and research was among the highest in the world. Its scientists even won a fair number of Nobel science prizes. Its leading companies were well known for their high quality. But Japan suffered from a lack of appreciation of the importance of creativity at the highest levels. In the final analysis, creativity meant going beyond the past, even rebelling against it, a concept that was difficult for most Japanese to understand.[9]

The Japanese, who clung to the popular myth of their nation as uniformly middle class, were shocked to discover that the country's poverty rate, at 15.7 percent, was close to the 17.1 percent of the United States, which allegedly represented a more ruthless capitalist model.[10] Women were discriminated

---

[9] I have vivid memories of Nobel conferences in Tokyo and Kyoto in 2002. The topic was creativity. The Japanese Nobel laureates present were almost without exception very harsh in their ciriticism of Japanese education on this point. Several of them had done much of their work in the United States. One of them, Susumu Tonegawa (Nobel Prize for medicine in 1987), had chosen to become an American citizen. See also Aurelia George Mulgan, "Why Japan Can't Lead," *World Policy Journal* (Summer 2009), 101–10.

[10] Martin Fackler, "New Openness in Japan Leads Nation to Wake Up to Poverty," *International Herald Tribune* (April 21, 2010), 1.

against in many different ways, and breaking through the "bamboo ceiling" was a slow process. As a consequence many women married late or not at all. The banking sector badly needed reform, but it came only slowly. The pride of the country—the car companies—also ran into problems. No sooner had Toyota become the world's largest car company than it had to recall large numbers of the cars produced.

Japan's economic problems were closely related to its political ones. In its heyday the Japanese model of close cooperation among politicians, bureaucrats, and businessmen had been seen as the recipe for the country's success. Resources were allegedly not wasted, as was presumably the case in more purely capitalist countries. There may possibly have been some truth to this, but over time this cooperation deteriorated into conformism and corruption. Reform became increasingly difficult, and even reformist prime minister Junichiro Koizumi achieved only rather limited results. The Liberal–Democrats, who had ruled Japan virtually without interruption for more than 50 years, were in an ever deeper crisis. Again, the opposition Democrats, who triumphed in the August 2009 elections, promised reform. Very little actually happened. In a consensus-oriented society such as Japan's it was exceedingly difficult to bring about substantial reform to deal with Japan's deep economic and political problems. Expectations of dramatic change were soon downplayed. In June 2010 the new prime minister, Yokio Hatoyama, resigned after some turbulent months in office, leaving the crisis as deep as ever. New Japanese governments now came and went in rapid order. Japan had six prime ministers in five years. It was obvious that such governments were utterly unable to deal with the many problems Japan was now facing.

In the past, when crises were sufficiently deep—such as after Japan's opening to the world in the 1850s, after 1945 and the end of the Second World War, and even, in a much more limited form, after the oil crisis of the 1970s—Japan had been able to undertake large-scale reform. Then change had been both comprehensive and swift. The problem now seems to be that while there is a definite need for change, not everybody recognizes this. There is no consensus in favor of dramatic reform. Some parts of the Japanese economy still function reasonably well; many earn a very good living. There was no total collapse as there had been in the 1850s and after 1945. While the triple catastrophe of earthquake/tsunami/nuclear reactor problems in March 2011 threatened to set Japan back considerably, at least in the short run, it was possible that the crisis would also provide the shock that could finally bring about a new reform period.

Japan still limited its defense spending to 1 percent of GNP, although this included some statistical tricks to keep it under the limit. As long as the economy had grown, this 1 percent had meant a rapid increase. With no or only modest growth, the situation changed. Japan's will to play an international role outside the economic field was also limited. Only very slowly did it agree to take on international missions and, when it reluctantly did, everything possible was done to restrict the loss of life, including undertaking few if any real military activities. Japan's lingering unwillingness to deal with the legacy of the Second World War still harmed its standing with neighbors China and South Korea. The lack of support in its own region, and the uniqueness of Japanese culture, limited Japan's popularity in many parts of the world. Its discrimination against non-Japanese groups, some of whom had lived in Japan for a very long time, did not give a good impression of the country abroad. In a world of growing global interdependence, pluralism was not something the Japanese really appreciated, much less welcomed. They remained convinced that only the Japanese could understand Japan and point the way forward. It was unclear what Japan's message to the world was. For some time now it had been hard work and material rewards, but despite the Japanese still working fairly hard, although not quite as hard as they used to, the results were not as impressive as they had been in the past. In a few areas, however, such as consumer technology, automobiles and, increasingly limited kinds of food, Japan exerted considerable influence.

THE EUROPEAN UNION

For some years after the turn of the millennium the European Union (EU) was seen by many as the most likely challenger to the United States. The book titles told the story: *The European Superpower: The New Europe and its Challenge to America; Why Europe will run the 21st Century; The United States of Europe: The New Superpower and the End of American Supremacy*.[11] In 2011 the EU had a population that was two hundred million larger than that of the United States. It also had a combined GDP slightly larger than that of the US. The EU was trying to develop approaches to international relations based on norms and rules that were attractive to states and individuals around the world. Over time the EU had managed to combine geographical widening and a deepening of content. It had gone from six to nine to twelve, and then on to twenty-five and the current twenty-seven members. Additional states were hoping to get in. European integration had started with limited economic cooperation, then evolved

---

[11] John McCormick, *The European Superpower: The New Europe and its Challenge to America* (Basingstoke: Palgrave, 1997); Charles Kupchan, *The End of the American Era: U.S. Foreign Policy and the Geopolitics of the Twenty-first Century* (New York: Knopf, 2002); Stephen Haseler, *Super-State: The New Europe and its Challenge to America* (London: Tauris, 2004); T. R. Reid, *The United States of Europe: The New Superpower and the End of American Supremacy* (Penguin, 2004); Jeremy Rifkin, *The European Dream, How Europe's Vision of the Future is Quietly Eclipsing the American Dream* (Penguin, 2004); Mark Leonard, *Why Europe will run the 21st Century* (London: Fourth Estate, 2005).

into a full-fledged single integrated market with a common currency for many of its members, and finally a Common Foreign and Security Policy (CFSP), now renamed the Common European Security and Defence Policy (CESDP).

The achievements were there for all to see. From a long-term historical perspective, against the background of two world wars with their focus on Europe, it was difficult to believe that European integration had developed as far as it had. Europe had become an ever-growing "zone of peace." Germany and France had become each other's closest partners; democracy had been consolidated in the Southern European countries with an authoritarian past; at the end of the Cold War Europe had become "whole and free" and almost all the countries of Central and Eastern Europe had been accepted as members of the EU. The requirement was that the new members become fully democratic and market-oriented. In the future, Turkey could become the EU's bridge between Europe and Asia, Christians and Muslims, although this prospect was highly controversial within the EU.

These achievements were frequently underestimated by impatient people, such as Americans and journalists. Yet the EU had obvious limitations. Its CESDP was more a proclamation of hope than a reality. The ever-growing number of members had different views on virtually any major foreign policy question, whether this was the EU's relationship with the United States or Russia, or the use of force in various parts of the world. While in the economic area the EU had gone far beyond the confines of the nation state, in the security area and in the inhabitants' own personal identification the nation state remained strong.

After the end of the Cold War defense budgets in Europe had declined in real terms, with a partial exception only for Britain and France, the two countries with the biggest military capacity. While there was a definite will to increase the EU's role in the world, the willingness to increase defense expenditures to achieve this goal was virtually non-existent. The EU countries combined actually had a larger military force than the United States, but with twenty-seven national armies, twenty-three air forces, and twenty navies— most of them still being rather national in their orientation—the EU's military strength was much smaller than that of the US. The EU did not live up to the various military objectives adopted for its force projection, and in fact had major difficulties undertaking any really significant military operations outside the borders of the member countries. The operations the EU countries did carry out were small in size and limited in scope; the bigger ones, such as in Bosnia and in Afghanistan, were undertaken in cooperation with NATO.[12]

---

[12] For a recent survey of these operations, see Muriel Asseburg and Ronja Kempin, "ESDP in Practice: Crisis Management without Strategic Planning," *Journal of International Peacekeeping*, 15 (2011), 178–99.

Still, Robert Kagan's famous phrase that "Americans are from Mars, Europeans are from Venus" is clearly overstated.[13] America itself had often been reluctant to intervene, as could be seen in anything from its traditional isolationism, including the events leading up to the outbreak of the Second World War both in Asia and in Europe, to Bill Clinton's doubts about Bosnia, Haiti, and Rwanda. Correspondingly, while the EU countries were spending less than half of what the US was spending on defense, and even less on research and development, in combination the EU countries were spending more on defense than China, Russia, India, and Brazil did together.[14] Despite the EU's many crises, the Europeans were slowly doing more, even in the way of military operations. It was very easy to underestimate the effects of the many small steps taken. (See Table 3.)

If the United States wanted military partners—and it did—the most reliable and effective ones were still to be found in Europe. And, in fairness, almost to the end the Bush administration had been opposed to EU countries carrying out military operations on their own. Everything should be done inside NATO. Even the Clinton administration had warned against "duplication, decoupling, and discrimination" within NATO.[15] At the very end, however, the Bush administration had changed its tone. When America was so hard-pressed it was obviously a good idea for Europe to do more. The Obama administration felt the same to the extent that it was increasingly frustrated by the slow pace of the EU's efforts to strengthen its foreign policy role. There was little or no risk that the EU would gang up on the United States anyway. Too many members were too close to, and too dependent on, Washington for that to happen. In 2009 France even rejoined NATO's integrated military structure. However, in Libya in the spring of 2011, France and Britain took the lead in going to war against Gaddafi's regime in support of the beleaguered Libyan opposition. The US, so different from in previous crises, was determined to remain in the background. Germany and many other EU countries stayed out of the war. In September, Gaddafi had to give up power. It was far from clear what policies the new government would pursue.

Time and again the EU countries would stress the value of non-military means. Most important, inside Europe, the war-torn continent, the EU represented an ever-widening zone of peace. War among the member countries was unimaginable. This was something dramatically new in Europe's history.

[13] Robert Kagan, *Of Paradise and Power: America and Europe in the New World Order* (New York: Vintage, 2004).
[14] The positive version of the EU's development is found in Andrew Moravcsik, "Europe, the Second Superpower," *Current History*, 109 (March 2010), 91–8. See also Jolyon Howorth, *Security and defense policy in the European Union* (Basingstoke: Palgrave, 2007).
[15] For the United States and European integration, see my *"Empire" by Integration: The United States and European Integration, 1945–1997* (Oxford: Oxford University Press, 1998). For the treatment of the Clinton administration, see 17–25.

Table 3. The 15 countries with the highest military expenditure in 2010
Spending figures are in US$, at current prices and exchange rates. Countries are ranked according to military spending calculated using market exchange rates (MEW). Figures for military spending calculated using purchasing power parity (PPP) exchange rates are also given.

Rank	Country	Spending ($ b., MER)	Change, 2001–10 (%)	Share of GDP (%, estimate)[a]	WorldShare (%)	Spending ($ b., PPP)[b]
1	United States	698	81.3	4.8	43	698
2	China	[119]	189	[2.1]	[7.3]	[210]
3	United Kingdom	59.6	21.9	2.7	3.7	57.6
4	France	59.3	3.3	2.3	3.6	49.8
5	Russia	[58.7]	82.4	[4.0]	[3.6]	[88.2]
Subtotal top 5		995			61	
6	Japan	54.5	−1.7	1.0	3.3	43.6
7	Saudi Arabia[c]	45.2	63.0	10.4	2.8	64.6
8	Germany	[45.2]	−2.7	[1.3]	[2.8]	[40.0]
9	Indian	41.3	54.3	2.7	2.5	116
10	Italy	37.0	−5.8	[1.8]	[2.3]	[32.2]
Subtotal top 10		1218			75	
11	Brazil	33.5	29.6	1.6	2.1	36.2
12	South Korea	27.6	45.2	2.8	1.7	40.8
13	Australia	24.0	48.9	2.0	1.5	17.3
14	Canada	[22.8]	51.8	[1.5]	[1.4]	[19.4]
15	Turkey	[17.5]	−12.2	[2.4]	[1.1]	[23.9]
Subtotal top 15		1344			82	
World		1630	50.3	2.6	100	

[] = estimated figure; GDP = gross domestic product.
[a]The figures for national military expenditure as a share of GDP are based on estimates fro 2010 GDP from the IMF *World Economic Outlook*, October 2010.
[b]The figures for military expenditure at PPP exchange rates are estimates based on the ratio of PPP to MER-based GDP projections for 2010 implicit in the International Monetary Fund's *World Economic Outlook*. Thus, military expenditure figures at MER rates have been multiplied by the same ratio to obtain the PPP estimates.
[c]The figures for Saudi Arabia include expenditure on public order and safety and might be slight overestimates.
Source: SIPRI Yearbook, 2011 (Oxford: Oxford University Press, 2011), 183.

By holding out prospects for membership the EU could exert major influence on prospective new members. The problem was getting new members to live up to their obligations after they had joined. Thus, there was a widespread impression in many EU countries that Rumania and Bulgaria, in particular, had been admitted too early. With the EU now taking in few new members this instrument was also losing its force.

Many saw the EU as an increasingly separate pole in international relations, stressing international cooperation and law, the limits of national sovereignty, nonproliferation, trade liberalization, social justice, and environmental action. This list was also clearly meant to differentiate Europe from the United States. There was indeed support in Europe, and elsewhere, for such notions. But the trouble was that the most rapidly rising new states were even more nationalistic and state-centered than the United States; they normally reacted against any form of intervention from the outside, whether it fell under "the responsibility to protect" or not; they were in favor of building up their own defenses—for some of them this even included nuclear weapons; and they tended to downplay their own contributions to alleviating climate concerns, or promoting further trade liberalization. This certainly applied to China and India, and largely even to South Africa and Brazil.[16] None of the BRIC countries supported Western military action against Libya in the spring of 2011.

The EU countries combined gave much more development assistance than did the United States; they also contributed significant forces to peacekeeping after wars. Some talked about a division of labor, with the US doing most of the fighting and the EU most of the reconstruction after a war. There was a certain trend in this direction, but no clear-cut division was possible. With so few resources for non-territorial defense, and with very limited military integration, Europe's relative role was bound to be limited. It would also mean the continued dependence of most EU countries on the United States. If the EU were to develop into a new superpower, it could not continue to rely on the United States even for its own protection, as was evident in the European desire to continue the conventional American, and even nuclear, presence in Europe, although in a much reduced form compared to the Cold War decades.

The EU also had problems with its engine. Franco–German cooperation had been at the heart of Europe's integration. The duo had provided the necessary leadership on most occasions when integration was advanced. Giscard d'Estaing and Helmut Schmidt, François Mitterrand and Helmut Kohl—even Jacques Chirac and Gerhard Schröder—had worked closely together, despite their differences. Nicolas Sarkozy and Angela Merkel struggled more;[17] their personalities simply clashed, and the financial crisis exposed major differences in French and German economic thinking. The chaos on the European side over the Iraq War in 2003, and the collapse of the proposed European Constitutional treaty a few years later, illustrated that Franco–German leadership could take the EU only so far. In fact, a certain

---

[16] Castañeda, "Not Ready for Prime Time," 109–22.
[17] For an analysis of the Sarkozy–Merkel relationship, see Steven Erlanger, "The Odd Couple at Europe's Helm," *International Herald Tribune* (January 15–16, 2011), 1, 4.

dissatisfaction in other EU countries with this self-appointed Franco–German leadership added to the difficulties.

On the other hand, it was difficult to see what the alternative was. With its negative attitude to European political integration and to the euro, Britain had to a large extent tied its own hands. Italian, Spanish, and Polish claims to leadership made the situation even more unresolved. This emphasis on the member states further illustrated the limited competence of the EU Commission and the more supranational bodies outside the traditional economic area, although the European Parliament steadily increased its powers. The ultimate adoption of the Lisbon Treaty in 2009, after a second referendum in Ireland, finally gave the EU a president and a foreign minister, although the official title of the latter was the High Representative for Foreign and Security Policy. But both the selection process and the individuals chosen underlined the fact that the leading powers in the EU were not really going to yield to Brussels; they preferred to keep control of security matters in their own capitals, which was bound to limit the role of the EU. The number of top politicians who abandoned a national career for Brussels was small, particularly from the larger member countries.

The introduction of the euro had apparently gone remarkably well. It soon became clear, however, that problems were emerging, although they were offset by the general economic growth. Already debt-ridden countries in the South could continue borrowing because of the low interest rate they got in joining the euro. Even Germany and France broke the rules of the EU's Stability and Growth Pact to keep deficits down. In fighting the economic recession of 2008–11, most of the initiative remained with the nation states. Only slowly did the EU come to play a larger role. Most of the early crisis packages to stimulate demand and avoid bankruptcy were worked out in the national capitals, with the EU only augmenting and coordinating these.

With the huge new spending added to the already substantial debt problems of some EU countries, particularly Greece, Ireland, and Portugal, crises arose. The EU members had great difficulties coming up with the necessary assistance for the most threatened countries. And while the creditors deliberated— with Germany definitely in the lead, working with France, and the European Central Bank (ECB) playing an important role—the necessary economic packages to the debtors became even larger. The situation appeared to require new levels of EU solidarity, and strengthened powers for the authorities in Brussels, to prevent similar situations happening again. Bigger loans were needed; few yet talked about transferring tax money. A European Financial Stability Facility (EFSF) was set up. If the strong Northern countries did not support the weak Southern ones (and Ireland), the whole EU structure could be in trouble. But why should Germans support Greeks who retired at an earlier age than they did themselves (though the actual difference in the retirement age was smaller than most Germans thought)? Taxpayers in

Germany were strongly opposed to bailing out governments in the South that had shown such limited interest in efficient tax collection. Spain and Italy feared that the contagion would spread to them, as it actually did. In Greece there was a great deal of opposition to the tough measures that had to be undertaken in return for the loans. It was debatable whether they would actually take the recommended medicine. With a Greek economy in recession, the loans appeared unmanageable.[18]

In this situation, the EU either needed to move forward to new levels of coordination, or the achievements of the past—in the form of the euro—were threatened. That left Germany and the other creditors little choice. Germany and the ECB again and again had to take the lead, despite their natural caution, although there were certainly differences between the two; they were some-times backed by an impatient France, with the EU Commission largely on the outside. Berlin insisted that, in return, the debtors become more "German" in their economic policies. Deficits had to be cut, state property sold off, wage indexation ended, and the retirement age increased. Many members of the EU responded negatively to these far-reaching recommendations, and compro-mises had to be worked out.[19] These developments also created tension between those members of the EU that had adopted the euro and who made most of the financial decisions, and those left on the outside.

The situation in North Africa in early 2011 presented similar challenges to the EU. Thousands and thousands of refugees fled the countries in turmoil. Many of these individuals came to an Italy that was not in any way prepared to handle such large numbers. Many continued on to France. Again, the dilemma was the same. Either the EU had to handle the issue with some form of solidarity, or the whole 1985 Schengen Agreement for passport-free move-ment among the twenty-five participating countries could be threatened.

In *A Community of Europeans? Transnational Identities and Public Spheres*, Thomas Risse argued that the EU had indeed developed a sense of community. "More than 50 percent of European citizens hold . . . Europeanized national identities."[20] He also contended that a "common communicative space" was developing. European media were discussing the same issues at the same time in a common frame of reference. As was clear from Risse's own work, however, the importance of these findings could easily be overstated. For most of the 50 percent their own national identity came first; the European one a clear second. Forty percent held exclusively national identities. In some

---

[18] Landon Thomas Jr., "Market Fears Lead Spain and Italy to Assail Greece," *International Herald Tribune* (May 24, 2011), 1, 16.

[19] Paul Krugman, "The Triumph and Tragedy of the Euro," *International Herald Tribune* (January 14, 2011), 6, 8; Paul Taylor, "Berlin Flexes Muscles, and E.U. Chafes," *International Herald Tribune* (February 22, 2011), 21.

[20] Thomas Risse, *A Community of Europeans? Transnational Identities and Public Spheres* (Ithaca: Cornell University Press, 2010), 5.

EU countries, led by Britain, they constituted a definite majority. As has been argued, this was indeed a European "non-emotional identity," as opposed to the emotional identity attached to the nation states.[21] On the issue of communicative space it remained true that Europe had no common language, although English was making good progress in this respect. Media primarily had a national orientation. It may be true that certain quality papers were discussing the same European issues, but this fact did not really apply to television and tabloids. The attempt in the 1990s to establish a truly European newspaper, *The European*, had failed miserably. Sales dwindled and losses increased. With such a limited sense of community, it remained difficult to see how the EU could make further substantial progress toward integration.

The EU was finding it difficult to go beyond what it had already achieved in terms of integration. While, over several decades, it had been able to combine geographical widening with a deepening content, this was becoming increasingly difficult with twenty-seven members. The members were just too many and too different. Virtually nobody was prepared to make the big jump to a federalist structure. Helmut Kohl had, in a way, been the last leading politician to even sketch that goal.

The EU had to move on if it was going to solve the many substantial problems it faced. The nation states had insisted on keeping control over taxes and social benefits. Although, in theory, the EU had an integrated labor market, in practice only a very small segment of workers moved from one country to another. Some observers, particularly in the US, had argued that monetary union under such circumstances was almost impossible. In times of economic growth these structural problems were hardly noticed. With the recession they became urgent. The spirit of federalism was now virtually dead in Germany, but it was felt to be impossible to give up the euro. This meant that integration had to be continued in the form of additional financial contributions and new legislation to introduce some European oversight of national economies and avoid similar crises in the future.

To a lesser extent the same logic applied to the foreign and security policy. With ever new crises coming up the EU had to continue to respond; otherwise it would be giving up the effort to establish joint policies. But the intervention in Libya in March 2011 showed an EU in great disarray. France and Britain were now the two activists; Germany wanted no military role whatsoever, and even abstained at the UN Security Council, along with Russia and China, in giving the intervention force a mandate. Among the smaller EU countries, some supported the intervention, others did not. Britain and France were the two countries that counted militarily; they were used to intervening. The economic recession also stimulated further integration between the two

---

[21] Montserrat Guibernau, "The Birth of a United Europe: On Why the EU has Generated a 'Non-Emotional' Identity," *Nations and Nationalism*, 17:2 (2011), 302–15.

countries. Thus, in November 2010, financially hard-pressed Britain (under its new Conservative–Liberal government) and France launched ambitious plans for comprehensive military cooperation, including shared use of aircraft carriers and a joint expeditionary force.[22] However, this was more cooperation between the two most important military powers in the EU, than European integration as such. It also remained unclear exactly how far this cooperation would actually go. In the past, French–British military cooperation would have meant a major step forward for the EU; now, however, Germany was becoming increasingly skeptical of any such use of force.

There was little doubt that optimism concerning the EU's prospects was markedly declining. The emphasis was now definitely on the problems of the EU, not on its possibilities. Would some countries simply have to abandon the euro? There was little will to undertake further constitutional reform, although the various economic measures would sooner or later require such changes. Charles Kupchan, who had been among the first observers to raise the EU to potential superpower status, now predicted that "The European Union is dying—not a dramatic or sudden death, but one so slow and steady that we may look across the Atlantic one day soon and realize that the project of European integration that we've taken for granted over the past half-century is no more." Others saw the EU becoming and behaving as a small power in foreign policy, not exerting, and not really expecting to have, much influence on the world's basic security questions.[23]

Thus, the EU, as always, represented a work in progress. It would never reach the levels of integration of the United States. The European nation states had existed for hundreds of years; they were still the primary unit in the governing of the continent. In 1998, Jacques Chirac had stated that "we (are) not in the process of building the United States of Europe, but the united Europe of States."

There was still considerable truth to the saying that the EU was "an economic giant, but a political and military dwarf." It was also often treated as such by Russia and China, and even by the United States. Even internal EU documents stressed that the EU could only deal with its strategic partners "when the EU becomes a 'strategic' actor itself, i.e. develops a true strategic

---

[22] John F. Burns, "Britain and France Unite on Military Roles," *International Herald Tribune* (November 3, 2010), 1, 3; Ben Jones, *Franco–British Military Cooperation: A New Engine for European Defence?* (European Union Institute for Security Studies: Occasional Paper, February 2011).
[23] Charles Kupchan, "As Nationalism Rises, Will the European Union Fail?," *Washington Post* (August 29, 2010); Asle Toje, *The European Union as a Small Power: After the Post-Cold War* (Basingstoke: Palgrave, 2010). For a remarkable sign of continued optimism, see Steven Hill, *Europe's Promise: Why the European Way is the Best Hope in an Insecure Age* (Berkeley: University of California Press, 2010).

culture and global policies."[24] Many questioned the EU's lack of focus. And it turned out that in 2010 EU foreign ministers had only discussed China's international position once in the last four years. Under such circumstances, there was little reason for China to take the EU particularly seriously on the foreign policy front, as opposed to the economic side.[25] Instead of Germany working to give the EU a seat on the UN Security Council, Berlin pressed for a seat of its own; so the EU would be represented by three national countries.

But the EU had made remarkable progress in terms of integration. One step back most often led to two steps forward. From a historical perspective it was very impressive indeed that European countries had been able to reach such a level of integration. The EU had integrated Western Europe, helped consolidate democracy in Southern Europe, and made Europe whole and free through the inclusion of Central and Eastern Europe. Certain mechanisms left it virtually no alternative to continuing integration; otherwise there might be a partial collapse. And, after the United States, the EU countries still represented the second most powerful unit in the world, but definitely not the most dynamic one.

CHINA'S FUTURE

So, in 2011, China was undoubtedly perceived as the main challenger to the United States. China had much going for it. Since the change in economic policy started in 1978, China had experienced economic growth not seen before in history. The new policy had surpassed the wildest expectations and the most optimistic of Five-Year Plans. Deng Xiaoping had stressed the policy's improvisational nature—China would "cross the river by feeling for stones." His program was based on "the four modernizations" (industry, agriculture, science and technology, and national defense.) The possible "fifth modernization" (of the political system) was left out. Deng's overall guideline was announced in his famous "24-character statement": "Observe carefully; secure our position; cope with affairs calmly; hide our capacity and bide our time; be good at maintaining a low profile; and never claim leadership."[26] For decades these guidelines would be followed.

---

[24] Paper prepared for the European Council, Brussels, September 16, 2010.
[25] Stephen Castle, "Aiming to Amplify E.U.'s Global Voice," *International Herald Tribune*, (September 16, 2010), 4. See also Jonathan Holslag, "The Elusive Axis: Assessing the EU–China Strategic Partnership," *Journal of Common Market Studies*, 49:2 (2011), 293–313.
[26] Chen Jian, "China's Prolonged Rise: Legitimacy Challenges and Dilemmas in the Reform and Opening-Up Era," in Geir Lundestad, *International Relations Since the End of the Cold War* (forthcoming).

Despite definite doubts about the details of official Chinese statistics, there could be no question about the exceptional nature of this growth. On a purchasing power parity (PPP) basis China's growth was even more sensational. Although PPP is useful in measuring local living standards, particularly in less developed countries, it is generally seen to make less sense in comparisons of international economies. It is also difficult to establish the many numbers needed to make meaningful PPP comparisons. Most statistics are therefore based on current exchange rates. This method offers better indications of a country's international purchasing power and relative economic strength. The US position was roughly the same under both sets of calculations. In addition, many observers argued that China's currency was undervalued by anywhere from 15 to 40 percent. If this were to be corrected, its GDP would increase correspondingly, without the country's real living standards being directly affected at all. (See Tables 4 and 5.)

Year after year, decade after decade, China's GDP appeared to grow by 10 percent or more. In 2007 the size of China's economy surpassed that of Germany and became the third largest in the world. In 2009 China also surpassed Germany as the world's biggest exporter. It was the second biggest importer after the United States, and was overtaking the US as the world's leading manufacturer and producer of climate gases. Then, in the second quarter of 2010, China overtook Japan as the second largest economy in the world.

As with Japan and the EU, the book titles told it all: *The New Asian Hemisphere: The Irresistible Shift of Global Power to the East; When China Rules the World: The Rise of the Middle Kingdom and the End of the Western World; The Beijing Consensus: How China's Authoritarian Model Will Dominate the Twenty-First Century.*[27] Growth curves were extended into the future, and depending on exactly what numbers you put in, China's GDP would surpass that of the United States sometime in the 2020s, if not earlier. If the Chinese and American economies continued to grow at the same pace as over the past 10 years (10.5 and 1.7 percent respectively), and nothing else changed, China's GDP would overtake America's in 2022.[28] With virtually no growth in the US, this date was constantly being brought forward, first to 2019, then even to 2016. According

---

[27] Kishore Mahbubani, *The New Asian Hemisphere: The Irresistible Shift of Global Power to the East* (New York: Public Affairs, 2008); Martin Jacques, *When China Rules the World: The Rise of the Middle Kingdom and the End of the Western World* (London: Allen Lane, 2009); Stefan Halper, *The Beijing Consensus: How China's Authoritarian Model Will Dominate the Twenty-First Century* (New York: Basic Books, 2010). See also Ted C. Fishman, *China Inc.: How the Rise of the Next Superpower Challenges America and the World* (New York: Scribner, 2005). For a useful survey of the new literature about China, see Stein Tønnesson, "Hvor går Kina?" ["Where is China headed?"], unpublished manuscript, 2010.

[28] "The World's Biggest Economy: Dating Game," *The Economist* (December 18, 2010), 129.

Table 4. List of countries by GDP (Nominal)

2010 List by the International Monetary Fund			2010 List by the World Bank			2010 List by the CIA World Factbook		
Rank	Country	GDP (millions of US$)	Rank	Country	GDP (millions of US$)	Rank	Country	GDP (millions of US$)
—	*World*	62,911,253	—	*World*	63,048,823	—	*World*	63,170,000
—	European Union	16,242,256	1	United States	14,582,400	—	European Union	16,070,000
1	United States	14,526,550	—	*Eurozone*	12,174,523	1	United States	14,660,000
2	People's Republic of China	5,878,257	2	People's Republic of China	5,878,629	2	People's Republic of China	5,878,000
3	Japan	5,458,797	3	Japan	5,497,813	3	Japan	5,459,000
4	Germany	3,286,451	4	Germany	3,309,669	4	Germany	3,316,000
5	France	2,562,742	5	France	2,560,002	5	France	2,583,000
6	United Kingdom	2,250,209	6	United Kingdom	2,246,079	6	United Kingdom	2,247,000
7	Brazil	2,090,314	7	Brazil	2,087,890	7	Brazil	2,090,000
8	Italy	2,055,114	8	Italy	2,051,412	8	Italy	2,055,000
9	India	1,631,970	9	India	1,729,010	9	Canada	1,574,000
10	Canada	1,577,040	10	Canada	1,574,052	10	India	1,538,000
11	Russia	1,479,825	11	Russia	1,479,819	11	Russia	1,465,000
12	Spain	1,409,946	12	Spain	1,407,405	12	Spain	1,410,000
13	Australia	1,237,363	13	Mexico	1,039,662	13	Australia	1,236,000
14	Mexico	1,034,308	14	South Korea	1,014,483	14	Mexico	1,039,000
15	South Korea	1,014,482	15	Australia	924,843	15	South Korea	1,007,300

Source: Wikipedia.

to one PPP estimate, China's GDP had actually surpassed that of the United States in 2010.[29]

This transfer of leadership was far from certain, however, as China's GDP today, in market exchange terms, is still only 40 percent that of the US. And it should be remembered that if and when China's GDP does surpass that of the US, China will still be a relatively poor country. In fact, with a population more than four times that of the United States, per capita income would be only one-fourth of what it would be in the US. Despite the tremendous progress made, China today is still relatively poor. On a list of countries ranked by GDP per capita, China comes in at around number 90, roughly at the same level as

[29] Yao Yang, "When Will China's Economy Overtake America's?," Yao Yang Project Syndicate (June 2, 2011); "Economics Focus: The Celestial Economy," *The Economist* (September 10, 2011), 78.

Table 5. GDP (PPP) per capita list

GDP (PPP) per capita list (in international dollars)							
Country	2011	2012	2013	2014	2015	2016	Estimate as of
Qatar	102.275.695	107.840.919	109.172.175	110.865.145	113.053.080	115.533.346	April 2011
Luxembourg	83.437.850	85.835.213	88.285.561	90.982.815	93.829.844	96.873.899	April 2011
Singapore	59.123.686	61.527.772	63.953.851	66.570.257	69.310.519	72.178.819	April 2011
Norway	53.738.052	55.398.065	56.945.625	58.606.295	60.406.351	62.317.756	April 2011
Brunei Darussalam	49.719.344	50.515.519	51.108.742	52.542.689	53.602.662	55.089.095	April 2011
United Arab Emirates	49.499.516	50.549.584	51.712.810	53.134.919	54.776.768	56.516.200	April 2011
United States	48.665.805	50.273.201	51.810.462	53.499.313	55.361.154	57.319.743	April 2011
Hong Kong	48.347.105	50.659.520	53.045.273	55.648.606	58.535.595	61.667.986	April 2011
Switzerland	42.857.726	43.966.293	45.061.844	46.272.467	47.615.897	49.051.800	April 2011
Netherlands	41.691.100	42.777.930	43.909.170	45.194.994	46.635.714	48.213.086	April 2011
Austria	40.978.714	42.412.512	43.817.378	45.343.312	46.970.587	48.595.444	April 2011
Australia	40.816.409	42.291.416	43.801.370	45.327.989	46.976.420	48.669.205	April 2011
Canada	39.981.631	40.978.464	41.913.546	42.837.552	43.919.849	45.108.041	April 2011
Sweden	39.847.085	41.694.237	43.583.032	45.662.643	47.915.411	50.318.583	April 2011
Kuwait	39.497.707	41.276.659	42.441.647	44.483.539	46.756.096	49.204.236	April 2011
Ireland	39.311.805	40.746.364	41.953.253	43.529.869	45.420.589	47.474.913	April 2011
Denmark	37.585.034	38.778.631	40.002.546	41.323.287	42.729.769	44.220.681	April 2011
Iceland	37.504.027	38.708.686	39.861.636	41.329.650	43.096.711	44.946.583	April 2011
Germany	37.428.520	38.815.316	40.133.746	41.530.741	42.917.765	44.364.826	April 2011
Taiwan	37.208.709	39.318.388	41.476.248	43.792.685	46.316.511	49.023.356	April 2011
Belgium	36.834.391	37.777.865	38.673.637	39.687.526	40.881.028	42.065.232	April 2011
Finland	35.885.066	37.100.465	38.219.212	39.447.916	40.771.298	42.154.319	April 2011
United Kingdom	35.645.803	36.731.807	37.879.128	39.134.921	40.545.945	40.058.019	April 2011
France	34.858.085	35.804.821	36.821.070	37.962.812	39.222.562	40.567.714	April 2011
Japan	34.645.985	35.907.131	37.054.953	38.254.611	39.499.749	40.806.315	April 2011
South korea	31.410.470	33.072.463	34.784.891	36.612.498	38.616.003	40.777.069	April 2011
Israel	30.347.324	31.268.100	32.172.527	33.187.233	34.189.236	35.202.462	April 2011
Spain	30.233.772	31.067.864	31.954.516	32.978.989	34.073.360	35.213.742	April 2011
Italy	29.888.874	30.563.775	31.253.002	32.032.744	32.917.742	33.884.253	April 2011
Russia	16.840.802	17.904.352	18.986.139	20.152.217	21.385.706	22.717.455	April 2011
Brazil	11.767.155	12.320.792	12.892.226	13.527.702	14.328.543	15.193.354	April 2011
China	8.288.818	9.157.407	10.103.254	11.172.768	12.374.793	13.729.025	April 2011
Bosnia and Herzegovina	8.063.111	8.517.368	9.021.885	9.598.156	10.229.919	10.967.101	April 2011
Ecuador	7.995.004	8.211.359	8.401.185	8.603.333	8.820.318	9.052.643	April 2011

Source: Wikipedia.

Ecuador, Bosnia and Herzegovina, and Albania, even in PPP terms. Although there are a few countries in the world with a higher GDP per person than the United States—such as Qatar, Luxembourg, Singapore, Norway, and Brunei—none of them counts in the Great Power game.

The economic crisis of 2007–10 promised to speed up China's rise considerably. Growth fell noticeably, but only down to 6–8 percent for a year or two.

The government worked out substantial infrastructure packages to pick up the pace again, and China was soon back to its normal rapid rate. In the United States there was virtually no growth at all until well into 2011. The US was also becoming increasingly dependent on China to finance its two huge deficits, in the federal budget and in its current accounts. China's growth had been facilitated by the open American market. In turn, its huge surplus financed huge US deficits. China's savings paid for America's debts. As long as America's growth had been strong, the system worked reasonably well; with limited growth, America had to work harder to attract China's money. China was now suggesting that the end of the dollar's domination might be approaching. There could be no doubt about the basic direction: China was rapidly becoming a key economic player.

Many other factors also worked in China's favor. Its population, at more than 1.3 billion, was still the largest in the world, although it would soon be surpassed by that of India. McKinsey projected that by 2030 there will be 221 cities in China with a population over one million; there are ten such cities in the United States today.[30] Over a 50-year period, life expectancy had increased from the 40s to the 70s. The population is expected to peak at around 1.4 billion, but it will then decline due to the one-child policy. In fact, from a long-term perspective, the rapidly aging Chinese population will not be conducive to economic growth. The prospects are that China is likely to be one of the few countries where the population becomes old before it becomes rich; it will turn from a relatively young country to an old one. In 25 years' time there will be only three workers to each retired person; with a retirement age of 60 (and in many cases even lower), this is bound to present problems, despite pensions being small, and in many cases non-existent, which will of course become a problem in itself. The number of people over 65 will rise to 300 million by 2050—a threefold increase. The preference for boys meant that the current ratio between male and female babies is 119 to 100; there are 32 million more males under the age of 20. This is bound to result in a great deal of frustration.[31]

Geographically, China's location is favorable as the country has easy access to important regions such as Central and South (East) Asia, as well as the Pacific. It was both a land power and a sea power, with the advantages that brought to the country.[32] From about 1500 BC, China had a centralized, rather unified culture, so unlike the diversity of India. For centuries it also had a

---

[30] *Foreign Policy* (September/October 2010), 1.

[31] Wang Feng and Mara Hvistendahl, "China's Population Destiny: The Looming Crisis," *Current History*, 109 (September 2010), 244–51; Ted C. Fishman, "Graying Nations, Shifting Power," *International Herald Tribune* (October 16–17, 2010), 10, 12; Torbjørn Peterson, "For mange eldre kinesere" ["Too Many Old Chinese"], *Aftenposten* (September 28, 2010), 16.

[32] Robert D. Kaplan, "The Geography of Chinese Power," *Foreign Affairs* (May/June 2010), 22–41.

highly developed culture, in many ways leading the world in inventions and sophistication, although signs of decline could be seen as early as the end of the Ming dynasty (1368–1644), and then multiplying under the Qing or Manchu dynasties (1644–1912). More than 90 percent of the population is Han Chinese. Although Han is sometimes rather broadly interpreted, this fact still clearly strengthens the unity of the country.

After the turbulence of the 1970s, and even 1989, China's political leadership now appears quite unified. The torch of leadership was peacefully passed from one generation to the next. Rapid economic growth, and the stress on Chinese nationalism and culture, had made the Chinese rather proud of their country's achievements. The Communist Party emphasized its ability to reform itself from within, taking into account the interests of ever wider groups of the people, including even those of leading business people.[33] The Olympics in Beijing in 2008, and the World Expo in Shanghai in 2010, represented great triumphs. Historically, the Chinese were used to seeing themselves as the center of the universe—as the leaders in East Asia (if not the world), with various vassals paying different forms of tribute to the ruler in Beijing, and with relationships varying from total subjugation to equality. "Barbarian" superiority did not come naturally to the Chinese;[34] now China seemed to be regaining its traditional historic role.

China was also increasing its defense budget rapidly. While the US defense budget had increased by 81.3 percent from 2001 to 2010, the Chinese budget had increased by 189 percent, faster than any other Great Power. China had the world's second largest defense budget. It grew even more rapidly than the country's economy. China had a small, but modern, nuclear force. It had demonstrated its capacity to shoot down satellites in space. And its ambitious space program aimed to put a man on the moon. China was developing a jet fighter with stealth technology, though doubts were expressed in the US about exactly how "stealthy" this technology actually was. Its navy was beginning to appear further and further out in the Pacific, even in waters it had not been in before, at least not for many centuries and in such numbers. China was trying, although with considerable difficulty, to develop a modern aircraft carrier. It launched its first one in 2011. Its armed forces were the largest in the world, with around two million troops, although they were being reduced and modernized. While the role of its armed forces had long been to defend "Chinese territory," it was now, more broadly, to protect "Chinese interests." China took part in UN-led operations.

---

[33] Heike Holbig and Bruce Gilley, "Reclaiming Legitimacy in China," *Politics and Policy*, 38:3 (June 2010), 395–422.
[34] Giovanni Andornino, "The Nature and Linkages of China's Tributary System under the Ming and Qing Dynasties," Working Papers of the Global Economic History Network (GEHN), 21/06 (March 2006), 15.

Again, there was talk of China surpassing the United States in defense spending in a few decades' time, but the military gap was much larger in America's favor than the economic one. After all, China was still spending only about 2 percent of GNP on defense, more than the European average, but less than Britain and France, at least until now, and quite a bit less than the US at around 4–5 percent. China was actually spending only one-sixth of what the US was spending on defense. Its nuclear force was probably too small to survive an American first strike. The United States had 11 aircraft carrier groups and many other forms of offensive power. It could project its force virtually anywhere in the world. As Secretary of Defense, Robert Gates stated in May 2010 when concern was expressed about the state of the US Navy: its displacement exceeds "at least the next 13 navies in the world combined, of which 11 are our allies or partners."[35]

While the United States had allies and bases all over the world, China had few, if any, traditional allies and true bases abroad—though it was developing port facilities in a few countries such as Pakistan, Burma, and Sri Lanka. China did not really have the capabilities for global power projection, at least not yet, as was seen in the considerable problems it had developing its first aircraft carrier, and its lack of long-range bombers. In August 2010 even the Pentagon concluded that "China's ability to sustain military power at a distance, today, remains limited."[36] It was, however, an increasingly important regional actor, also militarily. And the Pacific, particularly the Western part, could no longer simply be considered an American lake.

Commercially, and in part diplomatically—but not militarily—China was becoming an active player virtually all over the world. Its rapidly expanding economy required immense resources, particularly energy, though China had vast coal and even oil reserves. Still, this was not in any way enough, and even factories had to close due to the lack of energy. China had been an important oil exporter; it started importing oil in 1993, and its production now represents less than half of its consumption. Energy needs dictated much of China's foreign policy. Demand for energy in China is expected to rise by 75 percent by 2035, and China will then account for 22 percent of world demand for energy, up from 17 percent currently.[37] It imported more oil from the Middle East than did the United States.

China's huge current accounts surplus was invested in a rapidly increasing number of countries all over the world. Even in Europe China was becoming

---

[35] Robert Gates, speech given to the Navy League on May 3, 2010, at National Harbor, Maryland.

[36] *SIPRI Yearbook, 2010*, (Oxford: Oxford University Press, 2010), particularly 201–7. The quotation is from CNN.com, August 18, 2010.

[37] Julia Werdigier, "China Will Lead Surge in Energy Demand," *International Herald Tribune* (November 10, 2010), 19; Chris V. Nicholson, "A Globe-Trotting China Scouts Oil Deals," *International Herald Tribune* (March 15, 2011), 20.

an important economic actor in virtually all countries, from Greece to Iceland. Beijing's stress on non-intervention in domestic affairs made it popular, not only among relative outcasts such as North Korea, Iran, Burma, Zimbabwe, Sudan, Venezuela, and others, but also in many other countries in Africa, Asia, and Latin America. While, traditionally, China played no significant role in Latin America, it is now Brazil and Chile's largest trade partner, although it is still far behind the US in total trade and investment in Latin America. Even in Antarctica China's new engagement showed.[38] Its rapid economic growth made it an attractive model in the many countries that longed for better living conditions. For some Third World leaders the control exerted by the Party was also a positive feature of China's growth model.

Still, in 2009, Chinese companies invested 48 billion dollars overseas, around 1 percent of China's GNP; US companies, on the other hand, invested 340 billion dollars, around 2.4 percent of its GNP. In total accumulated foreign direct investment (FDI) there was still no comparison: 211 billion dollars for China, as opposed to 3.245 trillion for the US.[39] Even Mao's China had become involved in the foreign aid business in the 1960s, particularly in Africa. Now China was becoming a much more important actor in this field. Its rapidly growing foreign aid was perceived quite positively, but it was still quite small compared to Western aid. Thus, in 2006, China's aid to Africa amounted to half a billion dollars; aid from the Organisation for Economic Co-operation and Development (OECD) countries to 30 billion. China later promised to double its aid.[40] Some of the Chinese projects were remarkably successful. The Chinese were also seen as a useful antidote to excessive dependence on the West. But the number of negative reports was also increasing: the Chinese put their own interests first, were too demanding as employers, did not respect local customs, brought in too many Chinese at the expense of local labor, and so on.

China also had a certain measure of "soft power." Features of its culture were exported to other parts of the world—arts, medicine, cuisine, sports, martial arts, and even language—as Chinese became more popular. Beijing worked hard through 24-hour news channels, news agencies, newspapers, and a rapidly increasing number of Confucius Institutes in cities around the world, to strengthen support for China's case in a wider sense. Respect for family, and

---

[38] Eric Farnsworth, "The New Mercantilism: China's Emerging Role in the Americas," *Current History*, 110 (February 2011), 56–61; Anne-Marie Brady, "China's Rise in Antarctica?," *Asian Survey*, 50:4 (July/August 2010), 759–85.

[39] Ken Miller, "Coping With China's Financial Power," *Foreign Affairs* (July/August 2010), 96–109, particularly 102.

[40] *Foreign Affairs*, Book review by Nicolas van de Walle, 88:6 (November/December 2009), 174; Deborah Brautigam, "Chinese Development Aid in Africa: What, Where, Why and How Much?," in Jane Golley and Ligang Song, eds., *China Update 2011* (Canberra: Australia National University, 2011), 203–22.

even for the state, was appreciated in many parts of the world. Most important, again, was China's economic success. A "Beijing consensus" was allegedly spreading around the developing world, and the Chinese growth model was proving its superiority. The country's favorability ratings increased dramatically in the years of George W. Bush—less so under Obama—and frequently surpassed those of the United States, not only in Africa, but also in some Asian, but only a few European, countries.[41]

Chinese culture was in many ways unique, and not as easily transferable as American culture and politics, or even Soviet culture had temporarily been. China's neo-Confucianism is rather diverse, but its present emphasis on obedience to authority and its anti-democratic vein is, after all, based on the country's own traditions. But its emphasis on meritocracy and harmony probably has a wider international appeal. On the whole, neo-Confucianism probably evoked sympathy in some parts of the world, but even more opposition. In Beijing's world view strong elements of ethno-centrism existed. China was the center; the rest of us were "barbarians." Beneath the surface of formal equality, even traditional elements of racism could be found in the Chinese population, primarily directed against black people. It was very difficult to become a naturalized Chinese citizen. In a world where the status of women was rapidly being upgraded, despite official strictures Chinese women were lagging behind, particularly in politics—less so in economic life. Beijing's insistence on non-intervention and national sovereignty might be attractive to many, but the question remained of how effective such an ideology would be in coping with the many challenges that could only be addressed at the global level, such as the environment, terrorism, disease, and even good governance.

Soft power is a popular concept, but often difficult to relate to other forms of power. Most countries of the world want to modernize and this often includes adopting the technology of the West and many aspects of its culture. Yet, cell phones, Coca-Cola, and blue jeans do not necessarily lead to human rights and a Western political orientation. Many countries, from China to Iran, prove the point. No one could, however, be certain of the borderlines. Even nationalistic Chinese youth argued, with reference to the United States: "But we can't do what they do culturally: produce things like Tom and Jerry cartoons, *Transformers, Avatar, Inception,* iPhones, Barbies. America has things we really, really like, on a cultural level."[42]

---

[41] David S. Mason, *The End of the American Century,* (Lanham: Rowman & Littlefield, 2009) 197; Andrew J. Nathan and Andrew Scobell, "Human Rights and China's Soft Power Expansion," *China Rights Forum* (2009, no. 4), 10–23; David Shambaugh, "China Flexes its Soft Power," *International Herald Tribune* (June 8, 2010), 6.

[42] Didi Kirsten Tatlow, "Confucius and iPhones in This Future," *International Herald Tribune* (January 13, 2010), 2. For an interesting discussion of China and soft power, see Alan Hunter, "Soft Power: China on the Global Stage," *Chinese Journal of International Politics,* 2:3 (2009), 373–98. The concept of soft power did of course originate with Joseph S. Nye.

China shared borders with fourteen countries. Historically there had been many border disputes. Now, however, it had sorted out most of these disputes, including the ones with Russia that had led to such serious conflicts in the 1960s and 1970s. China acted quite reasonably in solving these disputes, getting only 6 percent of the disputed territory with Nepal, 8 percent with Burma, and 29 percent with Mongolia. It was showing a great deal of interest in promoting cross-border networks, although from a position of strength.[43] The bitter conflict with India over substantial territories remained, however, preventing full rapprochement between the two countries; and there is conflict over the Paracel (with Taiwan and Vietnam), the Spratly Islands in the South China Sea (with Vietnam, Taiwan, the Philippines, Malaysia, and Brunei), and the Senkaku or Diaoyutai islands (with Japan). Chinese commentators began to describe the South China Sea as one of its "core interests," on a par with Taiwan, Xinjiang, and Tibet.[44] China was clearly on the offensive even in the East China and Yellow seas. In some of the island cases codes of conduct promoting peaceful solutions to limit conflict were attempted, but these were not really successful. Occasionally rather difficult incidents occurred which fired up public opinion, both in China and in the other countries involved. The issues involved not only ownership of the islands, but also control over sea lanes and potentially large reserves of oil and natural gas. China showed little willingness to compromise on these; neither did most of the other states involved. The US insisted on open shipping lanes, here as elsewhere.

A steep rise such as China's had to have repercussions for existing alliances and loyalties. The fall of the Soviet Union and the rise of China were important factors behind the rapprochement that took place, starting in the 1990s, between the United States and India. Some of the Association of Southeast Asian Nations (ASEAN) countries—such as Vietnam, the Philippines, and

[43] David C. Kang, *China Rising: Peace, Power, and Order in East Asia* (New York: Columbia University Press, 2010), 89–90; M. Taylor Fravel, "Regime Insecurity and International Cooperation: Explaining China's Compromises in Territorial Disputes," *International Security*, 30:2 (Fall 2005), 46–83; Jonathan Holslag, "China's Road to Influence", *Asian Survey*, 50:4 (July–August 2010), 641–62; David M. Malone and Rohan Mukherjee, "India and China: Conflict and Cooperation," *Survival*, 52:1 (February–March 2010), 137–58; Marvin C. Ott, "Deep Danger: Competing Claims in the South China Sea," *Current History*, 110 (September 2011), 236–241.

[44] *The Economist* (June 12, 2010), 65–6; Banyan, "Carps among the Spratlys," *The Economist* (March 12, 2011), 62; Banyan, "Not littorally Shangri-La," *The Economist* (June 11, 2011), 54. A prominent Chinese academic suggested that "these reckless statements, made with no official authorization, created a great deal of confusion." For this, see Wang Jisi, "China's Search for a Grand Strategy: A Rising Power Finds Its Way," *Foreign Affairs* (March/April 2011), 71. The truth is apparently that the statements did come from unofficial commentators, but were never denied by leading officials. A public denial would quite simply send the wrong signals. For this, see Edward Wong, "Beijing Lets a Delicate Issue Lie," *International Herald Tribune* (March 31, 2011), 2.

Singapore—strengthened their ties with Washington. They were particularly concerned about China's attempts to reinforce its role in the South China Sea, and encouraged the US Navy to show the American flag even there to counter any idea that the South China Sea was Chinese.

Allies in the area—Japan, and to some extent South Korea—moved even closer to the US, in part influenced by the increasingly worrisome situation in North Korea.[45] However, in South Korea, and even in Japan, foreign policy conclusions were also influenced by left–right political divisions, though in 2011 this factor appeared to diminish because of the seriousness of the outside threat. The left became less critical of the United States. In diplomacy vis-à-vis North Korea, China's role was crucial. Here the US and China cooperated to some extent. Both were concerned about North Korea developing its own nuclear weapons and means of delivery, but Beijing was much more protective of the continued existence of the North Korean regime than was Washington. And again, if proof were needed, North Korea's stubbornness illustrated that national and local factors frequently prevailed over Great Power considerations.

Few, if any, countries tried to actively create a balance against China. Not even the United States attempted to do this. Elements of containment and accommodation were clearly found alongside each other. Virtually all countries wanted good relations with the United States and China at the same time, for obvious economic, political, and military reasons. Since China was definitely rising, most countries in the region increasingly appreciated the United States providing some form of counterbalance. If forced to choose, which they were not, the guess was that some of the countries in Southeast Asia would probably opt for China.[46] Japan and South Korea of course already had their alliances with the US.

The rise of China to the status it had previously enjoyed had frequently been predicted, but something had always happened in the past to prevent it from truly happening. It is impossible to be precise about the future. My own guess is that the momentum in China's development is so dynamic that in some years' time its economy will become the largest in the world. From a long-term historical perspective that will appear quite dramatic. The United States has,

---

[45] Edward Wong, "Asians Look to the U.S. as Frictions Rise with China," *International Herald Tribune* (September 23, 2010); Mark Landler, Jim Yardley, and Michael Wines, "As China Rises, Neighbors Look to Alliances New and Old," *International Herald Tribune* (November 1, 2010), 8; Sheryl Gay Stolberg, "India Gets a Boost in Bid to Join Larger U.N. Council," *International Herald Tribune* (December 9, 2010), 1, 5; Noritmitsu Onishi, "U.S. and China Court Indonesia," *International Herald Tribune* (December 10–11, 2010), 1, 6; Martin Fackler, "Japan Shifts Defense Strategy as China Grows More Assertive," *International Herald Tribune* (March 1, 2011), 1, 8.

[46] Marvin Ott, "Asia's Clouded Horizon," *International Herald Tribune* (September 29, 2010), 8.

after all, had the largest economy in the world since around 1870. However, it is doubtful that China will then be able to move on to challenge the United States for the overall leadership position. China will still be lagging far behind the United States in military strength, in the wealth of its citizens on a per capita basis, in the number and strength of its allies, and in the attractiveness of its culture. Furthermore, in the long run, China is facing serious structural problems that will have to be addressed if its rapid growth in virtually all categories is to continue. It is far from clear that the country will be able to address these deficiencies in a satisfactory way.

There would seem to be three primary challenges to China's long-term rise to superpower status: the nature of the political system, China's ethnic-national composition, and the many tensions in China's economic policies.

First, China's political history combines long periods of great stability with various forms of outburst. The long-cherished American dream of the rise of a friendly China was crushed by the Communist Revolution of 1949. Under communism the swings of the pendulum have been wide, not to say wild. The Soviet model was tried; Mao's dramatic experiments ended in total failure. The fact that they had been tried at all said a lot about the unpredictability of China. The emphasis on economic growth has now been pursued for more than three decades, but has led to periodic tensions within the Communist Party, particularly in 1989. Then the leadership had been badly divided until Deng Xiaoping had taken command and clamped down both on leadership division and popular demonstrations.

The question of the long-term political legitimacy of the regime is still unresolved. The Communist Party remains firmly in power, but the communist fervor is largely gone. Although the authorities treasure "shengshi," the combination of peace and prosperity, it is evident that while China has now achieved material prosperity, there is not really much social peace. The overall priority is now to make money. As Deng had famously declared, "I don't care whether a cat is black or white. As long as it catches mice, it is a good cat." Or, as another less prominent leader had stated even more bluntly: "We are the Communist Party and we will decide what communism means."[47]

The regime undoubtedly gained legitimacy through the fast growth and the pride that most Chinese took in the country's rapidly increasing influence. The Party was also trying, with some success, to co-opt the rising new elites. But changes were being made with or without the permission of the authorities. The government could limit the role of Google, but not really of the Internet in general. Groups that had been frowned upon, such as homosexuals and lesbians, increasingly appeared in the open.

[47] *The Economist* (June 19, 2010), 75. See also Guoguang Wu, "Muddling Through Crises: China in 2009," *Asian Survey*, 50:1 (January/February 2010), 25–39.

The uprising in 1989 had involved many different cities; it was still a festering sore. The communist regimes in Eastern Europe and the Soviet Union had all collapsed. This made a great impression on the Chinese leadership who were determined to avoid any such outcome. Political reform was put on hold; virtually all the emphasis went into the economic side. Yet, ever new dissidents appeared on the scene. In other rapidly industrializing countries in Asia, in the long term economic growth had almost inevitably strengthened political democracy. Would not this happen at some stage even in China?

The authorities in Beijing displayed considerable nervousness about the political situation. The self-confidence of the leaders was perhaps not that great after all. Dissidents and activists of various kinds, including the religious Falun Gong, were given long prison sentences or sent into exile; all the various means of communication were closely supervised, although not always successfully. In December 2008 Charter 08 was publicized and signed by hundreds of critics of the Chinese regime, and also by ordinary citizens. It openly advocated a constitutional democracy. The awarding in 2010 of the Nobel Peace Prize to Liu Xiaobo, who had been sentenced to eleven years in prison, led the Chinese authorities to intervene against many human rights activists. Every effort was made to encourage foreign ambassadors to stay away from the Nobel ceremony in Oslo, with only limited success. The prize clearly touched a raw nerve.

The number of "mass incidents" told of a great deal of restlessness in the country. This number, as reported by the authorities themselves, increased rapidly to more than 87,000 in 2005. Numbers for later years were withheld, but a study indicates that it may have jumped to 280,000 in 2010.[48] Most of these protests were local and reflected accidents of several different sorts, property disputes, closed factories, increased prices. It did not remain out of the question, however, that the protests could coalesce and become more comprehensive in scope and better organized. Would not that restlessness only increase as the results of economic growth were more and more taken for granted, and as expectations had a tendency to increase even more quickly than economic results?[49]

---

[48] The 2010 number comes from a study by sociologist Sun Liping of Tsinghua University. For this, see Didi Kirsten Tatlow, "Indifference as a Mode of Operation at China Schools," *International Herald Tribune* (May 19, 2011), 2.

[49] At the somewhat less dramatic level, complaints about pollution simply exploded. The number of incidents about which people sent letters or visited Environmental Protection Bureaus increased from 111,359 in 1991, to 682,744 in 2004. There is reason to believe that the increase has continued. For this, see Anna Brettell, "Channeling Dissent: The Institutionalization of Environmental Complaint Resolution," in Peter Ho and Richard Louis Edmonds (eds.), *China's Embedded Activism: Opportunities and Constraints of a Social Movement* (London: Routledge, 2008), 111–50, particularly 113–21.

Because of the one-child policy China would also face serious problems, with a rapidly aging population and possibly also with the spoiled "little emperors" (the result of policy), as these youngsters were entering society with high expectations. They were individualistic, merit-focused and consumer-oriented. More and more of the many university graduates were having problems finding suitable jobs. Later, many of these spoiled children would have to support their parents in the care the latter required in their old age, since the government did so little in this field. In 2011 this private care was even made into a legal obligation. This was indeed, in Mao's terms, "managing contradictions." Recent research indicates that even if the authorities were to reverse the one-child policy, it is now so ingrained that it will be hard to change. It now represents the typical drop in birthrates that occurs as societies modernize.[50]

If major political change were to take place in China, many assumed it would come as a result of pressure from below. The masses would force the leadership to modify its policies. Yet this was not necessarily so; it could also happen because debates at the top of the political hierarchy would become so heated that one or more of the leaders would be tempted to take this debate to the masses in some way. This had been one aspect of the Cultural Revolution. It was of course possible that one-party rule would continue into an indefinite future. But why would China remain a permanent exception to the general trend of the people ultimately insisting on taking control in some form? In 2011 even the Arab Middle East, which had been one of the other major authoritarian holdouts in the world, was affected by large-scale protests and even revolutions in several countries. The Chinese had been much more economically successful than the Arabs, but they still had important features in common: corruption, growing inequality, and a lack of political reform.[51]

Second, another major challenge related to the fact that although (allegedly) more than 90 percent of the population is Han Chinese, close to 10 percent from 55 different nationalities is a vast number with a total population of more than 1,300 million. Beijing is very concerned about the situation in Xinjiang and Tibet. Depending on the exact definition of empire used, China's role in these provinces may be considered imperial. As had happened after 1949 in Inner Mongolia, Beijing was encouraging thousands and thousands of Han Chinese to move to the two provinces to shift the population balance against the minorities. Ethnic–national disputes fused with an economic growth that easily disturbed native cultures, although this growth was still considerably slower than along the coast. The outbursts in the two provinces

---

[50] Sharon LaFraniere, "For Families, Finances Beat the One-Child Rule in China," *International Herald Tribune* (April 7, 2011), 1, 7.
[51] Didi Kirsten Tatlow, "Arab Revolts Seen Through China's Prism," *International Herald Tribune*, (February 24, 2011), 2.

were treated with great severity by the Chinese authorities, but they seemed to flare up again at irregular intervals.

In this respect 2008 and 2009 were bad years for the Chinese authorities. The widespread rebellion in Tibet in 2008 illustrated that Tibetans had not become reconciled to China's rule, despite economic growth and the massive influx of Han Chinese into Tibet. The Dalai Lama was still a highly revered person in most of Tibet. The Uighur uprising in Xinjiang in 2009 was even more threatening. It was more violent, had connections with Muslim groups in other neighboring countries, and was better organized, despite repressive measures undertaken by the authorities.

Third, although the Chinese economic model has produced great results, the big question remains: can these results really be expected to continue in the future? Experience tells us that economic growth lines cannot be extended indefinitely. In the Soviet Union growth had been extremely high for several decades, until it slowed down dramatically in the 1970s and stopped entirely in the 1980s. The same had happened in Japan, where the growth of the 1950s–1980s had been replaced by slow and no growth since the 1990s. In less mature economies dramatic results could be achieved by relatively simple means. The transition from agriculture to industry almost always led to high growth. In mature economies it was much more difficult to maintain such high growth rates. This was particularly the case as the service sector replaced agriculture and even industry as the leading one.

As its economy grew from a relatively low base, and as it was no longer making up for the dramatic setbacks of Mao's long era—the Great Leap Forward (1958–61), and the Cultural Revolution (1966–76)—China's growth would also be harder to achieve. The country had actually been lagging far behind the modern tigers—South Korea, Taiwan, Hong Kong, and Singapore. Now it was beginning to catch up with them. No one could answer the question of how far into the future the growth lines could be extended. Japan's history provided a warning. After 40 years of explosive growth, the country's economy had ground to a screeching halt. Models that work exceedingly well at a certain level of development may work less well, or even be counter-productive, at a higher level. Thus, the same factors, whether they be elite cooperation in Japan or Confucianism in China, may in fact explain both rise and fall, although at different stages of development.[52]

Growth also created its own problems. In 2010–11 signs of stress were growing in the Chinese economy: many banks were experiencing problems, bubbles existed, particularly in the real estate market, with a growing number of properties remaining unsold, and, most ominously, inflation was definitely picking up and stayed high even after certain corrective actions had been

---

[52] Michael Wines, "For China, a Cautionary Tale from Japan," *International Herald Tribune* (May 27, 2010), 15; "BRIC Wall," *The Economist* (April 16, 2011), 76.

taken. The increase in food prices was particularly worrisome. The price of Chinese goods sold abroad was going up considerably. This was bound to have a negative impact on the export volume.[53] The Chinese authorities were beginning to address these problems, but priority was still given to the rapid rise in production, particularly in exports. The list of environmental problems was long and growing: mining accidents were frequent, water supplies were worryingly low (although they were even lower in India), air quality in virtually all big cities was terrible. The huge Three Gorges Dam project raised serious questions, certainly including environmental ones. The ultimate environmental question was, of course, what were the limits to growth? How long could the furious pace of growth be maintained simply from an environmental point of view?

Despite reforms, the legal system and the courts were still arbitrary and often corrupt; they had to be improved and, in particular, property rights respected, if investors were to feel secure. The vast corruption had to be limited. Sometimes the death penalty was imposed for some of the worst cases of corruption, but with very limited long-term effect.

China had made huge strides in education, including higher education. Over the past decade the number of Chinese who enrolled at a university quintupled. China was experiencing a "meteoric rise" in the publication of scientific papers. From 2004 to 2008, more than one in ten scientific articles came out of China, up from fewer than one in twenty the previous decade. China moved from sixth to second place on the world list. The United States definitely remained in first place, but its share of publications dropped from one in four to one in five.

There was reason to believe, however, that China's scientific influence was lagging behind its output.[54] As has been argued, "The traditional Asia approaches may work well for training engineers, but they are less suited for fostering innovation." Rote learning could take you only so far. Creativity at the highest levels was a problem in China, as in several other Asian countries. Progress flowed more from imitation, tinkering, and steady improvement; less from true creativity and originality. In pursuing one's intellectual interests, wherever they might lead, India may well have a long-term advantage over China. In sensitive areas the Chinese leadership set definite limits as to what kinds of research could be performed, and what conclusions should be reached.[55] China's many new universities had far to go before they could

---

[53] David Barboza, "Rapid Growth Breeds Host of Worries for China," *International Herald Tribune* (December 14, 2010), 17; Keith Bradsher, "Chinese Inflation Spreads Beyond its Borders," *International Herald Tribune* (January 13, 2011), 13; Keith Bradsher, "Rising Prices in China Send Ripples Around Globe," *International Herald Tribune* (January 31, 2011), 14, 16.
[54] "China Shoots up Rankings as Science Power, Study Finds" (March 30, 2011), CNN.com.
[55] Richard C. Levin, "The Rise of Asia's Universities," *International Herald Tribune* (April 21, 2010), 6; Don Durfee and James Pomfret, "China Struggles to Find a Formula for Innovation,"

rival good Western universities. Although the number of Chinese patents was growing rapidly, questions were raised about the quality of these inventions.[56] Not a single Chinese scientist was awarded any Nobel science prize.

China's record in protecting intellectual property rights was probably the worst in the world. Unlike Taiwan and Thailand, where counterfeiting was largely carried out in the private sector, in China the state sector also participated on a large scale. Various agreements between the US and China appeared to make little difference. And even counterfeiting could only take you so far. It has to be added that some of the more advanced products were simply assembled and stamped "Made in China"; they were not really developed there. Much of the advanced production going on in China involves export processing. Semi-finished and finished components are brought in from various countries and then assembled and exported at low cost and stamped. Path-breaking new research and development are seldom done in China; when the results are, with some delay, imported into China, the West has moved on to even more advanced products, though China is working hard to transfer as many of these processes as possible to China itself.[57] This is part of the process of the increasing globalization of production, which affects the entire world; but it also tells us something about China's role in this process, certainly compared to the United States.

It was true that China was making determined efforts to move up the industrial pyramid; also because wages were moving upwards and low-cost manufacturing was facing increased competition from other countries.[58] These efforts met with success in many areas (solar and other forms of alternative energy, high-speed trains). This was very impressive indeed, although there were incidents of grave pollution within the solar industry and several serious accidents with high-speed trains that slowed down this program. Western companies investing in China were not only encouraged, but pressured, to give up their most modern technology; for instance, General Electric was sharing its most sophisticated airplane electronics with a state-owned company.

International Herald Tribune (May 6, 2011), 16. In some sensitive fields debate was growing, as long as criticism of China's own policies was avoided. Thus, in the journal *Contemporary International Relations*, published by China's foreign policy institutes, different points of view could be found on overall issues of international affairs.

[56] Steve Lohr, "Building a More Innovative Society by Government Decree," *International Herald Tribune* (January 3, 2011), 14, 16; "Climbing Mount Publishable," *The Economist* (November 13, 2010), 89–90.

[57] Edward G. Steinfeld, *Playing Our Game: Why China's Rise Doesn't Threaten the West* (New York: Oxford University Press, 2010), 85–8; "Still full of ideas, but not making jobs," *The Economist* (April 30, 2011), 44–5; Schumpeter, "Bamboo Innovation," *The Economist* (May 7, 2011), 64.

[58] David Barboza, "Chinese Industry Seeks a New Edge," *International Herald Tribune* (September 17, 2010), 1.

China was even buying advanced American companies, in areas such as solar energy.[59]

Inequalities were deep and getting deeper, with some benefiting hugely from the economic growth, and others much less so, or not at all. This was also the pattern in many other developing countries. China was enormous, and that too encouraged huge variations. In China, the richest 10 percent of the population earned twenty-three times more than the poorest 10 percent. In the United States and Germany the corresponding numbers were 15.9 and 6.9 times respectively.[60]

Even in China the number of available workers would begin to decline by 2015, the result of the one-child policy and the drying up of youth escaping rural drudgery. In 2011 indications were that the low fertility had less to do with the one-child policy, and more with new attitudes to children evolving in other developing countries as well. Despite the general increase in wages, which could become a problem in itself, and the Party's supervision of work-places, industrial unrest was becoming increasingly frequent. Under the Hukou system, which binds the Chinese to a particular place and is only partially modified even now, migrant workers (in particular) did not receive fair treatment; neither did their children. In the spring and summer of 2011 there were several incidents involving protests from migrant workers. Strikes also erupted in modern factories paying relatively high wages. As long as these strikes took place in foreign-owned companies the authorities did little or nothing. There were even demands for free unions. Thousands and thousands of labor disputes were brought before the courts.[61]

As economies advance from a low base, growth rates almost always decline. If that happened China could have difficulties, since it was assumed that 6–8 percent growth was more or less required to avoid unemployment problems. Although there was a steep rise in the number of private companies, the Chinese economy was still very state-dominated. All the main "commanding heights" companies were state-owned—defense, energy, finance, telecommunications,

---

[59] Steve Lohr and David Barboza, "Worth Billions, G.E. Jet Engine Deal puts Secrets at Risk," *International Herald Tribune* (January 18, 2011), 1, 15; Keith Bradsher, "U.S. Solar Panel Producer Decides the Grass is Greener in China," *International Herald Tribune* (January 15–16, 2011), 1, 15.

[60] Didi Kirsten Tatlow, "Poor Hidden by Glare of New Wealth," *International Herald Tribune* (September 3, 2010), 2; Tatlow, "Costs Rise, and China's Poor Struggle, "*International Herald Tribune* (December 10, 2010), 2.

[61] Numerous articles were published about these matters. See for instance Philip Bowring, "China's Dwindling Resource," *International Herald Tribune* (June 4, 2010), 7; "Labor Strife in China Sends Ripples Worldwide," *International Herald Tribune* (May 31, 2010), 16; David Barboza, "China Workers' Gains Cause Global Ripples," *International Herald Tribune* (June 8, 2010), 17; Edward Wong, "In China, Workers' Voices Carry Only So Far," *International Herald Tribune* (June 22, 2010), 18; "The Rising Power of China's Workers," *The Economist* (July 31, 2010), 46–8; "The most surprising demographic crisis," *The Economist* (May 7, 2011), 52–3.

mining and metals, ports and railroads—and private companies largely dealt with clothing, food, and factory-assembled exports. China had some huge companies that had had spectacular success on foreign stock markets, but these were, almost without exception, only partially privatized quasi-state monopolies—certainly huge, but not very innovative.[62] The land was still largely state-owned, and farmers had to pay rent for it; price controls were prevalent; competition was quite limited. Could such an economy function effectively in the long run? If it did, many Western economic textbooks would have to be rewritten.

The economic model emphasized exports, and therefore insisted on a cheap yuan or renminbi. This led to rapidly rising dissatisfaction abroad as more and more companies lost out to Chinese competition; it was also domestically controversial in that it limited domestic spending and welfare. So, in this respect, the outside world and the Chinese consumer had a common interest. Household spending, at 36 percent of GDP, was at the lowest level by far for any major economy. In 2011 there were definite signs that investment, not only in housing, but also in education and even social welfare, was finally improving. This was badly needed as the system of social assistance in China was extremely limited.[63]

Sooner or later the expectation was that the Chinese economic model had to be transformed. The growth in wages meant not only that China would have to move up the industrial ladder as it faced competition from ever new competitors paying lower wages; it would probably also mean increased imports and a somewhat more balanced economic relationship with the outside world. When, in 2010, the authorities finally agreed to the appreciation of the yuan, the rise in its value was still quite limited, although the rise could be useful in combating the growing inflation. The slow but growing shift in favor of domestic consumption was important in itself, and would probably also have a gradual impact on the currency. In 2010–11 there were signs that China's trade surplus was beginning to come down. In the first quarter of 2011 China actually ran its first trade deficit since 2004, but this soon changed again. Beijing, however, made it clear that the exchange rate was an issue

[62] Michael Wines, "China Puts its Cash Where the State is," *International Herald Tribune* (August 31, 2010), 1, 15; Ian Johnson, "The Party: Impenetrable, All Powerful," *New York Review of Books*, 57 (September 30, 2010), 71; "Let a Million Flowers Bloom," *The Economist*, March 12, 2011, 71–4.

[63] Daniel R. Hammond, "Social Assistance in China, 1993–2002: Institutions, Feedback, and Policy Actors in the Chinese Policy Process," *Asian Politics & Policy*, 3:1 (January 2011), 69–93; Alan Wheatley, "Waiting for the Chinese Consumer," *International Herald Tribune* (September 14, 2010), 22; David Barboza, "Warming up Renminbi for World Stage," *International Herald Tribune* (February 12–13, 2011), 18; Alan Wheatley, "China's Plan for Creating Consumers," *International Herald Tribune* (March 15, 2011), 22.

the authorities would decide on their own.[64] And the experience with Japan in the 1970s proved that the appreciation of a currency did not necessarily lead to reduced deficits. Japan's surplus in its trade with the US had in fact increased rapidly, despite the appreciation of the yen. In both cases there were many other barriers to imports than simply the exchange rate, however skewed that might be. The effects of appreciation also depended very much on the nature of the goods being exported and imported. The yuan's appreciation 'could, under certain circumstances, actually work against the United States. Many saw the whole issue as a demonstration of the weakened position of the United States.[65]

If China were to play a larger role in international finance, and the role of the dollar were to diminish, China would sooner or later have to address the question of the yuan's convertibility. Yet, for the leadership in Beijing, convertibility would mean a loss of economic and even some political control. The authorities were simply not prepared to give up power over either the exchange rate or the interest level. At least not yet.

Many observers agreed on the list of long-term problems in the Chinese economy: the high number of unprofitable state companies, Party interference, in the economy, the Party's suspicion of private Chinese companies, insolvent banks, overcapacity in many sectors, corruption, inequalities. Even Prime Minister Wen Jiabao stated that China's growth was "unbalanced, uncoordinated and unsustainable."[66] The disagreement was about how serious these problems were. In fact, in 2002, Gordon Chang had predicted the imminent collapse of China, largely because of these problems. He was obviously wrong.[67] China actually made considerable progress in alleviating some of them. The state sector has been drastically reorganized and even downsized,

---

[64] David Leonhardt, "China Seeks Orderly Shift to Consumer Economy," *International Herald Tribune* (November 27–28, 2010), 1, 16; Sharon LaFraniere and Bettina Wassener, "China Trims Trade Surplus in Tilt Towards Consumers," *International Herald Tribune* (January 11, 2011), 14; from news reports, "Trade Deficit is China's First Since '04," *International Herald Tribune* (April 11, 2011), 18; Bettina Wassener, "Beijing Lets Renminbi Move Above Key Level," *International Herald Tribune* (April 30–May 1, 2011), 11; Floyd Norris, "As Pattern Shifts, China Surplus Falls," *International Herald Tribune* (September 17–18, 2011), 12. Some were quite optimistic about how China's economy would become more domestically directed. See for instance James Kynge, "China: An Inwardly-Animated Economy," *Asian Affairs*, 41:3 (November 2010), 436–43.

[65] Joseph A. Massey and Lee M. Sands, "The Yen's Lesson for the Yuan," *International Herald Tribune* (August 25, 2010), 6; David Leonhardt, "Chinese See a Lesson in the Yen's Tale," *International Herald Tribune* (September 23, 2010), 24; Paul Kennedy, "Don't Surrender U.S. Influence to Beijing," *International Herald Tribune* (September 30, 2010), 12.

[66] "China: Don't Worry, Be Happy," *The Economist* (March 19, 2011), 49.

[67] Tønnesson, "Hvor går Kina?," 18–25, suggested this line of thinking. See also Gordon Chang, *The Coming Collapse of China* (London: Arrow, 2002); Minxin Pei, *China's Trapped Transition: The Limits of Developmental Autocracy* (Cambridge, MA: Harvard University Press, 2006); Susan L. Shirk, *China: Fragile Superpower: How China's Internal Politics Could Derail Its Peaceful Rise* (New York: Oxford University Press, 2007); Carl E. Walter and Fraser J. T. Howie,

although there are many different forms of state ownership. Massive urban layoffs had created higher unemployment rates, which now seem to have passed. Rural markets for agricultural commodities worked much better. Ironically, many of the most serious problems now seemed to involve not so much the transition from a command to a market economy, but the authorities' inability to provide standard public goods. The health care system, environmental protection, and anti-corruption efforts were the most glaring examples.[68] Regardless of this, the problems were many and tangible. As yet, they were not of sufficient importance to slow down the rapid economic growth; but they could of course have a larger impact as the very high growth rates inevitably had to fall.

While China was becoming the primary challenger to the leadership of the United States, the two were also cooperating in different ways. While, in virtually all US campaigns since 1980, the new president had criticized his predecessor for having been too friendly toward the Chinese, even newcomers had soon come to favor cooperation with China. There were strong forces pulling the two giants together, and the United States and China were becoming increasingly interdependent. The US had supported China's successful membership of the World Trade Organization (WTO) in 2001. The open American market had been crucial to China's growth, as it had been in Japan's case as well. In 2008, Chinese exports to the United States amounted to almost 8 percent of China's GNP, and a significant share of these exports came from American companies that had been established in China. Virtually all the major US companies were represented there. In 2008, foreign enterprises accounted for 55 percent of China's total exports, and for 54 percent of its imports. What would happen to these numbers if American–Chinese relations seriously deteriorated?

The US was by far the world's largest importer, while China was surpassing Germany as the largest exporter. The huge surpluses China had in its foreign trade were then, to a large extent, invested in the US, so China was actually financing parts of America's rapidly growing debt[69]. When demand in the United States collapsed during the economic crisis of 2008–09, exports from China were badly hit too. This interdependence limited conflict; but it also cut

---

Red Capitalism: The Fragile Financial Foundation of China's Extraordinary Rise (Singapore: Wiley, 2011).

[68] Jean C. Oi, Scott Rozelle, and Xueguang Zhou (eds.), *Growing Pains: Tensions and Opportunity in China's Transformation* (Stanford: Shorenstein Center, 2010) particularly xxiii–xxiv.

[69] About one-third of the US deficit was financed from other US government sources (primarily social security), one-third came from US pension funds, and one-third from abroad, with China as the major funder with 16 percent of the overall total. For this, see Niall Ferguson, "Debt Debate: China's View," *Newsweek* (August 7, 2011), Internet.

so many different ways, and it could sometimes be difficult to tell who actually held the upper hand in this complex relationship.

There was no doubt that US economic policies increasingly had to be carried out with an eye on the likely response from Beijing. As Hillary Clinton asked the then Australian prime minister, Kevin Rudd: "How do you deal toughly with your bank?"[70] China's position as the world's largest creditor had strengthened its position tremendously. The US position as the world's largest debtor had weakened its role, although it still had few problems in financing its debt. The world was awash in cheap money in 2010–11, but that could easily change. International financial structures had to be adjusted, reflecting the rise of Asia, and especially China. And since China was also surpassing the United States as the world's greatest polluter, there could be no effective global environmental policy unless the two countries contributed.

It had to be remembered that while trade across the Pacific had surpassed that across the Atlantic in the late 1970s, and the gap had widened since, on the investment side the story was a different one. American investment in Europe and European investment in America were much larger than in China and East Asia.[71] Americans and Europeans, despite the problems they were facing, were also ideologically and culturally much closer to each other than they were to the Japanese, not to mention the Chinese.

The Chinese had probably started investing in size in the United States in the 1990s because of rapid US economic growth. In many ways the US still had the most advanced economy in the world, and there was also much to learn. As growth began to falter the Chinese may have emphasized the security of US Treasury bonds. In an uncertain world, when even the United States was hit, many still felt safest with America. There was also the problem of where else to go. As one Chinese official told an American audience in February 2009, "except for US Treasuries, what can you hold? . . . US Treasuries are the safe haven. For everyone, including China, it is the only option . . . We hate you guys. Once you start issuing 1–2 trillion dollars . . . we know that the dollar is going to depreciate, so we hate you guys, but there is nothing much we can do."[72] Finally, there was also the question of the political benefits for the Chinese in investing in the United States.

---

[70] Elise Labott, "Analysis: Keeping a Check on America's Banker," CNN.com, January 18, 2011.

[71] U.S. Bureau of the Census, *Statistical Abstract of the United States: 2010* (Washington, DC: Government Printing Office, 2009), 782.

[72] Daniel W. Drezner, "Bad Debts: Assessing China's Financial Influence in Great Power Politics," *International Security*, 34:2 (Fall 2009), 7–45. The quotation is from 41. See also Aaron L. Friedberg, "Implications of the Financial Crisis for the US–China Rivalry," *Survival*, 52:4 (August–September 2010), 31–54; Robert Skidelsky, "The World Finance Crisis & the American Mission," *New York Review of Books* (July 16, 2009), 31–3.

Many worried about what would happen if the Chinese stopped investing in the US. This would harm America, but would also certainly harm China as it would have a negative impact on Chinese exports to the US, and on the already huge Chinese investment in the US. Dependency cut both ways. If China started to dump dollars, it would also hurt itself. To translate John Maynard Keynes's famous quote: "If I owe you a pound I have a problem; but if I owe you a million, the problem is yours." When the United States owes China billions, that is Washington's problem. When it owes China trillions, such amounts quickly become Beijing's problem. If China dumped dollars, the greenback would fall in value. That would have a negative side, but it would also make American goods more competitive. Some argued that this effect might actually be desirable for the American economy. Finally, there was an overriding political interest in maintaining good relations with what were more and more clearly becoming the two most important powers in the world.

On her first visit to China as Secretary of State in the Obama administration, Hillary Clinton stated, with reference to issues such as human rights, Tibet, and Taiwan, that had traditionally plagued American–Chinese relations: "those issues can't interfere with the global economic crisis, the global climate change crisis, and the security crisis." This clearly illustrated how China had become a crucial partner in all the most important issues of today. Traditional issues had to be downplayed. It was indeed a dramatic new situation, and clearly strengthened China's hand.

Soon, however, the Obama administration was willing to take up the traditional issues as well. Washington wanted to counteract the impression that China could exploit US weaknesses. Arms were still exported to Taiwan; President Obama received the Dalai Lama; Washington protested against the treatment of Liu Xiaobo and other Chinese dissidents, and against the censorship of Google in China. There were also serious issues in the priority fields. First among them came the question of the low exchange rate of the yuan. As Chinese products flooded Western markets, and as China's current account surplus grew dramatically, irritation in Western capitals—certainly including Washington—rapidly increased.

In Pentagon circles, and among realist political scientists, the rise of China was seen as potentially destabilizing. In the past, such a rise of new powers had allegedly always created conflict, even war. The rise of France under Louis XIV and Napoleon had led to major European wars. The rise of Germany was generally perceived as the underlying factor behind the First and the Second World Wars. China did strengthen its military forces substantially. But realist models based on European history did not necessarily fit the situation in Asia where, as we have seen, a mixture of balancing and accommodation existed. For one thing, European countries were located close to each other; China and the United States were geographically far apart (although some of America's allies were close to China). In its National Security Strategy, from 2010, the

Obama administration vows to "monitor China's military modernization program", but also states that disagreements on human rights "should not prevent cooperation on issues of mutual interest."[73]

In most of the world the rise of China was primarily seen in economic terms. It was certainly a threat to established industries in the United States and in Europe. Trade disputes were proliferating. China had long seen itself as the victim of the actions of others and the spokesperson for the poor masses of the world. For more than a hundred years before the revolution in 1949 it had suffered "national humiliation"; the exploitation of China's territory by foreign powers.[74] Now, while insisting that China was still a developing country with many limitations, its leaders were more and more emphasizing the peaceful, and even inevitable, nature of its rise. While both Russia and China had a common interest in balancing America's great influence somewhat, they both (and certainly China) had an even stronger interest in cooperating with the United States. China was also interested in working with the EU to limit the influence of the American hegemon, but Beijing had apparent difficulties understanding what the EU was all about, and in political matters ended up mostly working with individual EU countries. Although references to the G-2 or to "Chinamerica" were to be avoided, the Chinese took considerable pleasure in moving up the power tables in the way they did. Hu Jintao's standard phrase was to talk about the "peaceful rise" of China, later modified to "peaceful development" to sound less offensive. Nevertheless, to describe the new world, Chinese academics came up with the following formula: "one superpower working together with several big powers," or even "World No. 1 vs World No. 2." In 2010 some Chinese leaders openly referred to the country as a Great Power, a "world power," and even a "quasi-superpower."[75]

---

[73] David Sanger and Peter Baker, "Obama Gives Broader View on National Security," *International Herald Tribune* (May 28, 2010), 1, 6. See also Charles Glaser, "Will China's Rise Lead to War?: Why Realism Does Not Mean Pessimism," *Foreign Affairs* (March/April 2011), 80–91.

[74] The most recent history takes 1832 as the starting point of foreign exploitation. Much of the system actually disintegrated at the time of the First World War. For this, see Robert Bickers, *The Scramble for China: Foreign Devils in the Qing Empire, 1832–1914* (London: Allen Lane, 2011).

[75] Halper, *The Beijing Consensus*, 143; Cui Liru, "A Multipolar World in the Globalization Era," *Contemporary International Relations (CIR)*, 20 (September 2010), 3; Yuan Peng, "Where are China–U.S. Relations Headed?," *CIR*, 20 (September 2010), 54–5; Nina Hachigian and Yuan Peng, "The US–China Expectations Gap: An Exchange," *Survival*, 52:4 (August–September 2010), 67–86, particularly 73–4. I had breakfast with the Chinese Vice Foreign Minister for Europe on June 7, 2010, where we discussed some of these matters in addition to the Nobel Peace Prize. For a recent interpretation stressing the moderate rise of China, see Liu Liping, "China Can Hardly Rule the World," *CIR*, 21:1 (January–February 2011), 4–10. See also Henry Kissinger, *On China* (New York: Penguin Press, 2011), 497–513; Aaron L. Friedberg, *A Contest for Supremacy. China, America, and the Struggle for Mastery in Asia* (New York: Norton, 2011), 120–41.

The big evolution was that while China had earlier seen itself as an outsider in opposition to the dominant powers and institutions, it was now becoming more of an insider, though certainly one that was trying to reform many aspects of the international system. China had to be given its due influence in the UN and the entire UN system; the International Monetary Fund had to be reformed to reflect China's rise and the fall not so much of the United States as of Europe; the G-20 was to be the new important forum at the expense of the dwindling G-7(8); and trade rounds and environmental agreements had to reflect China's importance. China did not present many concrete proposals to solve the world's problems; it still left that largely to others. Yet, more and more, no overall agreements could be worked out without China on board.

After Hong Kong and Macao had been brought into the "homeland," China's primary military concern still related to Taiwan's status and its potential for independence. While China held firm to the one-China policy, there was every reason to believe that Beijing understood that China's continued rapid economic growth depended on peace and stability in the region. In 2006–09 China adopted constructive policies on several international issues. It participated in crafting sanctions against North Korea, backed a UN plan for peace and stability in Darfur, sent peacekeepers to several places (including taking part in the international effort to counter piracy off the coast of Somalia), and made somewhat constructive moves as concerned Haiti, East Timor, and even Burma. In the UN debate on Responsibility to Protect, Beijing tried to avoid obstruction, although the emphasis was on preventing abuses from occurring in the first place. For a country that stressed non-interference in domestic matters, these were important developments.[76]

But by 2010–11 there were many signs that China was becoming more determined in international affairs, and that the United States was beginning to push back. China gave definite priority to its own interests in most of the growing financial disputes with the United States and much of the industrialized world, including the increasingly controversial currency question. The list of highly sensitive issues now also included China's intellectual property

For very different interpretations within the same issue of *CIR, 21:2, March/April 2011*, see Fu Mengzi, "China's International Influence," where he writes that the "Beijing Consensus" sees "the U.S. as still being at the top of the pyramid, followed by the UK, France, Germany, Japan, Russia, Brazil, India, and China." (8–9) and Lin Limin, "Chaos and Change in Symbiosis: The World in 2010," where the author states that "Europe is slumbering, if not moribund, while the Asia–Pacific is thriving. Therefore, the twenty-first century will belong to the latter region, rather than to Europe and America." (96)

[76] Thomas J. Christensen, "The Advantages of an Assertive China: Responding to Beijing's Abrasive Diplomacy," *Foreign Affairs* (March/April 2011), 54–67, particularly 55–7; Rosemary Foot and Andrew Walter, *China, the United States, and Global Order* (Cambridge: Cambridge University Press, 2011), 42–61.

theft and the myriad of small protectionist barriers China had erected to limit certain Western imports. The Obama administration, and, even more, the US Congress were becoming increasingly critical of China's policies, particularly anything that smacked of discrimination against the US. It was difficult for many Americans to accept that China was becoming a major exporter of technologically advanced products, such as solar panels.[77] It did not help that the United States itself discriminated against Chinese investment in areas of sensitive national interest, however that term happened to be interpreted in Washington.

China's firm line in the South China Sea was a dramatic indication of Beijing's new determination. In response, Vietnam invited the US Navy to visit the area, and the aircraft carrier *George Washington* did. In the territorial dispute with Japan, which actually led to minor skirmishes, China held back rare earth minerals in an effort to influence Japan's position, a break with China's principle of not mixing economic and political questions.[78] When the Chinese dissident Liu Xiaobo was awarded the Nobel Peace Prize in 2010, Beijing made it perfectly clear that it would tolerate no interference in domestic matters.[79] China's rearmament was continuing at a brisk pace, with the Chinese military occasionally taking great pride in showing off some of their latest weapons; this naturally had a negative effect in the United States. The Europeans, on the other hand, were continuing to discuss lifting restrictions on exports of military hardware to China, to Washington's disappointment.

In the events in Libya in February–March 2011, China played a more constructive role. While officially still abhorring interference in other countries' internal affairs, it voted for sanctions against Gaddafi's government, dispatched a warship and aircraft to evacuate Chinese citizens from Libya, and refrained from voting against the international military intervention.[80]

With China continuing its rapid growth—not only economically, but also militarily—the future did not look too bright. The United States was definitely not going to sit still while China improved its position. Was China, then, a status quo or a revisionist power? Clearly both elements were represented. China was both a "responsible stakeholder" and a revisionist power. Elizabeth Economy went further and argued, "Never mind notions of a responsible

---

[77] Keith Bradsher, "U.S. Throws Down Challenge to World's Leading Producer of Solar Panels," *International Herald Tribune* (January 10, 2011), 15; David Leonhardt, "Looking Past China's Grip on Currency," *International Herald Tribune* (January 13, 2011), 18.

[78] Keith Bradsher and Judy Dempsey, "China Curbs Flow of Crucial Minerals," *International Herald Tribune* (October 20, 2010), 1, 16.

[79] Christian Caryl, "Unveiling Hidden China," *New York Review of Books* (December 9, 2010), 32–7; Banyan, "Great Disorder Under Heaven," *The Economist* (December 18, 2010), 104; Mark Landler and Sewell Chan, "U.S. Takes Harder Line on a Bolder China," *International Herald Tribune* (October 26, 2010), 1, 5.

[80] Yan Xuetong, "How Assertive Should a Great Power Be?," *International Herald Tribune* (April 1, 2011), 6.

stakeholder; China has become a revolutionary power."[81] There could be little doubt that China was trying, with some success, to modify the international system. However, it was no longer revolutionary in the sense it had been under Mao, and that earlier Great Powers had been. Unlike the Soviet Union it did not have a revolutionary ideology, communism, under which the whole world was ultimately to be dominated. On the contrary, China insisted on non-interference in domestic matters, a position for which a great many other countries had considerable sympathy. It sometimes tried to contain international crises and play an internationally useful role vis-à-vis rogue states such as North Korea and even Iran, although naturally the United States would have liked it to be much more constructive. China did not try to establish colonies in the way so many European Great Powers had done. And it had stopped supporting insurgencies against its neighbors.[82]

China generally respected markets, international trade, and many international institutions. It coordinated its stimulus packages to turn the economic recession around. It did not withdraw its huge support for the United States through loans and investment, although there were vague signs that it could come to re-evaluate its policies. In fact China was taking over much of the traditional British, and then American, role as the lender of last resort, thus contributing to the stabilization of the world economy. When the debt crisis hit several EU countries in 2010–11, China offered substantial assistance in the form of buying bonds and investing in these countries too.[83] Naturally it did this for its own economic and political reasons, but it was still very much appreciated by the countries concerned. This was hardly the behavior of a revolutionary power.

China was eagerly joining a whole series of international organizations, some of which, such as the WTO, could influence even its domestic decision-making. A few of these organizations were skeptical toward the West. Thus, in 1996, the Chinese took the initiative in establishing the Shanghai Five which in 2001 evolved into the Shanghai Cooperation Organization. Despite the occasional denunciations of "hegemony" in the form of the United States, the organization played a limited role. China helped to create the more open

---

[81] Elizabeth Economy, "The Game Changer: Coping with China's Foreign Policy Revolution," *Foreign Affairs*, 89:6 (November/December 2010), 142–52. The quotation is from 142. For a less dramatic discussion, see Robert J. Art, "The United States and the Rise of China: Implications for the Long Haul," *Political Science Quarterly*, 125:3 (Fall 2010), 359–91.

[82] For a useful survey, see the special section in *The Economist* on China's place in the world, "Brushwood and Gall," *The Economist* (December 4, 2010), 1–16.

[83] In a series of articles, see, for instance, Liz Alderman, "Beijing Seen Striving for Influence in Europe," *International Herald Tribune* (November 2, 2010), 1, 18; Liz Alderman, "In Embracing Europe, China Helps Itself," *International Herald Tribune* (January 7, 2011), 1, 14; Charlemagne, "Mr China Goes Shopping," *The Economist* (January 15, 2011), 30; Keith Bradsher, "China Ready to Help Prop Up Europe—For a Price," *International Herald Tribune* (September 16, 2011), 15, 16.

ASEAN Plus Three (China, Japan, South Korea). It also contributed to many international relief efforts, even to non-combat peacekeeping operations, and cooperated with the United States in fighting terrorism and piracy.[84]

Nevertheless, China clearly disagreed with the West on sovereignty (although actually less with the US than with the EU countries), sanctions, and the use of force (the opposition to force was not very revolutionary). It even signed some significant human rights covenants, but did not really implement them. China limited use of the death penalty somewhat, and of torture in exacting confessions. It was out-investing the United States in clean-energy technologies, though its fundamental interest appeared to be increased energy security rather than the environment—for instance, it is not yet reducing its vast coal production. China was actually exporting solar panels to the US and European markets, although this was done through state subsidies that probably broke WTO rules.[85] In a rapidly globalizing world, China's insistence on its full sovereignty, desperately trying to build firewalls against anything that could threaten its political system, made the solution of global problems, from the environment to North Korea's puzzling actions, that more difficult to achieve.

Yet occasionally China was actually willing to modify this full sovereignty line ever so slightly. It accepted the dispute mechanism of the WTO, some international cooperation about the environment, and even some UN sanctions against Iran. And it could be helpful on North Korea, Darfur, the Gulf of Aden, and Libya.[86] China was therefore both nationalistic and marginally prepared to share certain global responsibilities. It had solved most of its historically difficult border issues, but Taiwan could still potentially lead to war, even with the United States. So could, in the worst-case scenario, the situation in North Korea.

In the near future China's emphasis seems likely to be on a peaceful environment for the country's rise to Great Power status. In the West the hope was that China could gradually be co-opted into a Western-dominated world order. G. John Ikenberry argues that neither Russia nor China are inevitable enemies of the existing hugely successful Western international order. The task ahead must be to make them become full members. The

---

[84] Deborah Welch Larson and Alexei Shevchenko, "Status Seekers: Chinese and Russian Responses to U.S. Primacy," *International Security*, 34:4 (Spring 2010), 63–95.

[85] Keith Bradsher, "China Builds Lead on Clean Energy," *International Herald Tribune* (September 9, 2010), 1, 16; Wilson Center, *Centerpoint* (July/August 2010); Keith Bradsher, "China Makes Wind Power on own Terms," *International Herald Tribune* (December 15, 2010), 1, 19.

[86] Thomas J. Christensen, "Why the World Needs an Assertive China," *International Herald Tribune* (February 21, 2011), 6.

only certain way to make China an enemy was to treat it as one.[87] Edward G. Steinfeld even contended that China was gradually joining an American-dominated global economic system and that its authoritarianism was "self-obsolescing." China would become just like Taiwan. That seemed much too optimistic.[88]

Henry Kissinger believed that the competition between the United States and China "is more likely to be economic and social than military. A country with huge domestic tasks is not going to throw itself into a strategic confrontation or a quest for world domination. Weapons of mass destruction define a key distinction from Europe's pre-World War I period."[89] Aaron Friedberg is less certain. In political science terms not only realism, but also liberalism, with its emphasis on the different political systems, would suggest there could be conflict. Friedberg thinks China's ultimate goal is to "win without fighting," displacing the United States as the leading power definitely in East Asia, perhaps even in all of Asia, while avoiding a direct confrontation with the United States. To prevent such a development the United States has to preserve "a favorable balance of power."[90]

But was any Chinese–American reconciliation really possible without some form of grand bargain with China? Such bargains seem to have fallen out of favor in the modern world; they simply sound too cynical. Ikenberry argues that "The big bargain that the United States will want to strike is this: to accommodate China by offering it status and position within the regional order in return for Beijing's acceptance and accommodation of Washington's core strategic interests, which include remaining a dominant security provider within East Asia."[91] In other words, a continuation of the status quo with the US as the only global power, and China strictly limited, even within its own region. This is probably not much of a bargain for the Chinese.

To some extent the United States and China actually shared a concern with national sovereignty, although China's extraordinary insistence on this clearly presented a special problem when most of the world's challenges could only be solved through forms of international cooperation. In the longer term nobody could really tell what would happen, particularly if the economic growth collapsed. On the one hand, China's economic and military growth would

---

[87] G. John Ikenberry, "The Liberal International Order and its Discontents," *Millennium*, 38: 3 (2010), 509–21.

[88] Steinfeld, *Playing Our Game*, 218–34; for an interesting discussion of China's role, see also Amitai Etzioni, "Is China a Responsible Stakeholder?," *International Affairs*, 87:3 (May 2011), 539–53.

[89] Kissinger, *On China*, 525–26.

[90] Friedberg, *A Contest for Supremacy*, 1–8, 264–84. See also Friedberg's "Hegemony with Chinese Characteristics," *The National Interest* (July/August 2011), 18–27.

[91] G. John Ikenberry, *Liberal Leviathan: The Origins, Crisis, and Transformation of the American World Order* (Princeton: Princeton University Press, 2011), 356. See also 342–8.

give it capabilities which could be more actively exploited, primarily regionally, but also elsewhere. On the other hand, why would the country do anything that could represent a risk to a successful economic model that was producing such good results?

This is speculation. There could be no doubt about China's rapidly increasing importance in international relations. A new world was being created; or rather, elements of the old world were re-emerging. The size of China's economy could well surpass that of the United States in a few years. Yet, there might still be reasons to hold off making the most optimistic predictions about the future of Asia and China. On a per capita basis China would still be a relatively poor country by the standards of Great Powers. Its military strength would probably also continue to lag far behind that of the United States. Its alliance structure would also be much weaker. Or, to be more precise, China had virtually no real allies. Yet, more and more, China was insisting that its voice be heard and respected, most clearly in East Asia, but also on global issues in general.

3

War, Realism, and Power Transitions

Niall Ferguson has argued that imperial collapses are very sudden.[1] The collapse of the Soviet Union would appear to be a case in point, although it reflected deep structural changes that had been going on for quite some time. When Britain had to withdraw from India, Palestine, Greece, and Turkey in 1946–48, this, again, was quite dramatic, but the result of long-term processes. Yet, we are certain of the results only when we see the consequences. Today the signs of American decline are obvious. Should we therefore conclude that America's days are already numbered? Many of us feel that it may still be a bit premature to make such a prediction, at least with relevance for the near future.

Small changes happen every day that affect the relative situation of the world's Great Powers. Certain developments speed up the process considerably. Major wars often transfer the mantle of leadership directly from one country to another. Some powers are defeated; sometimes the winners spend so much of their strength that even victory leads to decline. The wars of Louis XIV (1643–1713) and of the French Revolution and Napoleon (1792–1815) ended French attempts at dominating Europe and marked the rise of Britain and, in the Napoleonic wars, also Russia. Germany became the leading continental power after wars with Denmark (1864), Austria (1866), and France (1870–71). The First World War resulted in the fall of four empires, those of Germany, Russia, Austria–Hungary, and of the Ottoman Empire. The last two of these units never reappeared as Great Powers.

The Second World War led to similarly huge changes. Germany and Japan were on the losing side. Although they ultimately recovered from the war, it took several decades and their policies were strongly influenced by the negative experiences of the Second World War. France had suffered a loss of prestige in 1940, from which it never fully recovered, despite the strong exertions of Charles de Gaulle. Great Britain had fought longer than any other Great Power during the war, but its moral record could not hide its

---

[1] Niall Ferguson, "Complexity and Collapse: Empires on the Edge of Chaos," *Foreign Affairs* (March/April 2010).

economic sacrifices and political problems. After the war it soon became economically, politically, and militarily dependent on the United States. Japan's victories in the early phase of the Second World War stimulated the independence movements in Asia. The colonial magic was gone. The yellow, and presumably even the black, man could defeat the white. European colonialism crumbled with the concessions the British had to make in India. To the surprise of many, what the British gave in India could not long be withheld by others, even in Africa. The other colonial powers had to follow Britain's path, more or less willingly. So total was Europe's defeat that the continent was put under the supervision of the two new powers that really counted, relatively indirectly by the United States in the West, and more directly by the Soviet Union in the East.

The Cold War focused primarily on Europe, but its casualties were suffered in Korea, in Vietnam, and in other places in Asia and Africa. Although the Soviet Union participated largely by proxy in most of these Third World conflicts, its militarization was an important factor in its ultimate collapse. When the Soviet Union had, at least in the military respect, become almost the equal of the United States, its existence came to an end. This collapse was indeed sudden, although certain warning signs had long been evident, which only became obvious with hindsight. In the long run the Soviet Union could not be America's equal when its economy was so much smaller and in such decline. As we shall see, Moscow's military spending may well have amounted to more than 30 percent of its total gross national product, a definite example of "imperial overstretch" if there ever was one. The United States spent around 4–5 percent of its GNP on military and other "imperial" expenses; only for a few years during the Korean War did it spend more than 10 percent. Starting in the 1960s the communist ideology had also gradually lost its force; in the 1980s hardly anybody believed that the future of the world belonged to Soviet Communism. Mikhail Gorbachev's efforts to reform the system ended in the collapse not only of communism, but also of the Soviet Union itself. But nobody did more than Gorbachev to bring the Cold War to an end. For this he did indeed deserve the Nobel Peace Prize.

Economic depressions also affect the Great Powers differently. The Great Depression of the 1930s started in the United States, and the US was among those hardest hit; but from a longer-term perspective we see that it hastened the transition from Great Britain to the United States as the world's economic leader. Britain was no longer able to protect the hegemonic or imperial functions it had earlier undertaken. Growing protectionism and the troubles of the pound further undermined Britain's role. Although the United States was temperamentally and politically unable to supersede Britain in the 1930s, the experiences of Pearl Harbor and the Second World War finally ended these restraints.

The oil shocks of the 1970s shifted the balance away from the oil consumers to the oil producers. Creditors were definitely in a better position than debtors, although the debt of the United States was very different from that of the countries of the Third World. As long as its economy was so dynamic, many were still willing to invest in the US. Yet the fact that in the course of the 1980s the United States became the world's largest debtor was bound to influence its role negatively. As we have seen, the days of the United States telling the rest of the world how to behave economically are largely gone, although old habits do not disappear overnight. When all the old Great Powers of the world were so negatively affected by the recession of 2007–10, and China was able to resume its very high growth so quickly, historical processes are indeed greatly speeded up. By how much is gradually becoming clear to us all.

All in all, it is difficult to avoid the conclusion that the American position in the world is certainly relatively weaker today than it was in the first decades after 1945, and also weaker than at the end of the Cold War in the 1990s. America's financial and economic problems are so grave that they are bound to affect its overall role negatively. Still, no single power, or combination of powers, is yet able to challenge the United States for the top leadership position. The United States is still the world's only true superpower. All its challengers are really still regional Great Powers, although the size of their respective regions varies considerably.

Despite the dramatic effects of the asymmetric power experienced every day in Iraq and Afghanistan, the United States is still in a league of its own militarily.[2] It spends six times as much on defense as does the second largest military spender, China. The US does not have the largest forces, but it has the most advanced and the only ones with a global reach. It can transfer hundred of thousands of troops to almost any distant corner of the world, as was seen during the Vietnam, Gulf, and Iraq wars. In its National Security Strategy of 2010, the Obama administration proclaimed that "we will maintain the military superiority that has secured our country, and underpinned global security, for decades."[3]

China's People's Liberation Army (PLA) is still primarily concentrating on Taiwan and the South China Sea and, increasingly, the Western Pacific. India's forces focus heavily on Pakistan and China. Pakistan is, in turn, even more obsessed about India. Russia's strategic vision does not extend much beyond the "near abroad" of the old Soviet territory, with the emphasis on the Caucasus and Central Asia, and with some attention being paid to its old sphere of interest in Central and Eastern Europe. Japan is reluctant to

---

[2] The best military data are found in the *SIPRI Yearbook, 2011* (Oxford: Oxford University Press, 2011). See particularly 183.

[3] David E. Sanger and Peter Baker, "Obama Gives Broader View on National Security," *International Herald Tribune* (May 28, 2010), 1, 6.

undertake any mission whatsoever that can lead to the loss of life; so is Germany, although not quite to the same extreme extent. Britain and France, and thereby also the EU, still have some capacities for power projection, but their major missions are generally carried out in close cooperation with NATO and the United States. With huge debts and financial retrenchment, that will be the case even more in the future, unless Britain and France are really able to implement joint policies.[4] The war in Libya in 2011 showed their ambition to try to do so; it did, however, also show the limits of what they could accomplish. For many different kinds of resources they were dependent on the United States, even when the US, as in this case, was "leading from behind.[5]

Despite the problems of the dollar, it remained the only really global currency. The French, the Organization of Petroleum Exporting Countries (OPEC), the Chinese, and others had talked about alternatives, from the German mark, to special drawing rights, the euro, and the renminbi. However, the dollar was still used in 85 percent of all foreign exchange transactions worldwide; 62 percent of world currency reserves were held in dollars, although this was down from 73 percent in 2001; 65 percent of China's 2.5 trillion dollar reserves are in dollars; and fifty-four countries had their currencies pegged to the dollar—twenty-seven to the euro. There were many reasons for the dollar's predominance: the size of the US economy, its large and very liquid financial markets, the incumbency of the dollar, and the low risk associated with the US treasury market. The trend was in the direction of reductions in these numbers, but the trend was slow. The euro in particular was becoming more important; its share of total foreign currency reserves increased from 18 percent in 2001 to 26 percent in mid-2010. Yet, all the alternatives, in 2011 definitely including the euro, also had their drawbacks. It was therefore likely that the dollar would remain the first among equals, while the others would primarily be taking on added regional importance.[6]

At least in the immediate future the United States will continue to have the world's largest economy. In a few years China's gross domestic product may well come to surpass that of the US, although today China's GDP is still only equal to 40.2 percent of that of the US, up from 17.9 percent in 2005. If the day comes when China actually surpasses the US, it will, as we have seen, still be a relatively poor country since it will have a population four times larger than that of the US. America's vast military lead, and the fact that it still

[4] Thomas P. M. Barnett, *Great Powers. America and the World After Bush* (New York: Berkley, 2009).

[5] For a short summing up of the various contributions in the Libyan war, see *The Economist* (September 3, 2011), 51–2.

[6] Barry Eichengreen, *Exorbitant Privilege: The Rise and Fall of the Dollar* (Oxford: Oxford University Press, 2011), 2–4, 39–96, 121–52; Alfred E. Eckes, Jr., *The Contemporary Global Economy: A History Since 1980* (Chichester: Wiley–Blackwell, 2011), 196–9; James Saft, "Welcoming the Dollar's Demotion," *International Herald Tribune* (May 20, 2011), 18.

has a GDP so much larger than that of China, have led some realist observers to proclaim that "The main feature of the distribution of capabilities today is thus unprecedented American primacy."[7]

This realist case may appear to be strong, but it definitely needs considerable modification. It leaves the impression that little or nothing has happened to the American position since the end of the Second World War. First, as I have already tried to indicate, the American position was in most respects considerably stronger in the first decades after 1945 and in the 1990s. There can be little doubt that America's position today, however strong, is weaker than in the 1990s.

Second, it is always a question of which numbers you focus on. On the economic side, the United States has held up well as far as GDP numbers are concerned. But if you look at the deficits in the federal budget and in current accounts the story is quite different. These numbers are almost entirely overlooked by realists in their rather exclusive focus on GDP. America's deficit problems are grave and undoubtedly represent the most serious challenge to its supreme status. This is what Niall Ferguson refers to when he suggests that America's decline and fall may well be precipitous. Alarm bells should be ringing very loudly indeed since previous falls have almost all been associated with fiscal crises. These cases were all "marked by sharp imbalances between revenues and expenditures, as well as difficulties with financing public debt."[8] In debates, Ferguson suggested that the collapse could actually take place within the next two years. President Obama and the Republican House of Representatives are trying to bring about a more balanced federal budget, still with limited success. A downgrade of the US by one of the rating agencies is striking, although this is still primarily a warning of what could follow if the parties are not able to work out further compromise.[9]

Third, numbers and perceptions may well be quite different. Perceptions matter, whatever they are based on. Thus, Soviet power was overestimated because there was the expectation of what would happen in the future, which of course nobody could know for certain. The same is the case with China's position today. The big new factor in international relations is indeed the economic rise of China. It is most definitely real and can be witnessed every day all around the globe, but this rise is further reinforced by our perceptions about the future. Thus, even the official US National Intelligence Council, which in 2004 had foreseen the continued domination of the international system by the United States, argued in its November 2008 report *Global*

---

[7] Stephen G. Brooks and William C. Wohlforth, *World Out of Balance: International Relations and the Challenge of American Primacy* (Princeton: Princeton University Press, 2009), 35. For the most recent numbers, see CNN World, "China's world GDP rises," April 5, 2011.

[8] Ferguson, "Complexity and Collapse," 30.

[9] Christine Hauser and Matthew Saltmarsh, "U.S. Rating Threat Unsettles Markets," *International Herald Tribune*, (April 19, 2011), 1, 18.

.

Trends 2025 that "the international system—as constructed following the
Second World War—will be almost unrecognizable by 2025 ... (It) will be a
global multipolar one with gaps in national power continuing to narrow
between developed and developing countries." Similarly, when so many
more in East Asia believe that China rather than the United States will be
"Asia's future power center," this becomes a factor in itself, at least until this
prediction may be replaced by a newer one.[10]

[10] The NIC report is available on the Internet. See also David C. Kang, *China Rising: Peace,
Power, and Order in East Asia* (New York: Columbia University Press, 2010), 70.

4

Expansion

"EMPIRE"—A DISCUSSION OF THE TERM

The proper meaning of the term "empire" has long been debated.[1] Many want to reserve the term for its narrow use, referring to the formal political control of one state over another's external and internal policy. In this sense the term will most frequently be applied to the historical period often described as the "Age of Imperialism" (climaxing in the years from the 1870s to the First World War). Others favor a broader definition, where empire simply means a hierarchical system of relationships with one power clearly being much stronger than any other. The stronger power also has to exercise considerable influence in at least some areas outside its home territory. Under such a definition, not only the Soviet sphere of influence, but also the wider and looser American one, could be called an "empire." I have generally followed this latter usage.

The term is therefore meant as a descriptive one, although some continue to see it as negative. As Felipe Fernández-Armesto has observed, a few historians have seen empires as good, so the US is an empire after all (Ferguson); many more saw empires as bad, so the US is not an empire (Parsons).[2] This was not always so. George Washington referred to the newborn republic as "a rising empire." In its early history the United States was frequently referred to as an "empire of liberty." Thus, Thomas Jefferson saw this "empire of liberty" as a collection of states loosely bound together in a federal union. The term suggested size and strength, but for Jefferson and others "empire" did not have to signify oppression. That was just the British version. This internal empire soon spanned the entire American continent. The means of that dramatic expansion were many—military, diplomatic, political, economic, and cultural.

---

[1] An early discussion of the term is found in my *The American "Empire" and Other Studies of U.S. Foreign Policy in a Comparative Perspective* (Oxford–Oslo: Oxford University Press, 1990), 37–9. The current section is substantially revised and extended.

[2] Felipe Fernández-Armesto, "Imperial Measures," *Times Literary Supplement* (*TLS*) (September 24, 2010), 8–9.

Only with the Civil War and the later rise of the United States to a position similar to that of the leading European powers did "empire" take on more negative connotations.[3]

Many saw the role of the United States as imperial at the time of the Spanish–American War. Then, the United States did indeed acquire colonies on the European model. Later, however, America, with only a few exceptions, came to frown on the use of the term empire about the US role. Americans like to see their country as special—different from all other powers. The European powers were imperial; the United States was certainly not. Only with the presidency of George W. Bush and the Iraq War did this change, not at the official level (although some unauthorized usage could be found even here), but at the academic and popular level.

Zbigniew Brzezinski insisted that "empire" could be a descriptive, not a normative, term. It simply told us something about the supreme position of the United States: "I use the term "empire" as morally neutral to describe a hierarchical system of political relationships, radiating from a center. Such an empire's morality is defined by how its imperial power is wielded, with what degree of consent on the part of those within its scope, and to what ends. This is where the distinctions between the American and Soviet imperial systems are the sharpest."[4] Arthur Schlesinger, another friend of American power, asked "Who can doubt that there is an American empire?—an 'informal' empire, not colonial in polity, but still richly equipped with imperial paraphernalia: troops, ships, planes, bases, proconsuls, local collaborators, all spread wide around the luckless planet?"[5]

Americans have also frowned on the term "power politics," despite the United States undoubtedly undertaking such practices normally associated with the Old World. As we have already seen, no one captured the European reaction to such claims to special status better than Winston Churchill.

When I first started using the term "empire" in the 1980s, many expressed a strong dislike to such a term being applied also to the United States. Today the situation is significantly different. Many historians and political scientists are using the term; a few even see it as a term of approval. "Empire" allegedly brings more order into a chaotic world. Some political economists still prefer the term "hegemon," but they usually stress only the economic power of the country in question. When we study power, we should look at all its aspects, not only the economic side. By doing so, we are also encouraged to compare

---

[3] Richard H. Immerman, *Empire for Liberty: A History of American Imperialism from Benjamin Franklin to Paul Wolfowitz* (Princeton: Princeton University Press, 2010) 1–19; David Reynolds, *America, Empire of Liberty: A New History* (London: Allen Lane, 2009).

[4] Zbigniew Brzezinski, *Game Plan: How to Conduct the U.S.–Soviet Contest* (New York: Atlantic Monthly Press, 1986), 16.

[5] Immerman, *Empire for Liberty*, 12.

the ways in which the different powers exerted their power. The United States, like other Great Powers, was special in some respects, not in others.

My argument is that the United States was definitely a stronger power after 1945 than was the United Kingdom in the nineteenth century or the Soviet Union in the twentieth. Territorially all three powers expanded considerably, both directly and indirectly. If this were indeed the case, why then call only the British and the Soviet versions "empires"? It is true that in organizing its sphere of influence the United States, on the whole, used much less force than either the British or the Soviets, although this was a difference in degree, not in principle. Yet this fact did not necessarily take anything away from the effectiveness of US power; in some regions the American version clearly outlasted the Soviet one. Great Powers generally order their spheres in accordance with their own strong and weak sides and their ideals and values. There was a British version of empire, a Soviet one, and an American one. We should be able to say something about what characterized each of them.

The effectiveness of an outside power's control may be entirely separate from its more formal aspects. First, even within the formal British Empire there was sometimes the form without the reality. For most practical purposes the white dominions had all become independent states well before the Second World War. This was reflected in Arthur Balfour's formula from 1926, under which Britain and the dominions were stated to be "autonomous communities within the British Empire, equal in status, in no way subordinate one to another in any aspect of their domestic or external affairs, though united by a common allegiance to the Crown, and freely associated as members of the British Commonwealth of Nations."[6] Here it was considerably clearer what the Empire was not than what it actually was.

Second, there was the reality of empire without the form. Certain areas were formally outside the British Empire, but Britain could nevertheless be almost as influential there as in several of the formally ruled areas. British influence in parts of China, in parts of the Ottoman Empire (particularly in Egypt), and in Argentina ("the sixth dominion") at times rivaled that in the dominions. This is what historians Robinson and Gallagher have called Britain's "informal empire." British rule in India was quite complex; some areas were under direct British rule, others were ruled indirectly through local rulers. The same was the case in Africa. Although the distinction between direct and indirect rule could be more formal than real, it too underlines the diversity within the British Empire. Similar complexities had existed within other empires, such as

---

[6] For a good survey of British imperialism, see Bernard Porter, *The Lion's Share. A Short History of British Imperialism 1850–1970* (London: Longman, 1975 and later editions). The quotation is from 267–8.

the old Athenian and Roman ones. Formal political control thus becomes a somewhat incomplete criterion for empire.[7]

In this context it should be noted that most prominent British experts on the British Empire who have compared the roles of Britain and the United States show little or no hesitation in describing the US role after 1945 as an American empire. (Porter, Darwin, Ferguson, even Robinson and Gallagher.) With the diversities within the British Empire—direct and indirect rule, formal and informal empire—there were indeed marked similarities between the two empires. Most foreigners, and even some Americans, react negatively to reserving the term hegemony, instead of empire, for the American role. If this is done, "We arrive at the somewhat paradoxical conclusion that a hegemon can be more powerful than an empire."[8] In an effort to get away from these complexities John Darwin has started referring to "world systems"—i.e. the British world system, instead of empire. The new term is meant to convey that "British imperialism was a global phenomenon; that its fortunes were governed by global conditions; and that its power derived less from the assertion of imperial authority than from the fusing together of disparate elements."[9] It is highly doubtful that this new term will resolve the debate.

In his new book, *Liberal Leviathan*, G. John Ikenberry discusses the difference between liberal hegemony, the term he prefers for the American role, and empire, a term he rejects, although he has some sympathy for the use of the term. Among the differences he stresses that a liberal hegemon acts within a wider order of rules and institutions. Even "the leading state operates within

---

[7] R. Robinson and J. Gallagher, "The Partition of Africa," in F. H. Hinsley (ed.), *Material Progress and World-Wide Problems, 1870–1898,* The New Cambridge Modern History, Volume 11 (Cambridge: Cambridge University Press, 1970), 593–640.

[8] Bernard Porter, *Empire and Superempire: Britain, America and the World* (New Haven: Yale University Press, 2006), 93–133; John Darwin, *After Tamerlane: The Rise & Fall of Global Empires, 1400–2000* (Penguin Books, 2008), particularly 479–85; Niall Ferguson, *Colossus: The Rise and Fall of the American Empire* (Penguin Books, 2005), particularly 10.

[9] John Darwin, *The Empire Project: The Rise and Fall of the British World-System, 1830–1970* (Cambridge: Cambridge University Press, 2009), xi. Darwin also argues that the British system "embraced an extraordinary range of constitutional, diplomatic, political, commercial and cultural relationships. It contained colonies of rule (including the huge "sub-empire" of India), settlement colonies (mostly self-governing by the late nineteenth century), protectorates, condominia (like the Sudan), mandates (after 1920), naval and military fortresses (like Gibraltar and Malta), "occupations" (like Egypt and Cyprus), treaty-ports and "concessions" (Shanghai was the most famous), "informal" colonies of commercial pre-eminence (like Argentina), "spheres of interference" . . . like Iran, Afghanistan and the Persian Gulf, and (not least) a rebellious province at home." (1).

In an even later work, Darwin has written that "Lacking the means and the manpower to govern by force, the British almost invariably chose to seek out the local power-holders and offer a bargain. Emirs, sheikhs, pashas, chiefs, khans and zemindars could stay in their place and rule their own roost, so long as they offered (and sanctioned) no challenge to imperial authority." John Darwin, "Empire and Ethnicity," *Nations and Nationalism*, 16:3 (2010), 383–401. The quotation is from 386.

them. In an imperial order, the core state operates above the law—outside the hierarchical structures that shape and constrain weaker and peripheral units." This clearly is a matter of degree, not of principle, as it could be argued that the United States frequently acts outside the order (several interventions without international mandate, opposition to the International Criminal Court and to the Kyoto Protocol, non-ratification of many international conventions, ending the Anti-Ballistic Missile (ABM) Treaty, occasionally somewhat unilateral roles in NATO and other organizations, including vetoes in the Security Council).[10]

In the flood of new books on comparative aspects of empire, Timothy Parsons, in his *The Rule of Empires*, uses a very narrow definition—so narrow in fact that when the Roman Empire bestowed citizenship on all residents of the empire in AD 212 "Rome ceased to be truly imperial." Empire always involved suppression; "no one became an imperial subject voluntarily."[11] This naturally excludes any consideration of the United States as an empire. On the other hand, in their very comprehensive *Empires in World History*, Jane Burbank and Frederick Cooper take a different view. Throughout the long sweep of history empires were the norm and nation states "a blip on the historical horizon." Empires were remarkably durable and they "accommodated, created, and manipulated differences among populations." The United States had "its own imperial trajectory" and "deployed an array of imperial strategies abroad: it occupied countries, dispatched troops to dislodge hostile leaders, sponsored proxy wars against foes, made use of enclave colonies and military bases on foreign soil, sent out missionaries and, more recently, supplied development aid and expertise."[12]

There can be little doubt that the Soviet Union exerted far more effective control over Eastern Europe—particularly in the years 1948 to 1953, but also later—than Britain generally did over most areas of imperial rule. The non-contiguous parts of the Soviet Empire, such as Vietnam and Cuba, had a much freer position. Still, since the Eastern European countries were all formally fully independent, even the Soviet Empire could not be called one under the narrow definition of empire.

Robinson has worked out more timeless definitions of "informal empire," but they are probably too vague to be really useful. But the complexity of imperial rule remains. Within the American "empire" some important areas were, at least temporarily, under direct American occupation—Japan, the

---

[10] G. John Ikenberry, *Liberal Leviathan: The Origins, Crisis, and Transformation of the American World Order* (Princeton: Princeton University Press, 2011), particularly 71–5. The quotation is from 73.

[11] Timothy H. Parsons, *The Rule of Empires. Those Who Built Them, Those Who Endured Them, And Why They Always Fall* (New York: Oxford University Press, 2010), 8, 25.

[12] Jane Burbank and Frederick Cooper, *Empires in World History. Power and the Politics of Difference* (Princeton: Princeton University Press, 2010), inside jacket, 2, 3, 456–7.

American zone in Germany. There, and in certain Caribbean/Central American and Pacific states, the American role could be just as striking as in some of the more directly ruled parts of the British Empire. On the whole, however, Britain had a formal empire, but few imperial institutions. The United States had no formal empire, but more developed institutions—in the form of alliances, security treaties, and partly also economic arrangements—than the British.[13]

So when the term "empire" is used about the American role, it generally refers to an informal hierarchical structure and a large-scale expansion. (The quotation marks are to make it clear that the term is used in its widest sense.) The states within this empire were generally politically independent; many, if not most of them, were political democracies, but they were still tied to America through important military, political, and economic arrangements. The American influence was more pronounced in shaping the overall structure (in NATO, for instance, or the integration of Germany and Japan in a Western system) than in forcing individual countries to make specific policy choices they would not otherwise have made (for instance compelling them to do certain things in their domestic policy which they did not really want to do). The American "empire" generally implied America's "power to" do certain things, less often "power over" certain countries or outcomes.

The administration of George W. Bush frowned upon the use of the term "empire," although certain members, including Vice President Cheney, used it in less formal contexts, and then with admiration for what the United States could achieve if it exerted its full power. The Bush administration had ambitions worthy of an empire. Just as Ronald Reagan had allegedly liberated Eastern and Central Europe and the Soviet Union, thereby ending the Cold War, Bush would liberate Afghanistan and Iraq and, later, presumably Iran and North Korea. This would reorder not only the Middle East, but much of the world. America had the strength and the means necessary to carry out such a hugely ambitious mission. This was indeed empire, without inverted commas.[14]

---

[13] In his interesting article "Making America Safe for the World: Multilateralism and the Rehabilitation of US Authority," *Global Governance*, 16 (2010), 471–84, David A. Lake starts out in the following way: "The United States is not an empire. Over the past century, however, it has built and sustained informal empires over states in the Caribbean littoral, spheres of exclusive political and economic influence over countries in South America, and after 1945 protectorates over allies in Western Europe and Northeast Asia in which it controls key segments of their foreign policies." See also Dennis Florig, "Hegemonic Overreach vs. Imperial Overstretch," *Review of International Studies*, 36:4 (2010), 1103–19.

[14] For a fine account of the thinking in the Bush administration, see James Mann, *Rise of the Vulcans: The History of Bush's War Cabinet* (New York: Viking, 2004). See also C. Akça Ataç, "Re-entering the Cosmopolitan Phase of Imperium: Remarks on Obama's Presidency and Discussions of American Empire," *Perceptions, Journal of International Affairs*, 14:1–2, (Spring–Summer 2009), 1–23.

But it was not to be. After initial victories, America soon faced great problems, both in Afghanistan and in Iraq. So big were these problems that nothing became of the expected follow-up in Iran and North Korea; regime change had to be abandoned in these two countries. Instead, in its second term, the Bush administration needed the support of its allies to get out of some of the problems it had created in its first four years. In much of the world George W. Bush had become the most unpopular president in recent US history. Then the economic problems, that had gradually become more serious, took on an explosive character in 2007–08. America was definitely in decline. Barack Obama could bring back America's popularity, but not its economic strength. America was still the world's leading power, but it had to work in cooperation with its various allies around the world and reduce its number of enemies as best it could. The days of empire, in almost any form, were virtually gone.

WHAT RIGHT TO EXPAND?

In *A Good Speed to Virginia* in 1609, Robert Gray asked "By what right or warrant we can enter into the land of these Savages, take away their rightful inheritance from them, and plant ourselves in their place, being unwronged or unprovoked by them."[15] This was a crucial question, but virtually all Great Powers came to think they had the right to do so. Part of the answer lay in the simple fact that they had the power to expand; therefore they did so.

Another part lay in the rather untroubled conviction that although the expansion might benefit the home country, it would certainly also benefit the colony or the area in question. This quickly led to the idea of higher and lower civilizations which has been an element in Western thinking at least since the Crusades. Certain civilizations quite simply stood "higher" in their degree of development than did others. Therefore, they had not only the right, but also the obligation, to expand. In this way they could bring "the natives" definite advantages, whether they be political rights, material benefits, or religious conversion.[16] As Lord Palmerston stated about one of the most important elements in Britain's expansion, "Commerce is the best pioneer of civilization." Free trade would, in his view, lead "civilization with one hand,

---

[15] Anthony Pagden, "The Struggle for Legitimacy and the Image of Empire in the Atlantic to c.1700," in Nicholas Canny (ed.), *The Oxford History of the British Empire, Volume I: The Origins of Empire* (Oxford: Oxford University Press, 1998), 37.
[16] Brett Bowden, *The Empire of Civilization: The Evolution of an Imperial Idea* (Chicago: The University of Chicago Press, 2009).

and peace with the other to render mankind happier, wiser, better."[17] The Romans and the Chinese were preoccupied with fighting "the barbarians"; the British felt "the white man's burden" and the French the "mission civilisa-trice"; the Americans were spreading "peace and liberty" around the world. It would be a big mistake to write off such sentiments as self-delusional propa-ganda, although there could certainly be an element of that as well. Even the highest ideals can be influenced by the most material of interests.

Great Powers almost always expand, sooner or later, directly or indirectly, but they expand in ways which, at least in the longer run, are in accordance with the instruments available and the political and cultural values of the power in question. The way in which the Great Powers organize their spheres of influence—or their "empires," if you will—can thus be quite different. But what they have in common is that they, in some form or other, control, or at least have substantial influence on, the basic orientation of the areas in question.

As Thomas F. Madden has argued in *Empires of Trust*, there were striking similarities between the Roman Empire (particularly under the Republic up to 27 BC), and the American one (particularly after the Second World War). Both Rome and the United States were initially colonies themselves; their motives and means of expansion were similar, with the fear of outside threats a predominant factor; their military supremacy was definite, and in both cases the imperial capital, not the allies, paid most of the expenses for defense. They both showed an initial reluctance to expand at the expense of "civilized" powers (Greece and Western Europe respectively), not of more primitive societies (Spain and Gaul in the case of Rome, Indians and Mexicans in Washington's). There were gradations of control within the empire, from rather directly imposed rule, to invitations to the imperial capital to play a larger role. There were clear limits as to how Rome and Washington could behave toward their allies. The importance of alliances is remarkable. They institutionalized the supremacy of Rome and Washington, but also limited the freedom of action of the imperial capital. Therefore, they were "empires of trust." In fact, neither Rome nor Washington liked the term "empire." They saw themselves more as first among equals and the allies as free. However, there could little doubt about their respective supremacies. One of their most highly appreciated functions was to keep peace within their empires.[18]

In *Why America Is Not a New Rome* Vaclav Smil argues that it may be tempting to call America an empire because of its "political strength, cultural

[17] Martin Lynn, "British Policy, Trade, and Informal Empire in the Mid-Nineteenth Centu-ry," in Andrew Porter (ed.), *The Oxford History of the British Empire, Volume III: The Nineteenth Century* (Oxford: Oxford University Press, 1999), 107.
[18] Thomas F. Madden, *Empires of Trust: How Rome Built—and America is Building—a New World* (New York: Dutton, 2008). See also Ali Parchami, *Hegemonic Peace and Empire: The Pax Romana, Britannica, and Americana* (Abingdon: Routledge, 2009).

allure, strategic might, and economic weight . . ." Yet, he concludes, this label should be resisted. The United States was definitely not the new Rome. "Clearly, the United States does not rule and it does not command. It leads; it has allies, not subjects; and a leader, unlike an absolute sovereign, cannot demand submission." He, like many others, ends up calling the US role "hegemony."[19] There is certainly something to Smil's argument, but as we shall shortly see, and as Madden indicates, the difference between hegemony and empire may be less clear-cut than he thinks. Even empires come in different forms, reflecting the respective strengths and values of the powers in question.

In Rome's case the role of Greece was strikingly similar to Western Europe's role within the American empire. Thus, while Rome and Washington certainly dominated, Greek and European culture were in many ways considered superior, at least by those ruled, but sometimes even by the ruler. The Greek charges of arrogance and lack of consultation bore a striking resemblance to the European situation. Rome and Washington in turn felt that these allies could be rather tiresome. Greece's special and respected position within the Roman Empire was the background for the British desire to play the role of Greeks within the American empire.

Historical China also had its empire in the form of its tributary system. Korea, Burma, Thailand, Vietnam, and even the Ryukyu Islands were central parts of this system. Between 1662 and 1911 well over 500 tribute missions from some 60 different countries are said to have called at Beijing.[20] These countries were all heavily influenced by many different aspects of Chinese culture. China tried to control them without the use of excessive military expenditure or violence, although occasionally there would be a deliberate show of force. The states were expected to show their subservience in different ways, including the language of diplomatic documents and ritual prostrations (kowtow) before the Chinese emperor. Direct military intervention became part of this system only very late in China's imperial history. Despite the clear notions of hierarchy and inequality involved, the Chinese liked to emphasize the consensual nature of this system. In part the whole arrangement rested on the voluntary compliance of the East Asian kings. The geographical borders of the Chinese system could be quite fluid, occasionally going beyond even East and Southeast Asia.[21]

Britain possessed a strong navy and at least initially expanded primarily in areas that could be reached by the Royal Navy. It enjoyed an economic

[19] Vaclav Smil, *Why America Is Not a New Rome* (Cambridge, MA: MIT Press, 2010), 53–4.

[20] Giovanni Andornino, "The Nature and Linkages of China's Tributary System under the Ming and Qing Dynasties," Working Papers of the Global Economic History Network (GEHN), 21/06 (March 2006), 15–16.

[21] Andornino, "The Nature and Linkages"; Jonathan D. Spence, *The Search for Modern China* (New York: Norton, 1990), 117–36.

superiority and cultural notions that facilitated its expansion. The cultural side was often summed up as the "white man's burden" or, more narrowly, "the Westminster model." Britain would bring progress and civilization, British concepts of law and order, and various British standards—in anything from language to private deportment—to different parts of the world.

Britain's approach to ruling the Empire was flexible and pragmatic. There were direct and indirect rule. There were evolution and incremental steps vis-à-vis the dominions and, to a lesser extent, India. In hindsight this was often seen as preparations for independence. At the time when most of these measures were introduced they were primarily meant to strengthen Britain's long-term role. There was less evolution in Africa. As late as toward the end of the Second World War, Labour deputy leader Herbert Morrison affirmed that independence for African colonies would be "like giving a child of ten a latch-key, a bank account and a shotgun."[22]

The Soviet Union had a strong army and generally ruled where the Red Army had reached. In Marxism–Leninism it possessed an ideology that could at any time explain why it was expanding and had the right to do so. "The Kremlin model" required considerable loyalty, even obedience, to the Soviet rulers.

Under Stalin the Soviet demands for loyalty were very high indeed. After a period of transition in the years immediately after the Second World War purges took place, soon even inside the Communist Party. Thus, the domination of the Party became near total in Central and Eastern Europe. Those individuals who showed signs of independence were killed or imprisoned, or, if they could not be reached, like Tito, were denounced and isolated. Five-year models of industrialization were introduced and agriculture largely collectivized. Rarely were the connections between domestic and foreign policy as clearly seen as in the Soviet case under Stalin. Under Khrushchev and Brezhnev the main characteristics of the political and economic systems remained, although the element of force and violence was reduced.[23]

The United States had a wide assortment of instruments, certainly military, but also economic, political, and cultural, and expanded in many different ways.[24] America was to bring peace, liberty, and, at least after the 1930s, freer trade to the world. While the overall structure was flexible, limits did exist. After 1945 the most important requirement of "the Washington model" was that the country in question supported Washington over Moscow in the Cold War. The United States expected its friends to stand up and be counted. As the

[22] Colin Cross, *The Fall of the British Empire, 1918–1968* (London: Paladin, 1970), 270–1.
[23] The best recent account of Soviet foreign policy is Jonathan Haslam, *Russia's Cold War: From the October Revolution to the Fall of the Wall* (New Haven: Yale University Press, 2011).
[24] Much of what follows in this section is based on my *The American "Empire."* Fuller documentation and references will be found there.

history-conscious President Harry Truman put it: "We are faced with the most terrible responsibility that any nation ever faced. From Darius I's Persia, Alexander's Greece, Hadrian's Rome, Victoria's Britain, no nation or group of nations has had our responsibilities."[25] It was now America's task "to save the world from totalitarianism."

Domestically the United States was a federation. Within the overall US ideology and political structure, different approaches could be found in the forty-eight and, when Alaska and Hawaii were added, the fifty states. In addition there was a federal district, the capital Washington, DC, and a whole series of territories and islands in the Pacific and the Caribbean with different formal arrangements. This diversity made it relatively easy for Washington to add states to its "empire." West Germany and Japan were occupied states; most others were fully independent states, but in many ways dependent on the United States. Through the open American political system they could lobby for their requirements and desires. The United States was an incredibly strong power, but its political system was more open to outside influence than virtually any other.

Initially at least, after 1945, there were also forces on the right which Washington wanted to keep at bay, either because they had been tainted by collaboration with fascism during the Second World War, or because they were seen as extreme in their nationalism, such as was the case with Gaullism in France. Soon, however, the containment of the right lost out almost entirely to the containment of the left.

In Western Europe and a few other places Washington could cooperate with regimes that were democratic, anti-communist, and in favor of freer trade. This was the best of all worlds. In so many other parts of the world these basic values were frequently at odds with each other, as seen for instance in the civil war in China in the 1940s, or in Vietnam in the 1960s. This often led Washington to a rather desperate search for "a third road" that could combine these values, often to no avail, since this alternative was weak or even nonexistent in many places.

The United States had Great Power interests which sometimes clashed with the values it often proclaimed, even the support for democratic rule. This had happened for decades, even centuries, in America's domestic treatment of its Native and African Americans. The United States had long been the most democratic country on earth, in the rights enjoyed by its white, male population. But this had never prevented the country from discriminating against other groups.

The same discrepancy could be found in US foreign policy. There were cases where Washington did not support democracies when they were too far

---

[25] Walter Millis (ed.), *The Forrestal Diaries* (New York: Viking, 1951), 281.

to the left. Thus, in the fall of 1946 the broad-based coalition government in Czechoslovakia, with the communists in a prominent role, still had overwhelming local support. Nevertheless, Secretary of State James Byrnes decided to stop further aid to Prague.[26] The government was out of favor, primarily because it tended to support Moscow on foreign policy issues. About the situation in Indochina in 1954 President Eisenhower himself wrote in his memoirs that "I have never talked or corresponded with a person knowledgeable in Indochinese affairs who did not agree that had elections been held at the time of the fighting, possibly 80 percent of the population would have voted for the communist Ho Chi Minh as their leader rather than Chief of State Bao Dai."[27] This realization did not stop the Eisenhower administration from taking strong measures to prevent Ho's coming to power. In Chile in 1973 the CIA certainly played a role in the overthrow of democratically elected leftist President Salvador Allende, although he was supported by only a minority of Chileans.

On the right, particularly in Latin America and Asia, the United States frequently worked closely with non-democratic regimes. Occasionally this was the case even inside Europe. During the Cold War Portugal and Spain consistently fell short of democratic standards; Greece and Turkey often did so. Salazar's Portugal was still a founding member of the Organisation for European Economic Co-operation (OEEC) and NATO. Franco's Spain was not permitted to take part in either organization, but that was increasingly because of opposition from certain Western European countries. Thus, in 1951–52, the United States entered into bilateral agreements which made Spain an indirect member of the Western Alliance. In Greece, the Americans actually wrote both the Greek application for aid, and the thank-you notes in connection with the Truman Doctrine. In Greece and Turkey local administration had broken down to such an extent that under the Marshall Plan Americans were closely involved in running their national bureaucracies.

Occasionally the United States interfered covertly to influence developments. In Italy in 1947 Washington encouraged the non-communists to throw the communists out of the government, and in 1948 far exceeded normal limits in supporting the Christian Democrats in the election. There, as in several other European countries, Washington encouraged the breakup of unions and parties dominated by communists or "fellow travelers." In 1953 the CIA intervened to help overthrow the radical nationalist Mosaddeq in Iran, and the leftist Arbenz in Guatemala the following year. The situation in

---

[26] Geir Lundestad, *The American Non-Policy Towards Eastern Europe 1943–1947. Universalism in an Area Not of Essential Interest to the United States* (Oslo–Oxford: Oxford University Press, 1975), 167–73.

[27] Dwight D. Eisenhower, *Mandate for Change 1953–1956* (New York: Signet, 1965), 449. See also 409.

the Philippines was somewhat different in that here a combination of overt and covert means was used to support the American favorite, Magsaysay, and defeat the Huk rebels.

With the exception of the Philippines, these operations were all rather small scale; they were still successful from the American point of view. One reason they succeeded was that they could draw upon various local forces—often the army—and at least some popular support. So, in Iran, a few CIA agents and a few hundred thousand dollars helped bring the Shah back. The CIA–Guatemalan group that started the action against the Arbenz government comprised no more than 150–300 men.

Where the United States tried to overthrow either well-organized governments, and/or broadly supported ones, it failed, even in the heyday of American expansion. That was the case in Albania in 1951–52, in Tibet from the mid-1950s, in Indonesia in 1958, and in Cuba in 1961. In the Cuban case many policymakers had the parallel with Guatemala in 1954 very much in mind. Cuba, one of the countries where America's influence had traditionally been the strongest, was to illustrate the limits of Washington's power, even on its own doorstep.

THE EXPANSION OF THE UNITED STATES[28]

The First World War and the October Revolution actually resulted in a contraction of the new Soviet state (the independence of Poland, Finland, and the Baltic States, border changes with Rumania and Turkey.) In the interwar period the only significant expansion took place in Outer Mongolia. In 1944–45 the Soviet Union not only regained most of the territory it had lost after the First World War, but also expanded its rule considerably. The expansion was largely the work of the Red Army. Moscow came to exercise close control over Eastern Europe, and much looser control over North Korea. The communists won a momentous victory in China. That victory was based on only limited support from the Soviets, but it certainly strengthened the Soviet position, at least temporarily, i.e. in the 1950s. The communists also won in North Vietnam, but Soviet domination there was modified by Vietnam's distance from Moscow and by a strong nationalism. Since the Soviet Union by itself constituted one-sixth of the earth's land area, this could be regarded as the largest contiguous empire the world had ever seen. However, Soviet expansion was limited to its border areas. In the first ten to fifteen years after the Second World War the Soviet Union was not a global

---

[28] Much of what follows in this section and in the next on America's allies follows my *The American "Empire,"* 46–54, 62–70. Further documentation and references will be found there.

superpower at all. So Stalin did not really have a Latin American or African policy.[29]

In that respect the British Empire was different. Before the First World War Britain's Empire constituted 23 percent of the world's population and 20 percent of its area. (It actually grew somewhat after the First World War, but the signs of breakdown were becoming increasingly clear, as witnessed in Ireland and in India.) The British Empire was more than four times the size of the Roman one, and its population did not fall much short of the combined populations of the contemporary French, German, and Russian empires. Despite its vast complexities the British Empire basically fell into two categories, both scattered over very diverse areas. One was the white dominions: Canada, Australia, New Zealand, and South Africa; the other the "colored" colonies, with India as "the jewel in the crown." Britain also dominated the seas and most of the world's strategic strong points: Gibraltar, Cape Town, Suez, and Singapore.

The expansion of Great Britain in the eighteenth and nineteenth centuries was the result of Britain's strength and the weakness of the periphery. Manchu China was declining; so were Mogul India and the Ottoman Empire; Africa was "backward" and characterized by a high turnover of regimes. Before the Second World War at least one billion people outside Europe were controlled by a few Western states. As has so often been said, the sun never set on the British Empire, or even on the smaller French one.

The American "empire" after the Second World War was in important ways more comprehensive than either the Soviet or even the British Empire. American expansion was global, unlike Soviet expansion, which was limited to its border areas, however vast these border areas might be. Compared to the British Empire the American "empire" came to include units which were much more important strategically, politically, and economically. The British Empire was in most respects a coalition of peripheries, to overstate the case a little. India was celebrated for its importance. In Curzon's words, "as long as we rule India we are the greatest power in the world. If we lose it, we shall drop straight away to a third-rate power."[30] Despite such rhetoric even India was of limited importance in Great Power politics. Britain's influence was weakest in the very center of Great Power politics, on the European continent. Huge changes, such as the unification of Italy and Germany, took place without the United Kingdom being a major actor in these events.

Like the British Empire, the American one also reflected the strength of the mother country. But unlike the British Empire, the American "empire" did not

---

[29] Latin America and Africa are hardly mentioned in the Stalin years in the newest account of Soviet foreign policy, Haslam's fine *Russia's Cold War*.

[30] Aaron L. Friedberg, *The Weary Titan: Britain and the Experience of Relative Decline, 1895–1905* (Princeton: Princeton University Press, 1988), 218–20.

so much spring from the weakness of the periphery (although it did that too), as from the weakness of most of the traditional power centers. The American "empire" was geographically just as comprehensive as the British, and, what was more important, came to include four of the six power centers of the post-war years: The United States itself, Britain, Western Europe with most of Germany, and Japan. (The remaining two were the Soviet Union and China.) The American "empire" was also more impressive in that it emerged largely in the course of a ten-year period after the Second World War, while the British Empire developed gradually over two to three centuries.

The term "isolationism," as applied to the period up to the Second World War, may easily give the wrong impression of America's policies. It was certainly not isolated from the rest of the world; in most respects—for instance, immigration, culture, and trade—it was in close contact with most of the world. The United States did, however, stay out of alliances outside the Western hemisphere. "Unilateralism" was probably a better term. Republicans, from Henry Cabot Lodge after the First World War and Robert Taft after the Second, to even some neo-conservatives in the 1990s, disliked alliances since they limited US freedom of action. They wanted the United States to act on its own. Yet there is no doubt that the American role expanded tremendously after the Second World War. The expansion was military, political, economic, and cultural.

The United States had no allies before the war and no US troops were stationed on territory it did not directly control. After the war Washington entered into numerous alliances, and bases were established in different corners of the world. Geographically the postwar expansion was least notice-able in Latin America, because this had traditionally been the US backyard. The Monroe Doctrine had been Washington's unilateral proclamation of its special role in the Western hemisphere. In 1940–41, FDR extended the Doctrine hundreds of miles out to sea, implied that Canada fell under it, and even broadened it to cover Greenland (1940) and Iceland (1941). Private-ly, the president believed that the Canaries, the Azores, and even West Africa should be covered because of their strategic importance to the Western hemisphere.

After the war the special role of the United States was given at least indirect multilateral sanction in the form of the Act of Chapultepec (1945), the Rio Treaty (1947), and the Organization of American States (1948). Until the late 1950s American policymakers took Latin America for granted to such an extent that, for instance, all of the Western hemisphere received less economic assistance than did the Benelux countries alone. This began to change only in Eisenhower's last years and was speeded up with Kennedy and the Alliance for Progress, although, as so often happened under Kennedy, the rhetorical change was greater than the practical results. When needed to contain leftist challenges, Washington reinforced its position through military interventions, although not always with success (Guatemala, 1954; Cuba, 1961; Dominican Republic, 1965).

The American position in the Pacific had also been strong before the war, with the possession of Hawaii and the Philippines. After the war Ernest Bevin soon complained that the Monroe Doctrine was being extended to the Pacific. The Philippines were given their promised independence, but remained close-ly tied to the United States economically and militarily. The Japanese Man-dated Islands came under American control, with only the thinnest of concessions to the suzerainty of the United Nations. American influence in South Korea remained strong despite the US forces being pulled back in 1948. The Korean War brought the forces back, and the American commitment to South Korea's defense was now expressed in a long-term security treaty.

The new American role in Japan was the most important change brought about by the war in Asia. The United States was the sole occupier of Japan and the allies from the war had only the most limited influence on the American occupation. After the peace treaty of 1951 Japan was tied to the United States through a security treaty and comprehensive American base rights, under which Japan's defense became an American responsibility and Japan's foreign policy to a large extent an extension of Washington's.

The Second World War had indicated that both Australia and New Zealand would now look primarily to the United States, and not to Britain, for their defense. In 1951 this understanding was formalized through the Australia, New Zealand, United States Security Treaty (ANZUS). Britain was excluded from taking part, rather pointedly demonstrating the decline of Britain in this part of the world too.

The biggest overall change took place in the American–European relation-ship. The United States did not withdraw from Europe as it was generally, and somewhat simplistically, seen to have done after the First World War. The US first extended considerable bilateral aid to many European countries, primari-ly those in Western Europe; then this aid was given a dramatically new framework through the Marshall Plan, where practically all the Western European countries, including Sweden, Switzerland, and Austria, participated. In September 1946, Secretary of State James Byrnes made it clear that Ameri-can troops would remain in Germany for the duration of the occupation. The American commitment was then given a more lasting and multilateral form through NATO. The United States, Canada, and the ten founding European members were later joined by Greece and Turkey (1952), and West Germany (1955).

The United States was far and away the dominating member of NATO. Indeed the major point of the alliance was to tie the Americans as closely as possible to the defense of Western Europe. The original commitment was expanded in scope through the integrated military command, the increase in the American troop strength, and military assistance programs, all in turn based on the perception of an enhanced threat largely resulting from the outbreak of the Korean War. The integration of West Germany into a Western framework, just a few years after the war—first economically through the Marshall Plan, and then militarily through NATO—was a dramatic expression of the American role. So Washington's influence was predominant in both (most of) Germany and Japan, the two main aggressor states of the Second World War. The United States alone basically filled the vacuums in these two core countries.

The financially strapped British were leaving more and more of their commitments to the Americans. The organization of the Bizone in Germany was an indirect way of relieving the British burden. The Truman Doctrine in March 1947 represented the official proclamation that the United States was replacing Britain in Greece and Turkey. From a historical perspective, the United States was not only replacing Great Britain as the organizer of the European opposition to the strongest continental power, but was also playing a much more active role in shaping the continent than Britain had done even in its heyday. The United States helped to form a new Europe through the Marshall Plan and NATO, and in many other, both direct and indirect, ways.

In the Middle East the situation was considerably more complex than in Europe. Here too the Western mantle of leadership was being transferred from Britain to the United States, but the transfer was both slower and had stronger elements of conflict than in Europe. The various British withdrawals, starting with Palestine in 1948 and ending with the Persian Gulf in the late 1960s, left considerable bitterness between London and Washington. In American eyes the British were, in some cases, too slow in leaving (generally in the 1940s and 1950s); in others they were too quick (in the 1960s). The British frequently felt that they were being undercut either by the Jewish lobby or the big oil companies, or by both. The outbursts against Washington could be strong. Thus, in 1954, Foreign Secretary Anthony Eden felt that the Americans were not only trying to replace the French and run Indochina themselves, but that "they want to replace us in Egypt too. They want to run the world."

However, it soon proved impossible for policymakers in Washington to put the local situation in the Middle East, and even elsewhere, into the East–West framework which came so naturally in Europe. Strong American support for Israel did not preclude an expanding role toward the Arabs as well. Before the Second World War, American oil companies had been operating in Iraq, Bahrein, Kuwait, and Saudi Arabia. From at least 1943, Washington pursued an active policy toward Saudi Arabia in particular, and continued Lend–Lease aid after it had been cut to other countries. This led the British minister to Saudi Arabia comment that "it was too bad that an American oil company did not hold oil concessions in the United Kingdom," so that the British too could continue to receive Lend–Lease. The outcome of the American–British oil rivalry was a division of responsibility; American companies would control the fields in Saudi Arabia, while British companies would take the lead in Iraq and Iran. The United States also obtained base rights in Saudi Arabia, at first in direct competition with the British. Dhahran became a key base in the Middle East, and in return the US provided economic and military support. In 1946 the United States was to take over another traditional British function— namely the role of containing Russian/Soviet influence in Iran. After the overthrow of Mosaddeq in 1953 American oil companies even got a 40 percent interest in the oil fields there.

The United States became increasingly involved in extending economic and military assistance to Israel and to most Arab countries. The Truman, and particularly the Eisenhower, administration favored an extension of the pact system into the Middle East, but when the Baghdad Pact was finally created in 1955—with Britain, Turkey, Pakistan, Iran, and Iraq as members—the US formally remained on the outside, in part because of Washington's Israeli connection, in part because of the conflict between Britain and Egypt.

The Suez intervention sharply reduced British influence in the Middle East. Not only was the United States the main factor behind the British–French decision to halt the invasion, but, as in Greece in 1947, it also stepped in to try to fill the vacuum which the reduced British role created. This was the intention of the Eisenhower Doctrine of 1957. As Eisenhower himself stated, "the existing vacuum in the Middle East must be filled by the United States before it is filled by Russia."[31] Now the United States took over as the predominant Great Power in the region, although it could still cooperate with Britain, as the joint invasion of Lebanon–Jordan in 1958 demonstrated. Kennedy tried to improve relations even with Nasser's more radical Egypt, but these efforts to broaden the American role largely failed, partly because of American support for Israel, but probably even more because of rivalry between moderate and radical Arab forces, as revealed in the Saudi–Egyptian conflict in Yemen.

The dismantling of colonial empires was one of the most important and dramatic phenomena of the postwar years. It was the result of a complex interaction of forces on the international, metropolitan, and colonial levels. In some instances the United States actually tried to uphold the old order. This was particularly the case when the independence movement was seen as communist-dominated, as in Indochina. In most instances, however, Washington tried to bring about compromises which could provide for political stability, and generally such stability was identified with slow advances toward independence.

American anti-colonialism helped bring about a change in Britain, the key country in the decolonization process, and also the one closest to the US.

---

[31] Dwight D. Eisenhower, *Waging Peace 1956–61: The White House Years* (New York: Signet Books, 1965), 178.

Various impulses, from Franklin Roosevelt's rhetoric, to Washington's very direct pressure on the Netherlands over Indonesia, stimulated the conclusion that the age of the empire was over. And with colonial self-confidence also undermined in this way, the transfer of power became a much more rapid process than any had thought likely before, and even during, the Second World War. As Louis and Robinson have argued, "In the shadow of their powerful American ally the British followed certain golden rules more warily than ever: handle the colonies with kid gloves; concede to subjects rather than risk confrontation with them; and above all avoid all dangers of possible uprisings, armed repression, and colonial wars. Only thus could the possibility of American intervention in the African empire be averted."[32]

Similar reasoning of course applied to Asia. There too the American position expanded dramatically. In South Asia the United States played a role in encouraging the British to give up colonial rule, although Washington increasingly deferred to London as the independence process was speeded up. After having tried to balance India and Pakistan, the United States became exasperated with India's neutrality and Nehru's morality lectures and sided with pro-Western Pakistan. But the alliance with Pakistan, and Dulles's occasional denunciations of neutrality, should not hide the fact that the Eisenhower administration wanted to maintain fairly close ties even with India and, for instance, came to increase American economic assistance to New Delhi. Kennedy attempted to strengthen these ties further, through military aid against the Chinese and increased economic support, but India's neutral position and the American allegiance to Pakistan meant that there would be no dramatic improvement in US–Indian relations.

In Southeast Asia the interests of the United States had traditionally been limited to the Philippines and to rubber and tin imports from Malaya. Soon, however, Washington came to play an increasing role, first in Indonesia, where a small European power—the Netherlands—tried to defeat a non-communist nationalist movement, but then also in Indochina, where France was struggling to hold on against the communist-led Vietminh. In Indonesia, Washington's threat to suspend economic and military assistance was an important factor in the Dutch decision to finally give up. In the early years after the war the United States largely deferred to France, primarily because of the overriding importance of France in the Cold War in Europe. In Vietnam the United States tried to promote a nationalist alternative at the same time as it financed a rapidly increasing share of France's expenses in fighting the Vietminh. After the French defeat and the Geneva Conference of 1954,

---

[32] William Roger Louis and Ronald Robinson, "The United States and the Liquidation of the British Empire in Tropical Africa, 1941–1951" in Prosser Gifford and William Roger Louis, *The Transfer of Power in Africa: Decolonization 1940–1960* (New Haven: Yale University Press, 1982), 31–55. The quotation is from 49.

the United States took the initiative in creating the Southeast Asia Treaty
Organization (SEATO), with Pakistan, Thailand, the Philippines, Australia,
New Zealand, Britain, France, and the United States as members. In addition
came the separate security treaty with Taiwan (and the treaties with Japan and
South Korea).

In 1945–46 the Joint Chiefs' lists of essential bases illustrated how dramatically the war had expanded US security requirements. The six most essential
ones were found in widely scattered parts of the world: Greenland, Iceland, the
Azores, Casablanca, the Galapagos, and Panama. There is no agreed definition
of a base, but, by one count, in 1955 the United States had 450 bases in thirty-
six countries. In the late 1960s, at its maximum, the United States had one
million troops stationed abroad, far more than Britain had had at any time.[33]

While the United States emerged as the world's main creditor after the First
World War, both Britain and France were still creditor states at the time. After
the Second World War the United States was virtually the only major source
of credit. (Canada and Sweden represented much smaller sources.) Practically
every Western European country, certainly including Britain and France,
wanted fresh economic assistance from the US, in this case from the government. (The more limited American credits extended after the First World War
came largely from private sources.)

American expansion was, in some respects, least striking on the economic
side. In part this was because here, unlike in military and diplomatic matters,
the United States had played an important role even before the Second World
War. In absolute figures there was a tremendous increase in American exports
and imports. The United States became the world's largest trader, finally
surpassing the United Kingdom. In 1943–47 exports were above "normal" as
a percentage of gross national product, but they soon fell back to their
traditional 3–5 percent range. During, and immediately after, the war imports
remained below 3 percent of GNP; this was somewhat lower than the historical average, and extremely low by international standards. In most Western
European countries, including Britain, exports and imports regularly constituted 30–40 percent, or more, of GNP. Only socialist–autarchic countries like
the Soviet Union, and less developed and geographically isolated countries,
had lower percentages than the United States. A pronounced increase in
America's trading role would only take place in the 1970s, with its rapidly
increasing oil imports and, in part as a consequence of this, its growing
exports.

American investment abroad increased considerably, but well into the
1950s most of the growth was limited to the more traditional areas of the

[33] John Lewis Gaddis, "Was the Truman Doctrine a Real Turning Point?," *Foreign Affairs*, 52:2
(January 1974), 388–402; Friedberg, *The Weary Titan*, 220, 277; Geir Lundestad, *America,
Scandinavia, and the Cold War 1945–1949* (New York: Columbia University Press, 1980), 23–4.

Western hemisphere, Canada, and Latin America. In fact the growth in Europe was so slow that only in 1957 did American investments there surpass European ones in the United States. In the late 1950s, however, American investment in Western Europe started to grow rapidly.

THE IMPORTANCE OF AMERICA'S ALLIES

Britain had traditionally practiced a diplomacy of "splendid isolation." The fact that it stood alone could be seen as a sign of strength, but the lack of allies can also become a sign of weakness. In war and conflict the power with strong allies naturally has an advantage over one standing alone, other factors being equal. Gradually Britain's isolation was abandoned. The country could not be prepared for war in all parts of its far-flung empire. In 1894–95 London concluded that it did not have the power or the interest in going to war against the United States. And in 1902 it concluded its first Great Power alliance with Japan. Even in Europe London had to reduce its traditional political distance to the continent. Germany's rapid build-up led to understandings with France in 1904, and with Russia in 1907—not alliances as such, but definite modifications of past policies.

The Soviet Union also had its alliances and treaties, first with its Eastern and Central European partners, then with China under Mao. The fact that the Soviet Union and China, the world's most populous country, concluded an alliance in 1950, and cooperated relatively well throughout that decade, greatly helped the Soviet position. The alliance appeared to confirm Soviet claims that the future did indeed belong to communism. Correspondingly, when the alliance started to break up ten years later, and armed conflict between the two countries even occurred in the late 1960s, it severely weakened Moscow's position. Suddenly the United States could exploit the rivalry between the two communist giants. In the first years after 1945 the Soviet Union had exploited its allies in Eastern Europe; some decades later it had to subsidize these allies in various ways to keep them reasonably happy, in part because of the conflict with China.

The United States was considerably stronger than either Britain or the Soviet Union. Washington too had traditionally shunned alliances and also practiced a diplomacy of "isolationism." After 1945 it could probably have continued more or less on its own. Instead, it reversed course and was soon prepared to enter into a comprehensive system of alliances and treaties. This reflected the dramatic changes imposed by the Second World War and by the Soviet threat; it also illustrated America's new-found strength and self-confidence. No longer was there any danger of the Old World undermining the American experiment. Now the United States would dominate much of Europe.

The system of alliances greatly underpinned US strength. America cooperated with many of the leading powers of the world—Britain, France, West Germany, Italy, and Japan.[34] It did this from a position of strength. Their resources were, in some respects, added to the huge resources of the United States. Naturally Washington sometimes had to enter into compromises with the various capitals, but with America's strength so overwhelming, and the lack of alternative leaders for the West so obvious, its position was very strong indeed. As we shall see, it was in fact so strong that in many ways the Europeans invited the United States to assume the leading role it came to play after the Second World War. Similarly, illustrating the complementary nature of their interests, most administrations in Washington worked hard to build up a more integrated Europe, so clearly different from the divide-and-rule policies normally pursued by imperial powers. But the underlying assumption was always that even this more integrated Europe would be following America's lead in most basic matters.[35]

American–European cooperation was based on the shared assumption that Europe was the area of the world that mattered most. The struggle between East and West had long been primarily a struggle over Europe. The Cold War, just like the Second World War, would be won or lost in Europe. The less important non-European issues soon created conflict between the United States and some of its European allies. First the European allies felt they got too little support from Washington in upholding their colonial roles; then, when the US dominated in Asia and the Middle East, it in turn felt it did not get the assistance it deserved. Suez and Vietnam were expressions of this respective state of affairs.

On the security side, whenever NATO had to decide on one policy which simply had to commit all the member states, including the United States itself, the American voice would decide. Thus, NATO strategy became an extension of US strategy. Under Eisenhower massive retaliation was adopted first by Washington, then by NATO. Under Kennedy–Johnson flexible response became the new doctrine, both for the US and NATO. Although there was more of a time lag in the latter case, a fact which illustrated both the skepticism and the rising influence of the Europeans, particularly the French, there could be little doubt that American authorities would decide American strategy and thereby indirectly also NATO's strategy. On the other hand, in most imperial

[34] I have dealt with the alliance relationship in my *The United States and Western Europe Since 1945. From "Empire" by Invitation to Transatlantic Drift* (Oxford: Oxford University Press, 2003).

[35] Geir Lundestad, *"Empire" by Integration: The United States and European Integration, 1945–1997* (Oxford: Oxford University Press, 1998).

relationships the "vassals" would be called up to do much of the early fighting. In Western Europe, on the contrary, US troops would be in the first line of defense against any Red Army invasion. The combination of America's nuclear deterrence and its forces along the Iron Curtain was the guarantee against any Soviet attack.

In many other cases as well American domination could be rather striking. It is hard to imagine that, so soon after the war, the Europeans would have agreed to the reconstruction and rearming of West Germany, if it had not been both for America's insistence that this be done, and an American presence which could provide assurance against a renewed German threat. In East Asia it proved impossible to construct one comprehensive security arrangement, in great part because Japan could not be brought together with its former enemies. There, a complex network of separate alliances and security treaties was established. Again, the United States was the linchpin in all this.

When the United States really insisted on a certain course of action, the countries most dependent on it had little choice. This was, once more, best illustrated in the Japanese and German cases, the defeated countries. Thus, in 1950, and much to his dislike, Prime Minister Shigeru Yoshida had to promise to undertake a limited rearmament; and in 1951–52 he had little choice but to recognize Taiwan, and to severely curtail even economic contacts with "Red China." In 1956 the Japanese showed an interest in exploring the conditions under which a peace treaty could be concluded with the Soviet Union based on a compromise solution as far as the disputed northern islands were concerned. After John Foster Dulles made it clear that the formal cession of Kunashiri and Etorofu to the Soviets would mean that the United States could claim Okinawa, the Japanese reverted to their original position of claiming all the disputed northern islands.

In Germany, even after the Bonn–Paris conventions of 1952 and the Paris Agreements of 1954, restraints remained on German sovereignty. In the 1950s West Germany's foreign policy was formulated in close cooperation with the United States. In 1962–63 the Kennedy administration was able to stop German exports of oil and gas pipelines to the Soviet Union. When, in January 1963, after de Gaulle had said "No" to Britain's membership of the European Economic Community, France and West Germany concluded the Franco–German Élysée Treaty, Washington made it clear that Bonn had now gone too far. The treaty could only be ratified in the Bundestag after the necessary declarations of loyalty to NATO and to the US had been made in a new preamble to the treaty. Even after the conclusion of the treaty the United States clearly remained Bonn's most important reference point.

Naturally, America had less influence in the unoccupied countries. None the less Washington's attitude became an important element for policymakers in all the countries within the American "empire." This was especially true on the foreign policy side. Even Churchill, the senior Western statesman, was not able to bring about the three-power summit he ached to have after Stalin's death. When the British prime minister suggested that he would go alone to Moscow, Eisenhower responded that if he did, "the effect on Congress which is this week taking up consideration of our Mutual Defense Program and extension of our Reciprocal Trade Act would be unpredictable."[36] Churchill stayed at home. Frequently, allied governments kept an eye on Washington's reaction, even when they dealt with economic and social matters. Unless you had a good reason, actions which could be seen as offensive to America were to be avoided.

Suez provided the most dramatic example of the influence the United States could have on its two most important allies, Britain and France. The Eisenhower administration was unable to prevent the British–French–Israeli operation against Egypt. Washington was quite simply not asked, in large part due to the allies' faulty appraisal that the United States would come to accept the operation once it really got under way. That proved a serious misreading of Eisenhower's attitude. And when Washington instead refused financial support through the International Monetary Fund, threatened to withhold deliveries of oil and to cut off the supply of intelligence information in this tense period, the strong American response became the crucial factor in making the British, and then the French, halt their operation and pull out. The lesson was clear: Britain "could never again resort to military action outside British territories, without at least American acquiescence."[37]

After the uncertainties of the first years after 1945, the US had gradually developed clear-cut objectives vis-à-vis Western Europe. On the whole, it was able to secure these objectives. By far the single most important objective was to limit Soviet expansion. After the "fall" of Czechoslovakia in 1948, no European country joined the Soviet bloc. To fight "Soviet Communism" the resources of the United States and Western Europe had to be coordinated. To Washington this meant that Western Europe had to be fitted into an Atlantic framework, and NATO was the most important part of that framework. NATO was originally set up on European initiative, especially Britain's. But once London had persuaded Washington, in March 1948, to commit itself to the idea of an Atlantic security organization, the United States was to heavily influence—sometimes to decide more or less on its own—the policies of this organization: who the members were to be, its military strategy, its overall attitude toward the Soviet Union, and, to a much lesser extent, the level of defense spending in the member countries.

[36] Peter Boyle, "The 'Special' Relationship with Washington," in John Young (ed.), *The Foreign Policy of Churchill's Peacetime Administration 1951–55* (Leicester: Leicester University Press, 1988), 43.
[37] The quotation is from Geoffrey Warner, "The Anglo–American Special Relationship," *Diplomatic History*, 13:4 (October 1989), 487.

On the economic side the Atlantic framework was constituted primarily by the Organisation for European Economic Co-operation (OEEC), General Agreement on Tariffs and Trade (GATT), and Coordinating Committee for Multilateral Export Controls (CoCom). The OEEC had not become as strong an organization as the United States had hoped, but it still played a prominent role in administering American economic assistance and coordinating the overall economic policies of its members. The United States was not a direct member, but still exerted great influence on the organization, particularly during the Marshall Plan years. When, in 1961, the OEEC was transformed into the Organisation for Economic Co-operation and Development (OECD), the United States was brought directly into the organization (together with Canada). Through GATT, Washington could fit Europe's efforts at economic integration into the Atlantic framework in such a way that the integration did not hurt America's economic interests too much, although the GATT rounds of the 1940s and 1950s were rather modest affairs. CoCom regulated the trade of the NATO members, and to some extent even of the neutral European states, with the Soviet Union and its Eastern European allies. The US had been instrumental in setting up CoCom, but could not prevent a great reduction in the number of embargoed goods, particularly after Stalin's death in 1953.[38]

From 1950 it became essential for the United States to have the larger part of Germany—West Germany—on its side, even militarily. This could either take place directly, through West German membership of NATO, or, more indirectly, through membership of a European defense structure linked to NATO. Washington frequently pushed much harder for European integration than did even its continental allies. This could be seen in Washington's insistence on a joint economic plan to administer the Marshall money, in its emphasis, even its threats, to bring about the highly integrated European Defence Community in 1953–54, and in its consistent push for an economic, and even a political, structure in Europe that more resembled that in the United States.

On the domestic side, the overriding American goal was to keep the communists and their "fellow travelers" out of power. From 1947 on it became essential to keep the communists out. With the exception of Iceland in 1956–58, where a leftist bloc including communists actually participated in the government, the United States was able to fulfill this objective in all the NATO countries, until the revolution in Portugal in 1974. Iceland was so small, and such a special case, that this limited any fear of its example spreading to other countries; the American air base at Keflavik remained (despite its controversial nature in Iceland, especially at the time), and

---

[38] For the most recent historical account of CoCom, see Tor Egil Førland, *Cold Economic Warfare: CoCom and the Forging of Strategic Export Controls* (Dordrecht: Republic of letters, 2009).

measures were taken to keep particularly sensitive documents out of communist hands.

The United States also wanted to keep Western Europe—and the rest of the world for that matter—open to American culture. In this area too the US was quite successful. American movies, literature, music, and other forms of expression steadily spread. The United States became the country to visit for aspiring politicians, business people, scholars, and even artists.

These were all significant American successes. Within the Atlantic community everybody took it for granted that the United States was the leader. Whenever something important happened, the other countries looked to the US for guidance. By acting first, so to speak, Washington was normally able to set the parameters within which the other capitals determined their course of action. Even when the US did not speak first, the allies always had to figure out the American response before deciding how to act. This defining function was crucial. When capitals disagreed with Washington, they had to justify their actions to the US administration in power.

On the whole America secured its objectives through close cooperation with the Europeans. When the two sides of the Atlantic had strong common interests, there was normally little need for Washington to use its sharper instruments of influence. The deepest reason, however, for America's success in Europe was undoubtedly the fact that Washington's basic overall objectives were shared, to such a large extent, by most European governments and peoples.

WHY THE EUROPEAN INVITATIONS? DID THEY DETERMINE US POLICY?[39]

Almost any form of rule, even an empire, operates on the basis of some sort of consent from the ruled peoples. Within the Soviet Empire the communist parties enjoyed rather limited support in Poland, Rumania, and Hungary, despite the many individuals and organizations accommodating themselves to the new future; in Bulgaria and Czechoslovakia, where the communists and other pro-Soviet forces were considerably stronger, so was the support. Culturally and economically most Eastern Europeans considered the Soviets inferior to themselves. In most of Eastern Europe the basis for the consent of the population, however passive and indirect, was quite simply that they

---

[39] I have written about "empire" by invitation for almost 30 years. For some of my earlier efforts, see "Empire by Invitation? The United States and Western Europe, 1945–1952," *Journal of Peace Research*, 23:3 (September 1986), 263–77; *The American 'Empire,'* 54–62; "'Empire by Invitation' in the American Century," *Diplomatic History*, 23:2 (Spring 1999), 189–217.

saw no alternative to the Red Army. The Soviet presence was pervasive, and the people generally remained calm. When Soviet interests were threatened, Moscow intervened through the Red Army (East Germany, 1953, Hungary, 1956, and Czechoslovakia, 1968). Where the local communists had an independent power base, they soon broke away from Soviet rule, as in Yugoslavia, Albania, and China.

The British Empire rested on a somewhat different mixture of active support and passive loyalty. In most of the dominions, with their large populations of British descent, support could be strong, particularly if the dominions kept moving toward higher degrees of self-government. In the "colored" parts the situation was much more complex. Examples can be found of the British being explicitly invited to rule over certain areas. In the early phase the extension of British rule more generally rested on the conclusion of treaties with local rulers. This was the case in Africa, although these treaties were often "unequal." Later the British tended to "neglect" even such formalities, and opposition to British rule increased. Frequently they faced some form of active resistance. Then the threat, and the occasional use of armed force, became important for both the introduction and the maintenance of British rule.

Both the British and the local peoples generally believed in the superiority of the white man (and the Anglo-Saxons in particular). With Britain's political ideals and limited resources, imperial control had to be rather "thin." In 1909 the population of the Empire was 7.7 times greater than that of Britain itself; the area ratio was 1:94. In India an administration of 2,000–3,000, an armed force of 60,000–70,000 (and a slightly higher number of dependents) ruled over 200–300 million people. In Northern Nigeria, during the interwar period, more than 10 million people were ruled by some 250 administrative officers. There were areas where white men were hardly seen at all. When the local populations started actively to resist, British rule was more or less bound to collapse.

After 1945 foreign rule over other peoples was coming to be challenged almost everywhere it existed. Traditional superiority thinking had been shattered by the excesses of Hitler and the triumphs of the Japanese. In East Asia the yellow man had defeated the white. The magic of colonial rule was gone; it could not be restored. Colonialism was certainly out of favor in Washington. However, America was so strong, it could exert its influence more indirectly. Here the parallel to British informal rule in the 1840s–70s is evident. When Britain was at its peak, informal rule not only sufficed for British objectives, it often flowed, more or less naturally, from its position of supremacy. In this case, annexation became a sign of weakness, an admission that more direct means had to be used to control the local scene.

With certain exceptions, such as in the postwar occupations—in Vietnam in the 1960s, and in West Germany in general—the direct American military presence was generally rather limited. Occasionally the United States, too, intervened with direct force or through covert activities. Yet, on the whole, intervention was both undesirable and unnecessary. Washington's supremacy was more in accordance with the will of the local populations than was Moscow's, and even London's, authority. Soviet rule was to a large extent imposed; British rule survived as long as it did because it was not opposed. As I have frequently argued, American "rule" was frequently invited. In this sense the American "empire" can be called an empire by invitation. Power is often defined as the ability to get others to do what you want them to do. The most striking aspect of America's power after 1945 was the extent to which the Europeans actively worked to increase the US role in Western Europe. This was indeed "empire by invitation."

It is no mystery why the Europeans invited the Americans in. In fact, the reasons were rather obvious. First, as we have seen, Western Europe needed economic assistance, and only the United States could provide substantial assistance. Second, the forces of the political center in most Western European countries wanted American support to strengthen their position, both domestically vis-à-vis the more extreme forces on the left and right, and often also internationally vis-à-vis other countries. The challenge from the left was strongest in France and Italy, where the communists and their allies regularly polled more than 20 percent of the vote. The challenge from the right was also strongest in France, although the Gaullist vote fluctuated a great deal. Internationally, Alessandro Brogi has demonstrated how a complicated mixture of cooperation with the United States and independence of it characterized both France's constant search for *grandeur*, and even Italy's for *grandezza*. Washington had it in its power to promote or relegate countries in their constant struggle for prestige and status.[40] Third, the Europeans wanted as much military support and as strong military guarantees as possible to guard against Soviet–Communist expansion. Although Washington had no particular desire to give Europe billions of dollars in assistance, the Truman administration definitely shared Europe's desire to contain the Soviet–Communist threat.

The Western Europeans invited the Americans into Europe despite the conditions set by Washington, whether in the form of currency convertibility, as in the December 1945 loan to Britain, the freer import of Hollywood movies, as in the Blum–Byrnes Agreement, or special shipping clauses, as in most American loans to Western Europe. Under the Marshall Plan the Europeans had to agree to a stronger OEEC organization than some of them had wanted, and to a more restrictive level of trade between Western and Eastern Europe.

---

[40] Alessandro Brogi, *A Question of Self-Esteem: The United States and the Cold War Choices in France and Italy, 1944-1958* (Westport: Praeger, 2002).

On the military side, most European governments wanted a substantial American military presence. This presence could certainly expose them to risks, but sometimes, when the initiative came from Washington, as with the B-29 bombers stationed in Britain in response to the Berlin crisis of 1948, the British agreed so quickly and uncompromisingly that Secretary of State Marshall had to check with Bevin if London had actually fully considered the implications. (Only later did it become publicly known that the aircraft had not yet been modified to carry nuclear weapons.)

For the Europeans there was always the possibility that they would be overwhelmed by the formidable power of the United States. But the US was far away, and it was better to be controlled by somebody that far away than by some European competitor with whom you had experienced a rather mixed history. An additional reason why the Europeans confidently invited the Americans in was that the Europeans were consistently able to transform US initiatives into something less threatening than they at first seemed. True, the price might still be high, as in the American–British loan negotiations. But if the price were too high, reality would frequently intervene in the sense that the agreement would break down, as was seen in the collapse of the pound and the resulting suspension of the convertibility London had promised to undertake in return for the loan.

In the Marshall Plan negotiations the British successfully opposed American efforts to make the OEEC strong and supranational. London could not be forced to take part in supranational European integration, then or later, entirely against its own will. Britain was simply too strong, too important, too unified, and too highly considered in Washington to be directly pushed into such responsibilities. Scandinavians and other lukewarm integrationists could then hide behind the British.

Under the Marshall Plan the counterpart funds seemingly provided the best leverage for the Truman administration. Each government had to deposit local currency funds equal to the amount of dollar assistance received. These counterpart funds could only be used with the consent of the United States. In Germany, Austria, Turkey, and Greece the missions of the Economic Cooperation Administration (ECA) exerted a great deal of authority. Germany and Austria were occupied countries where naturally the occupying power would have considerable influence. In Greece and Turkey local administrations had broken down to such an extent that here too the US would be rather directly involved in running the countries. This was rather different from the situation in most Marshall Plan countries.

In Britain and Norway the counterpart funds were generally used for debt retirement, a fact that obviously gave the ECA little influence on where the money was invested. Certain concessions were gradually made to the ECA representatives' wish for a more investment-oriented policy, but the two countries were able to continue their basic policies. In Italy the government invested too little, in the opinion of ECA. Counterpart funds were held back to make the Italians perform better, with some, although limited, success. In France, ECA's complaints were the opposite: the Monnet Plan was too ambitious. In addition, fiscal reform was consistently postponed, communists were not purged, among other factors. Elaborate plans were drawn up to make Paris follow American desires, again with only limited success. In the end the Truman administration was caught between a rock and a hard place. If it did not push hard, the French, and the Italians, would do little or nothing; if it pushed hard, weak centrist governments might fall, and that was clearly even less acceptable to the US. In the flood of new American ideas and proposals to reform the European economies, the Europeans were frequently able to pick those they liked and reject those they liked less.[41]

The story was rather similar when it came to American efforts to limit trade with the Soviet Union and Eastern Europe. In December 1947 the Truman administration initiated a strategic embargo on trade in certain products with these countries (the A-1 list composed of military commodities, and the B-1 list containing semi-strategic or "dual-purpose" goods.) In the summer of 1948 Washington started work on having these lists adopted by the European Recovery Program (ERP) countries, and a permanent coordinating committee (CoCom) was set up to monitor trade with the communist countries. The American position was soon strengthened by the increased international tension as a result of the communist victory in the Chinese civil war, the Soviet explosion of its first atomic bomb, and the outbreak of the Korean War. Nevertheless, with Britain in the lead, egged on especially by Denmark and Norway, the Western Europeans were able to substantially modify both the A-1 and, particularly, the B-1 list to take account of European economic interests. One reason they succeeded as well as they did was that after 1952 President Dwight D. Eisenhower clearly saw himself in a middle position between most Europeans on the one hand, and a hard-line Congress on the other.

On the military side, the increases in European defense spending were generally smaller than Washington would have preferred. The European governments had their own interest in increasing defense expenditure, but the optimal combination was one of the Americans spending rather more, and the Europeans rather less. Those countries that were skeptical about an explicit American presence, such as exposed Norway and Denmark, could pursue a policy of no allied bases on their territory (except in crucial Greenland in Denmark's case). Initially, at least, Washington had considerable sympathy for their special needs. And all European governments seemingly had leverage with the United States. Strong governments had this because they

---

[41] Lundestad, *America, Scandinavia, and the Cold War*, 109–66.

were strong; weak governments had it precisely because they were weak—often so weak that they risked being replaced by alternatives considerably less to Washington's liking.

It is factors such as these that have led Alan Milward and others to argue not only that the Marshall Plan was not particularly important for the recovery of Western Europe, but also that America's design for Western Europe was largely defeated.[42] Similar comments have been made about some of the other American initiatives discussed.

But these arguments go only so far. Milward probably somewhat under-estimated the economic importance of the Marshall Plan. With the exception of agriculture, the European Recovery Program, as the Marshall Plan was officially known, actually reached or surpassed all its major production targets. The direct economic significance of the Marshall Plan was considerable, although it certainly did not "save" Western Europe single-handedly. Marshall funds did account for 10 to 20 percent of capital formation in the European countries in 1948–49, and less than 10 percent in 1950–51.

Milward definitely underestimated the plan's political and psychological importance. In this sense, many did believe it had saved Western Europe. Then this belief developed a reality of its own. The Marshall Plan also gave Europeans a more positive perception of the United States. George Kennan may have gone too far, but he was certainly on to something when he stated that "The psychological success at the outset was so amazing that we felt that the psychological effect was four-fifths accomplished before the first supplies arrived."[43] Even more important in this context, although the Truman admin-istration definitely did not achieve its maximum objectives, European govern-ments always had to keep at least one eye on Washington's response to the policies they pursued. Thus, in May 1949, the British Cabinet even feared that "increased investments in the social services might influence Congress in their appropriations from Marshall aid."[44]

At the more structural level, despite certain shortcomings the political success of the ERP was still spectacular. It helped achieve political stabilization in Western Europe, externally vis-à-vis the Soviet Union, and internally vis-à-vis local communists; it promoted some measure of European integration; it made the western zones of Germany part of this stabilization and integration;

[42] See Alan S. Milward *The Reconstruction of Western Europe, 1945–51* (Berkeley: University of California Press, 1984) and also Milward, George Brennan, and Federico Romero, *The European Rescue of the Nation-State* (London: Routledge, 1992).

[43] Charles L. Mee Jr., *The Marshall Plan: The Launching of the Pax Americana* (New York: Simon and Schuster, 1984), 246.

[44] The quotation is from Cabinet Papers, EPC 5 (49), 23.5.49, Cab 134/192, found in Teddy Brett, Steve Gilliat, and Andrew Pople, "Planned Trade, Labour Party Policy and US Interven-tion: The Successes and Failures of Post-war Reconstruction," *History Workshop*, 13 (Spring 1982), 138.

it changed European perceptions of the United States dramatically for the better, from Washington's point of view; and it mobilized the American public around a comprehensive US role in Europe. On this level, the success of the Truman administration could be seen as astounding. The same basic argument can be made with reference to NATO.

Naturally for the Europeans nothing beat having the United States involved without the Americans exerting much influence on national policies. But having one's cake and eating it is an impossible combination in international politics too. The United States would not have become involved in European politics after 1945 to the extent that it did unless Washington had had its own reasons to do so, and the Europeans had wanted this to happen. Agreements between free governments presuppose a mutuality of interests. Otherwise the agreements presumably would not have been concluded.

It has been argued that America's foreign policy was determined primarily by America's own interests, not by the invitations from outside. This point is obviously true, so true in fact that I have consistently made it explicitly clear myself: "I just take it for granted that the United States had important strategic, political, and economic motives of its own for taking on such a comprehensive world role."[45] Indeed, any invitations had to be combined with America's own interests. After 1945, European invitations were extended to a United States disposed to respond in a much more affirmative way than it had done in 1918–20 when Britain and France, in particular, had issued somewhat similar invitations.

At the same time, however, it should be stressed that the European invitations after the Second World War were definitely more insistent, lasted longer, and came from many more countries than on the earlier occasion. While little is really known about the state of public opinion in Europe after the First World War, if we are to generalize about public opinion after the Second World War the invitations extended to the United States by most Western European governments clearly came to receive the basic support of most of the populations involved.[46]

From the perspective of American–European relations it would have been interesting to study the European response to America's new role after 1945, even if the response had had little or no effect on US actions. Yet the invitations definitely did have an effect. Obviously there would not have been any economic assistance if the Europeans had not wanted it. Considering Washington's initially lukewarm response to Bevin's pleas for an Atlantic security system, it seems likely that the setting up of NATO would have been substantially delayed, at least, if it had not been for the European invitations. The heart of NATO, Article 5, would probably not have had

[45] Lundestad, "Empire by Invitation?," *Journal of Peace Research*, 268.
[46] Lundestad, "'Empire by Invitation' in the American Century," 189–217.

even its semi-automatic form if the Europeans had not pushed as hard as they did for an even more automatic American response to potential Soviet aggression.

The experience after the First World War indicated that European invitations alone were not enough to change America's attitude, although it is not really possible to tell what would have happened if the invitations then had been as insistent, lasted as long, and come from as many countries as they did after the Second World War. After 1945, with the United States determined to play a much more active role, the invitations did not force the Americans to do anything they did not really want to do, but they certainly influenced at least the timing and scope of America's actions toward Western Europe.

THE RELATIVE CONTRACTION OF THE UNITED STATES IN RECENT YEARS

In an absolute and literal sense it is difficult to argue that the United States has contracted in recent years. Its imports and exports are increasing virtually every year; so are its cultural contacts with the world. The number of immigrants coming into the country is still high, although it has not increased further, in part as a result of September 11 and a political climate less generous to immigration than before. The United States still plays a military role all over the world. "Friction," in the sense of the lingering effects of the past, was important, in that established organizations have a tendency to continue as before, even under dramatically changed circumstances. Few organizations just disappear from the face of the earth. Most of them continue to live on under new circumstances. So America's contraction is partial and relative, compared to the expansion of the new regional powers.

In 1967, at the peak of the Cold War, the United States had had 1,014 overseas military bases scattered all over the world. In 2009 it had 716 such bases, not counting those in the war zones in Iraq and Afghanistan.[47] The defeat in Vietnam had led to the end of the Southeast Asia Treaty Organization (SEATO), and the revolution in Iran a few years later to the end of the Central Treaty Organization (CENTO). The end of the Cold War led to a substantial decline in the number of US troops in Europe, from more than 400,000 at its highest to about 75,000 in 2010. The nuclear presence had been reduced to a very small number of bombs that could be dropped from aircraft. There is even talk about phasing these out entirely, but most Europeans,

---

[47] Chalmers Johnson, *Dismantling the Empire: America's Last Best Hope* (New York: Metropolitan Books, 2010), 110–13, 121, 127.

particularly in the East, want to maintain a minimum American nuclear presence in Europe.

However, NATO definitely continued to operate, and its membership increased from the traditional fifteen members in Western Europe, to the present twenty-eight (now including most of Europe), with around twenty additional countries working in cooperation with NATO in Afghanistan. Even France came back within the military structure of NATO. And the United States continued as the undisputed leader of the organization. However, all this could not hide the fact that NATO no longer had the crucial importance it had had during the Cold War. The Cold War had been based on the primacy of Europe. The central conflict area was in Central Europe, particularly Germany and Berlin; America's most important allies were also in Europe. Now "the Greater Middle East" was undoubtedly the crucial area, followed by East Asia, with Europe only in third place; and the emphasis within Europe had shifted on the military strategic side—not the economic one—further east to the Balkans and Turkey.

Article 5 had been the core of NATO, the principle of "all for one, one for all," in the event of a military attack. With the Soviet Union gone, there was less talk of Article 5, although attitudes varied widely inside the organization. Poland, Rumania, and the Baltic states were most skeptical of Russia and insistent on the continued importance of Article 5; the United States, Canada, and Britain generally took a middle position, while France, Germany, and Italy were generally more interested in consolidating ties with Russia. NATO became more of a political organization with the emphasis on providing, at the very least, coordination on relevant international issues. The war between Georgia and Russia in 2008 revived the military perspective somewhat. The result was, however, that membership in NATO for Georgia and Ukraine was indefinitely postponed. The United States could not offer these states guarantees when there was actually a substantial chance of war. The United States had shown some interest in making NATO a more global organization by taking in Australia, New Zealand, Japan, etc, but there was much opposition to this in Europe. The idea was dropped, although cooperation increased at a less formal level.[48] NATO was to some extent being replaced by coalitions of the willing. In Afghanistan virtually all the NATO allies participated, but so did about twenty other countries. The invasion of Libya in March 2011 showed a NATO in considerable disarray, although the organization did eventually coordinate most of the allied military action. Only nine of the member countries participated directly in military action.

---

[48] WikiLeaks had interesting reports on the state of affairs in NATO. For this, see Tron Strand and Per Anders Johansen, "Uforsonlig splittelse i NATO" ["Irreconcilable Division in NATO"], *Aftenposten*, February 12, 2011, 6–7 and "Advarte mot russiske kjemiske våpen" ["Warned Against Russian Chemical Weapons"], *Aftenposten*, February 13, 2011, 16–17.

The weakened interest in Europe was in part the result of the increased focus on the Greater Middle East. The idea of the Bush administration—that the United States could handle the military challenge in this region more or less on its own—was definitely gone, although even under Obama most of the heavy lifting was still done by the US. In Afghanistan about two-thirds of the troops were American, and they were the most active ones. But the most important point in this context was that, after the initial success, the wars in Afghanistan and Iraq demonstrated the weakness of the United States. In the new form of asymmetrical warfare destructive technology was available to even the smallest groups, and they could inflict substantial casualties. Hardly anything went according to plan. "The surge" did help to improve the situation in Iraq. The number of American troops was later substantially reduced; the Iraqis were able to take over most functions. Violence was reduced. Government services improved. Even here it was difficult to be entirely optimistic. There were still high levels of violence and political reconciliation was limited. In Afghanistan the situation was considerably bleaker. The increase in US troops again improved the military situation, but the political and economic problems persisted. Several countries were getting ready to pull their troops out of Afghanistan. Contrary to what had been Washington's purpose, Iran had strengthened its position in the region considerably, Pakistan's problems had gone from bad to worse, and Turkey was reviving its contacts with the Muslim world at the expense of the West.

The occasional pressure in the United States for democratic reform of the Arab world threatened to backfire in the sense that elections could bring more extreme elements to power, as seen with Hezbollah in Lebanon and Hamas in Gaza. The democratic uprisings in Tunisia, Egypt, and several other countries in early 2011 also seemed likely to strengthen forces that were more critical of the United States and the West than had been the authoritarian rulers of the past. The fact that the United States had, almost without exception, supported these rulers because of a mixture of strategic interests, oil, and Israel, at the expense of democracy was not a good starting point. Still, even the new authorities would presumably have an interest in acceptable relations with a US that was desperately trying to adjust to new circumstances. The fact that Washington had had some covert contact with the opposition even earlier helped in this context.

The wars in Iraq and Afghanistan had to diminish any further US interest in adventures in Iran, North Korea, and elsewhere. In Libya in 2011 the United States decided to "lead from behind." This was certainly something new. Europe had to take the lead. With America's debt problems there were bound to be reductions in US defense spending, despite the priority given to military over civilian expenditures. Yet the reductions in other forms of international spending, in the form of diplomacy and assistance, were also bound to reduce America's role in the world. Even other cuts, for instance in education and health, could also affect its international standing: America's universities had represented one of its most effective forms of soft power, and the public ones in particular were now facing serious problems.

No power could yet challenge the United States as the global leader. Militarily China was definitely a regional power. It pursued a policy of non-alignment which meant that it did not really have formal alliances with other countries, although it had a series of close partners such as North Korea, Pakistan, Myanmar. The Shanghai Cooperation Organization encompassed military, economic, and cultural cooperation, and clearly aimed at reducing the American role in Central Asia, but the structure was loose and the practical results limited. Even in East Asia, with its formal alliances with Japan, South Korea, and Taiwan, America's military position was at least as strong as China's.

Nevertheless, the rise of many different regional powers meant that the American role in the world was reduced. In every region of the world there was a power that limited US freedom of action. In the Western hemisphere Brazil in particular was rising rapidly; in Africa, South Africa and even Nigeria were taking on new roles; in Asia, China, India, and (still) Japan had to included; and in Europe, Germany, France, Britain, and the EU itself (on many issues) were the primary actors, as was Russia, particularly in the East.[49]

Africa, the weakest of the continents, was a case in point. On important issues for the United States, such as "the war on terror," the International Criminal Court, and the US Africa Command, the US faced opposition, even from its friends. Washington could actually dictate very little. The leading regional powers—South Africa, Nigeria, and Kenya—and even smaller countries such as Tanzania, Mali, Namibia, and Niger, have resisted US policies and refused to support key initiatives. The explanation was found in a complex combination of regional balance of power factors, domestic opposition to the US, and growing economic independence from the United States.[50]

The international structure was also shifting in favor of the new powers in Asia. Throughout several rounds, voting power within the World Bank and the International Monetary Fund was redistributed in their favor, although primarily at the expense of European powers, less the United States. International negotiations that had earlier been led to a considerable extent by the United States now often ended in standstill, or were even conducted entirely without the US. The Doha round in the World Trade Organization was never concluded, although many efforts were made to resuscitate it. Differences,

---

[49] For an interesting discussion of these shifts, see Andrew F. Hart and Bruce D. Jones, "How Do Rising Powers Rise?," *Survival*, 52:6 (December 2010–January 2011), 63–88.

[50] Beth Elise Whitaker, "Soft balancing among weak states? Evidence from Africa," *International Affairs*, 86:5 (2010), 1109–27.

particularly between the United States on the one hand and China and India on the other were too big to be bridged. The United States signed, but never ratified, the Kyoto Treaty on climate change; in the new rounds on climate change the United States again had to attempt to bring China and India along, otherwise there would be no new treaty. Treaties banning landmines and cluster munitions were worked out against the will not only of the United States but also of Russia, India, and China. This was also a trend of the times. Even when major powers were united they could not necessarily stop the rest of the world from proceeding.

Invitations were still being issued to the United States. Virtually all European countries still wanted the US to be active militarily, politically, economically, and culturally in their part of the world. In Asia, growing concern about the rise of China often led to renewed interest in ties with the United States—not at the expense of China, but to be on the safe side in case developments in China took a more ominous turn.[51] President Obama could count on widespread sympathy in Africa. The Arab world hoped that the US would force the necessary concessions from Israel so that a peace treaty could be worked out with the Palestinians. But despite the personal admiration for Obama, with the partial exception of invitations from a few countries in Asia, the new invitations to Washington lacked the strength and conviction typified by invitations from Western Europeans in the first years after the Second World War, and from many of the Eastern Europeans after the end of the Cold War.

[51] Aaron L. Friedberg, "Implications of the Financial Crisis for the US–China Rivalry," *Survival*, 52:4 (August–September 2010), 45–6.

Part II

The Limits of Power

5

The Impotence of Omnipotence

The Great Powers are indeed great powers. The military, economic, political, and cultural influence of the United States, the greatest of them all, is felt in every corner of the world. Through the process of globalization, which some incorrectly identify as almost the same as Americanization, impulses from one part of the world are carried to virtually all other parts. We all witness the big events live as they happen. Ideas and goods are quickly carried around the world. Languages, tribes, and groups disappear. In Thomas Friedman's term, the world is in many ways very "flat" indeed.[1]

It is easy to assume that some country or idea is virtually omnipotent. But if we look more closely we see that the world is also fragmenting. Empires are dissolved, more and more states are born. The most powerful idea of all may well be nationalism, the idea that more and more groups deserve their own country. The Internet is the supreme symbol of our time. We can communicate with almost anyone instantly, and are all part of the same virtual universe; yet, at the same time, we see how the smallest of groups can get together and use this universe for their own separate purposes. The Internet developed in the United States and the net carries America's influence around the world. Yet, tiny terrorist groups fighting the US use the same means of communication.

In the past the United States fought major territorial units like Nazi Germany and the Communist Soviet Union. It did not fight them alone. It was never omnipotent. During the Second World War America had Stalin's Soviet Union as a crucial ally. During the Cold War Washington was finally able to sign on Mao's China, at least as an indirect ally. Now small terrorist groups can inflict major damage on the United States, as so clearly demonstrated on September 11, 2001. In its worldwide struggle against these groups, the United States carries no guarantee of success. It needs all the allies it can get.

---

[1] Thomas L. Friedman, *The World is Flat: A Brief History of the Twenty-First Century* (New York: Farrar, Straus & Giroux, 2005).

One superpower, the Soviet Union, collapsed apparently almost overnight. One day it was the military equal of the US; the next day the country did not exist. The collapse had much to do with imperial overstretch. The world's more traditional empires have all disappeared. In the long run it was impossible for a limited mother country to rule over distant provinces. Sooner or later the imperial will to rule weakened; sooner or later the colonial subjects were able to cut the imperial connection.

In Great Power terms the United States was far stronger than both the Soviet Union and the various colonial empires. Yet America's rule was also quite vulnerable: it was indirect; the US influenced mostly independent countries; it could not long rule an area against the will of the people. Even the mightiest of US presidents could suddenly decide to pull out of countries they had just pronounced of national interest. And the groups that forced it to retreat could be very small indeed, as long as they possessed the relevant and most destructive technology.

The following parts offer some comments on the most intriguing of questions—the curious combination of power and impotence in the rule of the Great Powers, including that of the United States. Such questions cannot really be resolved, only illuminated.

IMPERIAL OVERSTRETCH AND THE FALL
OF THE SOVIET UNION

Sometimes the fall of a superpower can be very rapid, even in peacetime. The clearest example is undoubtedly what happened to the Soviet Union under Mikhail Gorbachev. Virtually nobody predicted such a fall. The few who did got the reasons wrong, whether referring to a war with China (Amalrik), the dissatisfaction of the Muslims (Carrere d'Encausse), or even the infant mortality rate (Emmanuel Todd). George Kennan and Zbigniew Brzezinski had also expected change, even collapse, as had Ronald Reagan and other politicians, but they were not very specific about what kind of change this would be and exactly when it would occur. Many reasons explain the Soviet fall: imperial overstretch, the erosion of the center's will to rule and the dissatisfaction of the nationalities in the Soviet Union—although this actually affected the Muslim groups much less than most others—and a long list of political, social, and economic problems. If we are to understand how superpowers can suddenly fall, some comments on the fall of the Soviet Union appear to be in order. For the second most important actor in international affairs simply to disappear so swiftly from the face of the earth was so spectacular that we all, not only political science realists, have had difficulties understanding what happened.[2]

Imperial overstretch would appear to be the theory most relevant to a general discussion of the fall of empires. In 1987 Paul Kennedy published his best-selling *The Rise and Fall of the Great Powers*.[3] The book was to popularize the term "imperial overstretch," although Kennedy generally used simply "overstretch." He did not really define what he meant by the term (and it is not found in the index of the book.) The closest he got to indicating the precise point at which "overstretch" occurs was in a footnote: ". . . the historical record suggests that if a particular nation is allocating *over the long term* (*sic*, GL) more than 10 percent (and in some cases—when it is structurally weak—more than 5 percent) of GNP to armaments, that is likely to limit its growth rate."[4] Kennedy's basic argument was that as new powers arose they tended to assume military expenses. "If, however, too large a proportion of the state's resources is diverted from wealth creation and allocated instead to military purposes, then that is likely to lead to a weakening of national power over the long run." Because of these extra military costs, which aspiring challengers did not have, the leading power(s) were eventually doomed to decline.[5]

The stunning sales of Kennedy's book were probably largely based on his analysis of the United States and his prediction that the US was bound to "fall" in the same way that earlier Great Powers had fallen. Kennedy was rather uninterested in how his "imperial overstretch" argument applied to the Soviet Union. In *The Rise and Fall* he certainly dealt with the problems of the Soviet Union, including the high percentage of the gross national product devoted to defense spending. He even argued that, in general, the problems of the United States "are probably nowhere near as great as those of its Soviet rival." At the same time, however, he concluded that "This does *not* mean that the USSR is close to collapse, any more than it should be viewed as a country of almost supernatural strength."[6] No sooner was the book out than the Soviet Union,

---

[2] For some of the many relevant books, see Andrei A. Amalrik, *Will the Soviet Union Survive Until 1984?* (New York: Harper & Row, 1970); Hélène Carrère d'Encausse, *L'Empire éclaté* (Paris: Flammarion, 1978); Emmanuel Todd, *The Final Fall: An Essay on the Decomposition of the Soviet Sphere* (New York: Karz, 1979).

[3] This and the next two sections basically follow my "'Imperial Overstretch', Mikhail Gorbachev and the End of the Cold War," *Cold War History*, 1:1 (August 2000), 1–20.

[4] Paul Kennedy, *The Rise and Fall of the Great Powers: Economic Change and Military Conflict from 1500 to 2000* (New York: Random House, 1987), 609, note 18. Kennedy also used the term "strategical overstretch."

A general definition of "overstretch" is given in Paul Kennedy, "Conclusions," in Geir Lundestad (ed.), *The Fall of Great Powers: Peace, Stability, and Legitimacy* (Oxford: Oxford University Press, 1994): it "merely means that there exists a mismatch between a Great Power's obligations and its capabilities, between its desired policies and its actual resources." (374)

[5] Kennedy, *The Rise and Fall*, xvi.

[6] Kennedy, *The Rise and Fall*, 513, 514.

not the United States, entered into its terminal phase. In an analysis published as late as 1992, Kennedy actually saw Gorbachev as an effective representative of the "managed decline," "a strategy to deal with the challenge of *relative* (*sic*, GL) decline in peacetime," that he advocated both for the Soviet Union and for the United States.[7]

While it is easy to criticize Kennedy's emphasis on the decline of the United States and his downplaying of the crisis in the Soviet Union[8], my purpose here is really to resurrect Kennedy's general argument about the importance of "imperial overstretch." The Soviet Union, not the United States, fits his theory almost perfectly. Although many different factors account for the collapse of the Soviet Union, in my opinion "imperial overstretch" clearly represents one of the most powerful explanations for the fall of the Soviet Union, and the most relevant in the context of this book.[9]

The present author is no great expert on the Soviet Union; the emphasis on "imperial overstretch" is borrowed from Kennedy. So what this section attempts to do, more than anything, is to synthesize the enormous literature on the fall of the Soviet Union and on the end of the Cold War in the light of Kennedy's thesis.

The argument comes in three parts: imperial expenses in the Soviet Union were extremely high; the need to reduce them was a prime motivation behind Gorbachev's increasingly drastic changes in Soviet domestic and foreign policy; these drastic changes were responsible, more than anything, for bringing first the Cold War, and then the Soviet Union, to an end.[10]

---

[7] Paul Kennedy, "Grand Strategies and Less-than-Grand Strategies: A Twentieth-Century Critique," in Lawrence Freedman, Paul Hayes, and Robert O'Neill (eds.), *War, Strategy, and International Politics: Essays in Honour of Sir Michael Howard* (Oxford: Clarendon Press, 1992), 239–40. See also Kennedy, *The Rise and Fall*, 534–5.

[8] I have written about the debate caused by the publication of *The Rise and Fall* in *The American "Empire" and Other Studies of U.S. Foreign Policy in a Comparative Perspective* (Oxford–Oslo: Oxford University Press, 1990), particularly 85–7, 105–15, and in "'Empire by Invitation' in the American Century," *Diplomatic History*, 23:2 (Spring 1999), 216–17.

[9] In the rapidly growing literature on Gorbachev and the fall of the Soviet Union I have used the following extensively: Archie Brown, *The Gorbachev Factor* (Oxford: Oxford University Press, 1996); Martin McCauley, *Gorbachev* (London: Longman, 1998); Anders Åslund, *Gorbachev's Struggle for Economic Reform* (London: Pinter Publishers, 1989); John B. Dunlop, *The Rise of Russia and the Fall of the Soviet Empire* (Princeton: Princeton University Press, 1993); Hélène Carrère d'Encausse, *The End of the Soviet Empire: The Triumph of the Nations* (New York: Basic books, 1993); Vladislav M. Zubok, *A Failed Empire: The Soviet Union in the Cold War from Stalin to Gorbachev* (Chapel Hill: University of North Carolina Press, 2007). Among more general accounts I have primarily used Ronald Grigor Suny, *The Soviet Experiment: Russia, the USSR, and the Successor States* (New York: Oxford University Press, 1998); Geoffrey Hosking, *A History of the Soviet Union 1917–1991* (Final edition, London: Fontana Press, 1992); Martin Malia, *The Soviet Tragedy: A History of Socialism in Russia, 1917–1991* (New York: The Free Press, 1994).

[10] My more general treatment of the end of the Cold War can be found in *East, West, North, South: Major Developments in International Politics since 1945* (Sixth edition, London: Sage, 2010), 101–8.

In the 1950s and 1960s economic growth had been rapid in the Soviet Union. Optimism about the future was considerable, as could be witnessed in Khrushchev's many statements about when the Soviet Union would overtake the United States in various fields, including even agriculture. These statements are easy to caricature in the light of the Soviet Union's eventual collapse, but in this period even many non-communists were exceedingly optimistic about the prospects of the Soviet Union. In the 1970s and 1980s economic growth began to taper off significantly, as could be seen even in official statistics. So, when Gorbachev took over in 1985 there was little or no growth in the Soviet economy, military expenses were high, and there was very little spillover from military to civilian technology.[11]

A more comprehensive public presentation of the Soviet defense budget was made only in 1989. Then the official budget figure was published at 77.3 billion rubles, but the lack of a realistic pricing system made the numbers a great deal less meaningful than they appeared to be. Similar problems apply to efforts to determine the size of the Soviet gross national product. Therefore, at present, no accurate figures can be given for imperial expenses as a percentage of GNP. In fact, it is unlikely that we will ever be able to give a precise answer to this question.[12]

From 1975 onwards, Soviet official statistics began to present Soviet national income as unchanged, at 67 percent of US national income. In the 1980s the Institute of World Economy and International Relations (IMEMO) in Moscow estimated Soviet national income to be only about 50 percent of US national income, and the percentage was seen as falling.[13]

Western estimates of the size of the Soviet GNP have varied widely. The Central Intelligence Agency (CIA) was long regarded as the leading authority on the size of the Soviet economy. In 1986 they estimated the Soviet economy at 57 percent of the US economy; by 1990 this percentage had allegedly fallen to 52. In hindsight it is obvious that the agency had a clear tendency to overestimate the size of the Soviet GNP and to underestimate the growing

---

[11] Soviet economic history through the Khrushchev years is well analyzed in Alec Nove, *An Economic History of the U.S.S.R.* (Harmondsworth: Penguin, 1969). The best account of the growing problems in the 1980s is probably Åslund, *Gorbachev's Struggle for Economic Reform.* For the limited spillover from the military to the civilian sector, see Clifford G. Gaddy, *The Price of the Past: Russia's Struggle with the Legacy of a Militarized Economy* (Washington, DC: Brookings, 1996).

[12] Noel E. Firth and James H. Noren, *Soviet Defense Spending: A History of CIA Estimates, 1950–1990* (College Station: Texas A&M University Press, 1998) 190–1.

[13] Hannes Adomeit, *Imperial Overstretch: Germany in Soviet Policy from Stalin to Gorbachev* (Baden–Baden: Nomos, 1998), 143.

Soviet definitions of national income differ from western definitions of GNP by excluding depreciation and the non-material components of services. During the 1980s, GNP may have been roughly one-third to two-fifths greater than national income. For this, see Firth and Noren, *Soviet Defense Spending,* 189.

difficulties in the Soviet economy in the 1980s. In his memoirs, even CIA director Robert Gates (1991–93) admits that the "CIA in its statistics over-stated the size of the Soviet economy and relatedly underestimated the burden of military expenditure on that economy and society."[14]

Other studies, for instance by Swedish expert Anders Åslund, suggested that the CIA's estimates of the size of the Soviet economy were at least 20 percentage points too high. In 1990 the chairman of the US Council of Economic Advisers, Michael Boskin, stated that "Soviet GNP is probably ... only about one-third of the GNP of the U.S." In 1997 the European Compari-son Project calculated Soviet GNP in 1990 to have been 32 percent of US GNP, although this was on a per capita basis. Later estimates by Russian economists have put the figures even lower than this. Noted Russian economist Girsh Khanin has calculated Soviet GNP in the mid-1980s to have been only 14 percent of the US one, but his dramatic conclusions have been challenged.[15]

Traditionally, Soviet government officials used to state that Soviet defense expenditure comprised less than 7–8 percent of total GNP, a figure which appears to have been chosen primarily because it corresponded roughly with that for the United States at the time.[16] According to the CIA's estimates, the military's share of Soviet GNP was calculated to have grown from 12–14 percent at the beginning of the 1970s, to 15–17 percent in the 1980s. This upward trend reflected more a downward revision of Soviet GNP than an upward revision of defense spending. Robert Gates writes that he himself mistrusted these figures, "I believed instinctively that, in this communist variant of Sparta, the burden of military-related spending was ... perhaps between 25 and 40 percent."[17]

In their detailed studies of Soviet imperial expenses, Henry Rowen and Charles Wolf concluded that such expenses were clearly higher than estimated

[14] Thus, in the 1980s, the CIA concluded that the Soviet Union had many serious economic problems, but nevertheless it continued to forecast that the Soviet economy would continue to grow at a 2 percent rate per year. For this, see Robert M. Gates, *From the Shadows: The Ultimate Insider's Story of Five Presidents and How They Won the Cold War* (New York: Simon & Schuster, 1996), 382–9. The quotation is from 564. For the numbers given, see also Daniel Patrick Moynihan, *Secrecy: The American Experience* (New Haven: Yale University Press, 1998), 196–8; Henry Rowen and Charles Wolf, Jr., "The CIA's Credibility," *The National Interest* (Winter 1995/96), 111–12; Melvin A. Goodman, "Ending the CIA's Cold War Legacy," *Foreign Policy*, 106 (Spring 1997), 141.
[15] Goodman, "Ending the CIA's Cold War Legacy," 141–2; Moynihan, *Secrecy*, 196–8; Rowen and Wolf, "The CIA's Credibility," 112; Odd Arne Westad, "Secrets of the Second World: The Russian Archives and the Reinterpretation of Cold War History," *Diplomatic History*, 21:2 (Spring 1997), 261–2. A discussion of Khanin's work is found in Richard E. Ericson, "The Soviet Statistical Debate: Khanin vs. TsSU" in Henry Rowen and Charles Wolf, Jr. (eds.), *The Impoverished Superpower: Perestroika and the Soviet Military Burden* (San Francisco: Institute for Contemporary Studies, 1990), 63–92.
[16] Dmitri Steinberg, "The Soviet Defence Burden: Estimating Hidden Defence Costs," *Soviet Studies*, 44:2 (1992), 237.
[17] Gates, *From the Shadows*, 318–19; Adomeit, *Imperial Overstretch*, 147.

by the CIA. They set the figure at 25–30 percent of Soviet GNP. Two factors explain the higher estimate as compared with that of the CIA. First, Rowen and Wolf argued that the CIA both clearly underestimated defense expenditure, and overestimated the Soviet GNP. Second, in their calculations of Soviet imperial expenses Rowen and Wolf included other expenses than simply the defense budget, such as trade subsidies, trade credits, economic aid, military aid, covert and destabilization activities, and, from 1979, the costs of the operation in Afghanistan. These other costs fluctuated a great deal over time, but Rowen and Wolf estimated them at an average of 3–4 percent of Soviet GNP between 1970 and 1983. After that they declined appreciably.[18]

HOW TO REDUCE SOVIET DEFENSE SPENDING?

It is probably impossible to establish the correct figure for Soviet imperial expenditures, as a percentage of Soviet GNP, in the early 1980s. Most likely it was in the 25–40 percent range. If the lowest estimates of Soviet GNP are accepted, then the imperial burden may have reached 35–40 percent of Soviet GNP. In this context, however, what is even more important than reality itself is what the Soviet leaders themselves actually believed were the effects of the high defense spending.

When Mikhail Gorbachev came to power in March 1985, there already seems to have been, or at least there soon developed, a widespread feeling within the political and even the military leadership that the Soviet Union was devoting too much money to defense spending. Anatoly Dobrynin reports from his first private meeting with Gorbachev in April 1985 that Gorbachev "strongly believed that we could not gain victory 'over imperialism' by force of arms, nor could we solve our domestic problems without ending the arms race."[19]

The "real" size of the Soviet defense budget was a closely guarded secret, known only to a few people. (Gorbachev states that only "two or three people had access to data on the military–industrial complex.") In his memoirs, Gorbachev also writes that after he became General Secretary it turned out to his surprise that "military expenditure was not 16 percent of the state budget, as we had been told, but rather 40 percent; and its production was

[18] Henry S. Rowen and Charles Wolf, Jr. (eds.), *The Future of the Soviet Empire* (New York: St. Martin's, 1987), 121–40; Rowen and Wolf, *The Impoverished Superpower*, 1–12; Rowen and Wolf, "The CIA's Credibility," 112.
[19] Anatoly Dobrynin, *In Confidence: Moscow's Ambassador to America's Six Cold War Presidents* (New York: Random House, 1995), 570.

not 6 percent but 20 percent of the gross national product."[20] While the security of the Soviet Union had to be maintained, Gorbachev also emphasized "the need drastically to reduce our defence budget—an indispensable condition for improving our economy."[21]

On July 2, 1985, the inexperienced Eduard Shevardnadze was chosen to succeed the old veteran Andrej Gromyko as Soviet foreign minister. Shevardnadze also quickly came to the conclusion that something had to be done with the huge defense budget. With apparent reference to his thinking in 1986, he writes that "We became a superpower largely because of our military might. But the bloated size and unrestricted escalation of this military might was reducing us to the level of a Third World country, unleashing processes that pushed us to the brink of catastrophe."[22]

The consensus on the need to reduce defense expenditure included Yegor Ligachev, who soon became Gorbachev's de facto number two, and then his conservative rival. Ligachev writes that "After April 1985 we faced the task of curtailing military spending. Without this, large-scale social programs would not have been implemented; the economy could not breathe normally with a military budget that comprised 18 percent of the national income."[23] Marshal Sergei Akromeyev and Vice Foreign Minister Georgii Kornienko similarly indicated in their joint memoirs that "the USSR was not able to continue after 1985 the military confrontation with the USA and NATO. The economic possibilities for such a policy were exhausted." It is not entirely clear, however, whether this was an opinion they held in 1985, or whether it was something they concluded a few years later.[24]

Some Soviet officials estimated defense spending as a percentage of GNP even higher than Gorbachev's 20 percent. By 1991, Chief of the Soviet General Staff V. N. Lobov apparently put the military's share at one-third, or possibly even higher.[25] In his *The Collapse of the Soviet Military*, William Odom therefore concludes that "A surprisingly broad consensus existed among

---

[20] Mikhail Gorbachev, *Memoirs* (New York: Bantam Books, 1997), 277; Adomeit, *Imperial Overstretch*, 147–8. For the secrecy, see also Dobrynin, *In Confidence*, 618.

[21] Gorbachev, *Memoirs*, 564.

[22] Eduard Shevardnadze, *The Future Belongs to Freedom* (London: Sinclair–Stevenson, 1991), 54. See also Carolyn McGiffert Ekedahl and Melvin A. Goodman, *The Wars of Eduard Shevardnadze* (London: Hurst & Company, 1997), 52–3, 58–61. Eduard Shevardnadze had no previous experience in foreign policy. Thus, his appointment came as a great surprise, not least to Anatoly Dobrynin who told Secretary of State George Shultz that "Our foreign policy is going down the drain. They have named an agricultural type." For this, see George Shultz, *Turmoil and Triumph: My Years as Secretary of State* (New York: Charles Scribner's Sons, 1993), 572.

[23] Yegor K. Ligachev, *Inside Gorbachev's Kremlin* (New York: Pantheon, 1993), 329. Ligachev's 18 percent of the national income was considerably below Gorbachev's 20 percent of GNP. Still even Ligachev clearly thought the defense burden excessive.

[24] Michael Ellman and Vladimir Kontorovich, "The Collapse of the Soviet System and the Memoir Literature," *Europe–Asia Studies*, 49:2 (1997), 261.

[25] William T. Lee, "The CIA's Credibility," *The National Interest* (Winter 1995/96), 113.

most of the Soviet elite that the Soviet economy was in serious trouble and that the burden of military expenditure was much to blame."[26]

The conclusion seemed obvious: the Soviet economy was in dire straits. The burden of military spending was, to a large extent, to blame. To reduce this burden arms control and disarmament had to be promoted. That in turn implied a basic change in Soviet foreign policy in general, particularly toward the West.[27]

Gorbachev certainly represented a huge difference in style compared to his predecessors. He was much younger, and much more open to new ideas and to dialogue with Western politicians. Initially, however, in defense as in other fields, Gorbachev's reforms were cautious. There was the belief that modest reform would suffice to solve whatever problems the socialist system had. In chief reformer Alexander Yakovlev's words about the situation in 1985 and the need for perestroika: "The idea of acceleration was not oriented to abrupt social changes . . . The dominating opinion was that in the huge organism (of the socialist system) it was necessary to turn on some 'taps' and to turn off others, to replace this and to repair that, and then everything would go well."[28]

In recommending Gorbachev for the post of General Secretary, Foreign Minister Andrej Gromyko had not only stated that he had "teeth of steel," but also that for Gorbachev "defense and vigilance are a sacred matter. In current circumstances this is the holy of the holies." In the initial Five-Year Plan for 1986–90, military expenditure was to grow faster than the "net material product"; even the latter was supposed to accelerate significantly. To the extent that one could hope for a reduction in Soviet military spending, this should preferably take place in tandem with a reduction in the American defense budget, although Gorbachev was more willing than Ligachev and the military to go below strict parity with the United States.[29]

More generally, Gorbachev himself refers to the fact that "The inertia of paternalism made itself felt for a long time." As late as at the Polish party congress in June 1986, Gorbachev stated that "threatening the socialist system, attempting to undermine it from the outside and tear a country out of the socialist fold, means violating not only the will of the people, but also the entire order since the Second World War, and in the final analysis, peace itself."

[26] William E. Odom, *The Collapse of the Soviet Military* (New Haven: Yale University Press, 2000), 115. See also ibid., 104, 118–19, 442, note 59; Ellman and Kontorovich, "The Collapse of the Soviet System and the Memoir Literature," 261–2.
[27] This point is most succinctly summed up in Odom, *The Collapse of the Soviet Military*, 115.
[28] Ellman and Kontorovich, "The Collapse of the Soviet System and the Memoir Literature," 262.
[29] Odom, *The Collapse of the Soviet Military*, 91–2; Ellman and Kontorovich, "The Collapse of the Soviet System and the Memoir Literature," 267; Gaddy, *The Price of the Past*, 56, 62. For Gromyko's account of Gorbachev's early days, see Andrei Gromyko, *Memories: From Stalin to Gorbachev* (London: Arrow Books, 1989), 437–40.

Gorbachev's initial idea was to see whether it was possible to end the war in Afghanistan through one last concerted military effort.[30]

Some of Gorbachev's early ideas for disarmament clearly had a tactical dimension. From his first conversation with Gorbachev, Dobrynin reported that the General Secretary was interested in ousting as many American troops as possible from Europe. A stage-by-stage withdrawal of US and Soviet troops from Europe would take the Americans back across the Atlantic, while "the presence of our troops would be felt most palpably by European states."[31] In his first two years, Gorbachev had a rather low opinion about the possibility of cooperating with Reagan; Soviet disarmament proposals could then serve to increase the split between the United States and Western Europe.[32]

Still, Gorbachev believed, in the words of his close adviser Anatoly Chernyaev, that "scaling down the Cold War basically meant scaling down the arms race."[33] The idea of a nuclear-free world came up in April 1985, and it surfaced as an official Soviet proposal in January 1986. The proposal was actually made by Akromeyev, but the inspiration obviously came from political circles. Moscow had presented similar ideas in the past; the purpose had then been largely propagandistic in the sense that nobody expected any such nuclear disarmament to take place. While Gorbachev may well have been sincere in presenting the proposal, the Soviet military apparently still did not expect it to go very far.[34] It is another matter that with the proposal on the table, and with developments moving as quickly as they did, it soon came to take on a force of its own.

In the same way that domestic reforms were rather limited in the first two years after his coming to power, so foreign policy change too was moderate in 1985–86. In his memoirs, Gorbachev thus writes about his first meeting with Reagan, in Geneva in November 1985, that "As I reread the minutes, I am amazed at the extremely ideological stands taken by both partners. In retrospect, they read more like the 'No. 1 Communist' and the 'No. 1 Imperialist' trying to out-argue each other, rather than a business-like talk between the leaders of the two superpowers."[35]

---

[30] Gorbachev, *Memoirs*, 599–602, the quotation is from 601; Odom, *The Collapse of the Soviet Military*, 102–4; Ellman and Kontorovich, "The Collapse of the Soviet System and the Memoir Literature," 267. See also my *East, West, North, South*, 208–11.

[31] Dobrynin, *In Confidence*, 570.

[32] William D. Jackson, "Soviet Reassessment of Ronald Reagan, 1985–1988," *Political Science Quarterly*, 113:4 (1998–9), 621–2.

[33] William Wohlforth (ed.), *Witnesses to the End of the Cold War* (Baltimore: Johns Hopkins, 1996), 15, 166.

[34] Wohlforth, *Witnesses to the End of the Cold War*, 164; Dobrynin, *In Confidence*, 596–8; Nina Tannenwald, "Conference on Understanding the End of the Cold War," *Cold War International History Project Bulletin*, 11 (Winter 1998), 11.

[35] Gorbachev, *Memoirs*, 523. Despite his appraisal of the Geneva meeting, Gorbachev did not find Reagan "as hopeless as some believed." For this, see Dobrynin, *In Confidence*, 592–3.

At the next summit, in Reykjavik in October 1986, Reagan and Gorbachev apparently got close to agreeing on the elimination of all nuclear weapons. The two leaders shared a vision of a nuclear-free world. The difference in views on the Strategic Defense Initiative (SDI) prevented an agreement between them. It was also obvious that few of the other negotiators on the two sides fully shared the abolitionist views of their leaders. In the short term, Reykjavik was a disappointment.[36]

In the Politburo meeting after Reykjavik, Gorbachev affirmed that "It is impossible to expect any constructive actions or suggestions from the U.S. administration." The Soviet Union needed to show that "the American side is responsible for the breakdown in the agreement over the questions of reduction and liquidation of nuclear weapons." It should be demonstrated that the Reagan administration "bears full responsibility for the failure of the agreement at Reykjavik." Reagan could not control his "gang"; he appeared to be a "liar"; "the normalization of Soviet–American relations is the business of future generations."[37]

THE SMELL OF SUCCESS

None the less, the ground had been laid for huge changes, earlier and more dramatically on the foreign policy than on the domestic side. The domestic reforms of 1985–86 produced relatively few significant results; from the spring and summer of 1987 there was a definite shift in the direction of more comprehensive reform, particularly as far as glasnost was concerned. This was to produce a growing split between Gorbachev and Ligachev. Only more glasnost could produce perestroika, given the entrenched nature of the Soviet bureaucracy. Yakovlev even concluded that limited reform was impossible; it was necessary to dismantle the socialist system as such.

Gorbachev's problem on the domestic side was that he was so uncertain about where he actually wanted to take the Soviet Union. Perestroika was to take place within a basically socialist structure of ownership, and without dramatically modifying the artificial price structure; glasnost was still to

[36] There are many accounts of the Reykjavik meeting. See, for instance, Don Oberdorfer, *From the Cold War to a New Era: The United States and the Soviet Union, 1983–1991* (Baltimore: Johns Hopkins, 1998), 155–209. For versions presented by some of the leading participants, see Wohlforth, *Witnesses to the End of the Cold War*, 163–88; Gorbachev, *Memoirs*, 534–42; Shultz, *Turmoil and Triumph*, 751–80.

[37] *Cold War International History Project*, 4 (Fall 1994), 84–5. See also Diane P. Koenker and Ronald D. Bachman (eds.), *Revelations from the Russian Archives: Documents in English Translation* (Washington, D.C.: Library of Congress, 1997), 705–7; Jackson, "Soviet Reassessment of Ronald Reagan, 1985–1988," 625–34.

occur within the confines of the Party's, and particularly Gorbachev's own, unchallenged leadership.[38]

On the foreign policy side it was much easier. Gorbachev may not have known exactly where he was heading, even in foreign policy, but if he wanted to end the arms race and transform the East–West climate, the solution was obvious: he could do this simply by agreeing to Western proposals that were already on the table. Bureaucratically, Gorbachev had much greater freedom to maneuver on the foreign rather than the domestic side, since many fewer actors were involved on the Soviet side here.

It can be argued that the theoretical breakthrough for a new foreign policy came at the 27th party congress (February 25 to March 6, 1986). Robert Gates writes that "March 6, 1986, should be marked as the beginning of the end of the Cold War," although this became apparent only in retrospect "because the next months were filled with events that kept suspicion alive on both sides."[39] For generations, communist thinking had been based on the view that international relations were dominated by the interests and laws of class warfare. Periods of peaceful coexistence might be possible between communist and capitalist states, but even this represented the continuation of the international class struggle in another form. Now, suddenly, universal values were to take priority over the class struggle.

The overall tone was set, although it took time to work out concrete agreements. The earliest and strongest signs of change were seen in Afghanistan. At the party congress Gorbachev had described the situation there as a "bleeding wound." In July 1986 the first Soviet forces were withdrawn, and in September 1987 Shevardnadze privately told Secretary of State George Shultz that all Soviet forces would leave Afghanistan soon. On February 8, 1988, Gorbachev announced to the Soviet people that the Soviet forces would start withdrawing from Afghanistan by May 15, and would complete their withdrawal in 10 months.[40]

It was also important that the Soviet Union changed its position on the crucial question of verification of arms control agreements. A system of on-site inspections was accepted which would have been unthinkable only a few

---

[38] For a summing up of the memoir literature on the 1987 change, see Ellman and Kontorovich, "The Collapse of the Soviet System and the Memoir Literature," 262, 271, 272. For more general studies, see Åslund, *Gorbachev's Struggle for Economic Reform*, 25–37; Brown, *The Gorbachev Factor*, 147–50, 160–9; Dunlop, *The Rise of Russia and the Fall of the Soviet Empire*, 6–16; McCauley, *Gorbachev*, 50–132; Zubok, *A Failed Empire*, 294–302.

[39] Gates, *From the Shadows*, 380. See also ibid., 381–2.

[40] According to later figures more than 13,000 servicemen lost their lives in combat in the war in Afghanistan; the financial cost was about 5 billion rubles annually. For this, see Odom, *The Collapse of the Soviet Military*, 102–4, 247–51; Stephen White, *After Gorbachev* (Third edition, Cambridge: Cambridge University Press, 1993), 212. See also Koenker and Bachman, *Revelations from the Russian Archives*, 765–6; Shevardnadze, *The Future Belongs to Freedom*, 26, 47–8; Shultz, *Turmoil and Triumph*, 1086–92; Wohlforth, *Witnesses to the End of the Cold War*, 141–5.

years earlier. The new system was spelled out in September 1986 in the Stockholm Document of the Conference on Disarmament in Europe (CDE).[41]

Although the Reykjavik summit was a short-term failure, it proved a long-term success. Nuclear weapons were not to be abolished, but a series of concrete agreements were soon worked out. When Shevardnadze came to Washington in September 1987, he brought with him a letter containing proposals which were to lead to the treaty banning intermediate-range nuclear missiles (INF).[42]

With the signing of the INF treaty, the Washington summit of December 1987 was guaranteed to be a success. "Gorbymania" was beginning to break out in the West. Gorbachev told the Politburo that while, until now, Reagan had been seen as "the expression of the most conservative section of American capitalism and the master of the military industrial complex," he and the American leadership had now been transformed into individuals with "very normal feelings and anxieties."[43]

Gorbachev's speech at the UN in December 1988 provided the most dramatic evidence of his impatience to reduce military expenditure and end the Cold War. The speech's main intent "was to show the international community that mankind was on the threshold of a fundamentally new era, the traditional principles governing international relations, which were based on the balance of power and rivalry, to be superseded by relations founded on creative cooperation and joint development."[44]

In the speech, Gorbachev informed the world that Soviet armed forces would be unilaterally cut by 500,000, out of a total of five million, and by the corresponding number of weapons and equipment; six armored divisions were to be withdrawn from East Germany, Czechoslovakia, and Hungary, thus providing a good basis for the agreement on Conventional Forces in Europe (CFE) which was signed in Paris in November 1990.

Gorbachev had obviously decided that unilateral action was necessary to end the bureaucratic foot-dragging on both sides. In May 1989 the Soviet Union, for the first time, published a realistic defense budget. This budget was to be cut by 14.2 percent, and defense procurement by 19.5 percent. In 1989, conversion from military to civilian production finally started in earnest.[45]

---

[41] Raymond L. Garthoff, *The Great Transition: American–Soviet Relations and the End of the Cold War* (Washington, D.C: Brookings, 1994), 275–6, 284.

[42] Shultz, *Turmoil and Triumph*, 985–6. See also Jackson, "Soviet Reassessment of Ronald Reagan, 1985–1988," 634–7.

[43] Jackson, "Soviet Reassessment of Ronald Reagan, 1985–1988," 637–43. The quotation is from 637. See also Jack F. Matlock, Jr., *Autopsy on an Empire: The American Ambassador's Account of the Collapse of the Soviet Union* (New York: Random House, 1995), 150–2.

[44] Gorbachev, *Memoirs*, 594. See also Ellman and Kontorovich, "The Collapse of the Soviet System and the Memoir Literature," 267; Odom, *The Collapse of the Soviet Military*, 115, 144–6.

[45] Odom, *The Collapse of the Soviet Military*, 231–3; Gaddy, *The Price of the Past*, 61–2.

Why had Gorbachev decided to move ahead at such a rapid pace? First, the period from March 1985 had not yielded the results an impatient Gorbachev had hoped for. Economic growth may have picked up somewhat in 1985–86, but only marginally. But no real cuts had been made in Soviet defense spending; and no significant progress had been made in arms control.

Second, Gorbachev had strengthened his control of the government and the party considerably. He had had the chance to fill senior positions with more of his own appointments. Shevardnadze kept pushing for ever more comprehensive understandings with the West. On May 28, 1987, Mathias Rust landed his small Cessna aircraft virtually on Red Square, thereby hugely embarrassing the Soviet military. Gorbachev was furious. By the end of 1988, the traditionalist Minister of Defense, Sokolov, had been replaced by middle-of-the-roader Yazov, and all but two deputy defense ministers, all the first deputy chiefs of the General Staff, the commander and the chief of staff of the Warsaw Pact forces, all the commanders of the groups of forces and fleets, and all of the district commanders, had been changed. In October 1988 Gorbachev became president of the USSR, thereby giving himself an additional power base outside the party. Ligachev, who insisted that the class struggle ought still to form the basis of international relations, was demoted.[46]

Third, although Gorbachev was basically in control of foreign policy in 1987–88, he still faced resistance. His greatest opponent, however, was the lack of concrete results domestically. More and more, Gorbachev came to appreciate foreign policy, both because it could achieve more rapid results, and because the growing "Gorbymania" in the West provided him with additional strength domestically. In his memoirs Gorbachev writes, with reference to the UN speech, that "I will not deny that I also hoped that a positive international response to my programme would strengthen my position and help overcome the growing resistance to change in the Soviet Union."[47]

Related to this—as we have already seen, and shall shortly return to—when Gorbachev became willing to make dramatic concessions, he then met with a favorable response from the West, a response which, in turn, changed his appraisal of Reagan and other Western leaders, and contributed to further agreements and reforms.

Many books and articles have been written about the end of the Cold War.[48] On the American side, the many participant writers who helped formulate

---

[46] Odom, *The Collapse of the Soviet Military*, 107–11.

[47] Gorbachev, *Memoirs*, 593–4.

[48] I have presented a short survey of these writings in my *East, West, North, South*, 101–8; Vladislav M. Zubok, "Why Did the Cold War End in 1989? Explanations of 'The Turn'" in Odd Arne Westad (ed.), *Reviewing the Cold War: Approaches, Interpretations, Theory* (London: Frank Cass, 2000), 343–67. See also John Lewis Gaddis, *The Cold War* (London: Allen Lane, 2005) and Melvyn P. Leffler, *For the Soul of Mankind: The United States, the Soviet Union, and the Cold War* (New York: Hill and Wang, 2007).

Washington's foreign policy naturally want to stress the contributions made by Presidents Reagan and Bush, and thereby indirectly by themselves. They have received some support from old-style Russian writers who see the collapse of the Soviet Union as the result of Western machinations.

Most historians and political scientists who have written about the end of the Cold War place primary emphasis on the contributions made by Gorbachev. In his detailed study of the end of the Cold War, Raymond Garthoff thus argues that

> "The West did not, as is widely believed, win the Cold War through geopolitical containment and military deterrence. Still less was the Cold War won by the Reagan build-up and the Reagan Doctrine, as some have suggested. Instead 'victory' came when a new generation of Soviet leaders realized how badly their system at home and their policies abroad had failed."[49]

In any bipolar relationship the attitudes of both sides count. In general terms, the West certainly influenced Soviet actions by its political and economic success. As Gorbachev told a Central Committee Conference in May 1986, "We are encircled not by invincible armies but by superior economies."[50] In comparison with the West it was becoming increasingly evident that the Soviet Union was in an economic, social, and moral crisis; détente robbed the Soviets of an enemy which had meant much for the cohesion of the Eastern bloc; and the Helsinki Process set certain standards of human rights which had important long-term effects in the Soviet Union.

The containment policy of the United States in particular also greatly increased the costs of Soviet foreign policy, given the Soviet desire to act as its military equal. The already expensive arms race threatened to become even more expensive with the Strategic Defense Initiative. Dobrynin writes that the Soviet leadership "... was convinced that the great technical potential of the United States had scored again and treated Reagan's statement (on SDI, GL) as a real threat."[51] Shultz saw SDI as "a terrific bargaining chip." This it may well have been, though in the short term it probably also stimulated the further development of offensive weapons on the Soviet side.[52] The cost of the war in Afghanistan steadily escalated. The "success" of the Soviet Union in the Third World was ambiguous indeed. The new allies did not necessarily prove so loyal, and they all definitely came with a considerable price tag attached.

---

[49] Garthoff, *The Great Transition*, 751–78, the quotation is from 753.
[50] Quoted in Dusko Doder and Louise Branson, *Gorbachev: Heretic in the Kremlin* (New York: Viking, 1990), 207.
[51] Dobrynin, *In Confidence*, 526–32, the quotation is from 528. See also Ellman and Kontorovich, "The Collapse of the Soviet System and the Memoir Literature," 261–2.
[52] Shultz, *Turmoil and Triumph*, 701–2, 710, 716–17; Wohlforth, *Witnesses to the End of the Cold War*, 5–6, 31–3, 48. Gorbachev states with reference to SDI that "Even today I must not initiate the reader into certain detail." For this, see Ellman and Kontorovich, "The Collapse of the Soviet System and the Memoir Literature," 267.

For Gorbachev's foreign policy to succeed the West had to cooperate. Western Europe clearly was prepared to do so. Even Margaret Thatcher's Britain occasionally felt that in 1981–83 Ronald Reagan went too far in his anti-Soviet policies. In 1983–84 Reagan's attitude to the Soviet Union changed. He became willing to meet and have serious discussions with Soviet leaders. The harshness of his Cold War rhetoric was toned down. This change started well before Gorbachev came to power. As Beth Fischer argues, the change may have been influenced by the Soviet shooting down of a Korean airliner, by the war scare in September 1983 (when, for a while, the Kremlin actually appeared to believe that NATO might attack the Soviet Union), and by the anti-nuclear movie *The Day After*.[53] Other considerations probably also played their part: the American build-up had been going on for some time and Reagan could see the new policy as a reflection of that; a more flexible policy would stimulate cooperation, both with Congress and with Western Europe; and opinion polls indicated that the American people wanted both "strength" and "peace."[54]

On the American side, some soon felt that Ronald Reagan was advancing too fast, and that he was making too many concessions to Gorbachev. We tend to forget the opposition to the new policy. Even Nixon and Kissinger, who had worked so hard for détente in the 1970s, thought Reagan was too impulsive in his cooperation with the Kremlin.[55] Still, the concessions which led to the end of the Cold War were definitely made by Gorbachev and the Soviet Union. On the arms control side, the INF treaty became possible when Moscow gave up the linkage to SDI and to British and French weapons and agreed to dismantle the SS-20s already deployed. Under the CFE treaty of 1990, the principle of equal ceilings meant that the Eastern side gave up 50 percent of its tanks and heavy artillery while the Western side gave up only 10 percent. Later, the Soviet Union even conceded the United States the right to have the same number of troops in Europe as did the Soviet Union. And in all the various disarmament treaties the Soviet Union agreed to a comprehensive system of verification which would have been unthinkable in the old days.

Gorbachev's more political concessions were even more far-reaching. Moscow agreed to pull out of Afghanistan. In Eastern Europe the Brezhnev Doctrine was abandoned, and although Gorbachev clearly hoped that reform communists would be able to hold power, he refused to intervene militarily, and to a large extent even politically, when the old order was swept away in

---

[53] Beth A. Fischer, *The Reagan Reversal: Foreign Policy and the End of the Cold War* (Columbia: University of Missouri Press, 1997). For the war scare, see also Gates, *From the Shadows*, 270–3.

[54] Garthoff, *The Great Transition*, 142–68; Dobrynin, *In Confidence*, 563; Lundestad, *East, West, North, South*, 106–7.

[55] Leffler, *For the Soul of Mankind*, 338–450; James Mann, *The Rebellion of Ronald Reagan: A History of the End of the Cold War* (New York: Viking, 2009).

that momentous half-year in 1989, from the parliamentary elections in Poland in June, to the fall of Ceauşescu in December.[56] In Germany, Gorbachev eventually agreed not only to the unification of Germany, but even to the inclusion of the eastern part of Germany in NATO, although certain restrictions were set on NATO's presence in the eastern part.[57] In the Soviet Union itself, Gorbachev was behind the limited use of force in Baku in April 1989, and possibly also Vilnius in January 1991. In the end, however, he, as opposed to the coup leaders of August 1991 who were clearly planning a tougher policy to hold the Soviet Union together, resisted the violent option.[58]

Under Gorbachev massive historical changes were taking place. The outer Soviet empire was dismantled; even the Soviet Union was dissolved, although Gorbachev did his best to prevent an outcome which was clearly more the result of Boris Yeltsin's desires than his own; communism was replaced by a new form of Russian democracy; in the place of the centrally planned economy came a much more market-oriented system.

Gorbachev set all these changes in motion. But he clearly did not foresee the result of the changes he started, and may not even have favored any of the outcomes mentioned. Yet, by not using force on a significant scale to hold back change, he accepted the outcomes. Gorbachev turned more conservative from October 1990 to April 1991. In the end, however, unlike Czar Alexander II and Khrushchev, he did not reverse course when the reforms produced results very different from those he intended.[59]

By behaving in a constructive and sympathetic way, by showering Gorbachev with praise and stressing his many foreign policy "successes," rather than his domestic failures, the West, and Reagan in particular, stimulated

---

[56] The best account of the events in Eastern Europe is found in Jacques Lévesque, *The Enigma of 1989: The USSR and the Liberation of Eastern Europe* (Berkeley: University of California Press, 1997). In his memoirs Gorbachev writes that "It goes without saying that the events in Hungary and Czechoslovakia, and later in Rumania and Bulgaria, caused us great concern. However, not once did we contemplate the possibility of going back on the fundamental principles of the new political thinking—freedom of choice and non-interference in other countries' domestic affairs." For this, see Gorbachev, *Memoirs*, 674.

[57] A good account of the unification of Germany is still found in Philip Zelikow and Condoleezza Rice, *Germany Unified and Europe Transformed: A Study in Statecraft* (Cambridge, Mass.: Harvard University Press, 1995). See also Adomeit, *Imperial Overstretch*; Angela E. Stent, *Russia and Germany Reborn: Unification, the Soviet Collapse, and the New Europe* (Princeton: Princeton University Press, 1999); Hans-Hermann Hertle, *Der Fall der Mauer: Die Unbeabsichtigte Selbstauflösung des SED–Staates* (Opladen: Westdeutscher Verlag, 1996); Mary Elise Sarotte, *1989: The Struggle to Create Post-Cold War Europe* (Princeton: Princeton University Press, 2009).

[58] For a short discussion of Gorbachev's use of force inside the Soviet Union, see McCauley, *Gorbachev*, 273–5. By August 1991 the Soviet Union had probably disintegrated too far for the coup to have been successful. For this point of view, see Odom, *The Collapse of the Soviet Military*, 392–7.

[59] The most recent favorable treatment of Gorbachev in long-term perspective is Archie Brown, *The Rise and Fall of Communism* (London: Bodley Head, 2009), part 5.

Gorbachev to make the choices he did.[60] But in realpolitik terms the job of the West was easy: basically to cash in on all the various concessions Gorbachev made, concessions which resulted in the end of the Cold War and, ultimately, the collapse of the Soviet Union.

THE UNITED STATES AND OVERSTRETCH

Paul Kennedy's application of the "imperial overstretch" argument in *The Rise and Fall of the Great Powers* was curiously flawed. First, it might be argued that the 5–10 percent definition of armaments as a percentage of GNP, hidden in a footnote, was rather strange in that the qualification about structural weakness appears to be more important for the fall of a state than the specific percentage it spent on armaments. Second, Kennedy used his argument to explain in part the historical fall of Great Britain, but primarily the coming fall of the United States. In a slightly later study Kennedy has shown that for much of its imperial history it is highly doubtful that Britain's rather low imperial expenses met even the minimum 5 percent definition he presented in the footnote, let alone the 10 percent.[61] After 1945 the United States only spent more than 10 percent of its GNP on defense during and immediately after the Korean War (fiscal years 1952–55), and at no other time. On the prediction side (which was so important both for Kennedy's argument and for his sales), in the 1990s US defense expenditure even fell well below 5 percent, a fact which suggests that the United States was no longer negatively affected by its defense spending.[62]

However, the overall argument of overstretch would seem to be valid in explaining not only the fall of the Soviet Union, but also the end of the Cold War. Kennedy just focused on the wrong cases. Overstretch was acute for the Soviet Union, much more limited for Great Britain, and certainly for the United States.

[60] Dobrynin, *In Confidence*, 611; Matlock, *Autopsy on an Empire*, 667–70.

[61] Paul Kennedy, "The Costs and Benefits of British Imperialism 1846–1914: Comment," *Past & Present*, 125 (November 1989), 186–92. See also Patrick K. O'Brien, "The Costs and Benefits of British Imperialism 1846–1914," *Past & Present*, 120 (August 1988), 163–99 and O'Brien's reply to Kennedy's comment in *Past & Present*, 125 (November 1989), 192–9; Lance E. Davis and Robert A. Huttenback, *Mammon and the Pursuit of Empire: The Political Economy of British Imperialism, 1860–1912* (Cambridge: Cambridge University Press, 1986), particularly 304–5, 315–16.

[62] See for instance the statistics in John Lewis Gaddis, *Strategies of Containment: A Critical Appraisal of Postwar American National Security Policy* (Oxford: Oxford University Press, 1982), 359. For later years see, for instance, U.S. Bureau of the Census, *Statistical Abstract of the United States: 2011* (Washington, D.C.: Government Printing Office, 2010), 332.

Niall Ferguson has suggested that the fall of empires, even the current American one, can be precipitous.[63] It is difficult to believe that in the American case this would be because of imperial overstretch in Kennedy's narrow sense. Despite America spending more on defense than all of its major challengers added together, the total amount does not come to more than 4–5 percent of its GNP, higher than in all of its likely competitors, but still fairly limited.

Yet defense spending is of course part of the wider picture of the US deficit in federal spending and, more indirectly, its current accounts. Spending 4–5 percent on defense when everybody else spends considerably less, and when public debt is the overriding issue, is not a good situation to be in. Defense spending will undoubtedly be cut, but probably not severely as the Republicans want to maintain the high spending level. In several EU countries we see these very days how rapidly the situation can change, from years of uncontrolled deficit spending, to rapid and dramatic cuts in their budgets. The markets demand action. It is not likely, but far from unimaginable, that Washington may be forced to undertake similar actions, with the consequences this could entail for America's standing in the world. Larry H. Summer's question remains of how long the world's biggest borrower can also be the world's leading power. Others ask what kind of superpower the United States would be when it spends more on interest payments than on defense, a condition that is likely to occur in a few years' time.

[63] Niall Ferguson, "Complexity and Collapse: Empires on the Edge of Chaos," *Foreign Affairs* (March/April 2010).

6

The Long Lines of History

Globalization would seem to encourage the idea that we are all not only living in the same world, but that we are being influenced by the same forces emanating from one geographical center. The United States is usually seen as this center. Globalization and Americanization are often seen as very closely related phenomena, but this is too simplistic a view. Globalization flows from many sources; it is also accompanied by fragmentation. From a historical perspective we can see how almost all the old imperial units have been dissolved, and a rapidly increasing number of nation states has taken over. These nation states have become smaller and smaller in terms of territory and population. Imperial rule broke down due to emerging new standards of legitimacy at an international, national, and local level. Gradually the Great Powers—including the Soviet Union—lost their will to rule "the distant provinces." The new states became an important force in international relations, reducing the influence of the Great Powers, even including the United States. The US generally favored decolonization, but once they were free, most of the new states chose an independent course.

GLOBALIZATION[1]

Globalization was certainly not a new phenomenon after 1945. Throughout the centuries cultures all around the world had established contact with other cultures. The world religions illustrated how this happened. Judaism, Christianity, and Islam all originated in the Middle East. Then they spread to

---

[1] I have written somewhat more extensively about globalization and fragmentation in my "Why Does Globalization Encourage Fragmentation?," *International Politics*, 41 (2004), 265–76. Many of the statements that follow are further documented there. Among the enormous literature, I have found Ian Clark, *Globalization and Fragmentation: International Relations in the Twentieth Century* (Oxford: Oxford University Press, 1997), and John Baylis, Steve Smith, and Patricia Owens (eds.), *The Globalization of World Politics* (Oxford: Oxford University Press, 2008) particularly useful.

the most distant corners of the world. Pests and plagues illustrated the same basic development, as did economic transfers, in the form of technological inventions and economic cycles. The pre-1914 world was in some ways more integrated than the world of today. Workers could travel much more freely from country to country, practically all around the world, than they can today. The Great Depression after 1929 clearly illustrated the economic interdependence of the world; as such it had a great influence on the way in which policymakers after 1945 thought about these issues.

What was new after 1945 was the rapid improvement in communications of all types. Soon we could fly to practically anywhere in the world, and many of us did travel to ever more distant destinations. On television we could watch major events unfold almost anywhere as they happened. Exports and imports rapidly increased, although for decades they did not exceed the levels before the First World War, adjusted for the size of the economy. For centuries there had been multinational companies, such as the British, French, Dutch, and even other East India Companies, although they had, as their names indicated, a firm national basis. The number of multinational companies exploded from 3,500 in 1960 to 40,000 in 1995. The global currency turnover grew exponentially. Globalization helped to bring rapid economic growth to most countries of the world. The emergence first of Japan, then China, and to some extent even India, illustrated this—or rather their re-emergence, since China and India had, a few centuries ago, been leading economies and cultures. The housing and banking crisis that originated in the United States in 2007–08, and then turned into a semi-global economic crisis, showed the more problematic side of globalization.

Ideologies and religions of all kinds spread quickly—democratic or totalitarian, violent or non-violent. In the interwar years totalitarian regimes had been on the offensive. Democracy was found largely in North America and most of Western Europe. Today, almost 60 percent of the world's population lives under democratic rule. The main exceptions are China and large parts of the Muslim world, although important changes were taking place in 2011 in the Arab world.[2] We could all cross borders as salespeople and tourists, but so could terrorists; goods and, to a lesser extent, labor could also travel relatively freely, but so could pollution.

After the creation of the railroads in the nineteenth century it was said that the small German states had lost their relevance since you could pass through some of them in half an hour. Germany simply had to be united. With modern aircraft we can fly across many, if not most, of the world's states in that time. Although one overall government has not developed, many global institutions have evolved. The United Nations became a stronger and geographically much

---

[2] The best account is still Samuel P. Huntington, *The Third Wave: Democratization in the Late Twentieth Century* (Norman: University of Oklahoma Press, 1991).

more comprehensive organization than the interwar League of Nations. The General Agreement on Tariffs and Trade (GATT) has developed into the more effective World Trade Organization. A whole series of transnational, non-governmental organizations have become influential (Amnesty International, Greenpeace, the International Campaign to Ban Landmines. Some observers even started referring to the development of a "global society" or a "global consciousness," even the "global village."

The nation state was also being challenged by developments at the regional level. The European Union was the most successful and comprehensive of these regional institutions. The EU came to include a rapidly increasing number of new members, and integration spread to ever new areas. Similar, if not quite so strong, institutions were evolving in many regions of the world.

Technological improvements are constantly being made which will improve communication across the world. This aspect of globalization may well be inevitable and irreversible. Other parts of the process are clearly more politically driven. Thus, in the 1930s, under the influence of the Great Depression and totalitarian ideologies, globalization slowed down considerably. Today, with rising economic problems, there are signs that the pace might be slowing somewhat, although protectionism has been better contained than many observers had expected.

FRAGMENTATION

The extent of globalization may easily be exaggerated. Only 2 percent of students study at universities outside their home countries; only 3 percent of people live outside their country of birth; less than 1 percent of all American companies have any foreign operations; and the vast majority of goods are not traded across international borders.[3] If we look more closely, we can even see that the world has, in some respects, become larger and more fragmented than it used to be, rather than smaller and more globalized.

In 1945 the United Nations had fifty-one members, fewer than the number of countries in Africa today; it now has 193 members. Then there is the small number of states that do not want, or do not feel financially able, to join. So, depending on the definition used, today there are at least 200 states. The fate of modern empires and other large territorial units illustrates the point. The colonial empires were amazingly quickly dissolved after the Second World War. In 1945 virtually no one, including most colonial leaders, really had any idea about the dramatic developments that would take place in the ensuing

---

[3] Schumpeter, "The Case Against Globaloney," *The Economist* (April 23, 2011), 65.

decades. What the British started in India spread with amazing speed to the distant colonies of France, the Netherlands, Belgium, and Portugal. The Soviet Union was anti-colonial, but this did not prevent it from having its own "colonies." In 1989 the Soviet Empire in Central and Eastern Europe disappeared in the course of half a year. In 1990–91 even the Soviet Union itself was dissolved into its fifteen constituent republics.

In Europe we have not only seen the breakup of the Soviet Union, but Yugoslavia split into seven parts (so far), and Czechoslovakia into two. In Africa the creation of Eritrea represented the first break with the arbitrary imperial borders—borders which are strongly protected also by the new rulers. South Sudan followed in 2011. Once the dam breaks, no one can be sure where the water will flow. In China, more than 90 percent of the population is Han Chinese, but the status of Xinkian and Tibet (not to mention Taiwan) is still a matter of contention. East Timor has broken away from Indonesia; Bangladesh has split from Pakistan, and many questions still remain about Pakistan's future. India has been threatened by separatism ever since its creation. Even in liberal–democratic Canada the Quebec question long remained a festering sore. And, most paradoxically, the old colonial powers that spread from their small territories to encompass huge swaths of land are now themselves threatened by division. Belgium is in great trouble. Spain has its rebellious provinces. In Britain, Scotland's independence is hotly discussed. France has its Corsica. The United States had its Civil War that almost broke the union apart. Today the US is virtually alone among the big powers in that virtually nobody questions its territorial unity.

Nobody knows how many "nations" there are in the world since it is up to the various inhabitants to decide how they want to define themselves , but it has been estimated that there are at least 3,500. In only half of the world's states is there a single ethnic group that comprises at least 75 percent of the population. If, eventually, most "nations" are to have their own states, then the process has only just begun. In the early nineteenth century many thought Belgium and Greece too small to become independent; in the early twentieth century many thought Iceland and Malta too small. Today there are at least eighty-seven countries with a population under five million; thirty-five have fewer than 500,000 inhabitants. Some of the most populous states in the world, such as China, India, Indonesia, Pakistan, and Nigeria, are all poorer than the microstates of Nauru, St Kitts and Nevis (which might split up), Antigua and Barbuda, Dominica, Seychelles, and Grenada.

In field after field the many different needs of globalization will challenge the borders of the nation state. In highly developed service economies borders will generally mean less than in economies dominated by industry and agriculture. The challenges of terrorism and tourism, immigration and climate change will all break down borders. Interest groups of all different sorts will play an even larger part in international diplomacy than they have done so far.

Yet, in the foreseeable future, the nation state will remain the basic unit. Inside the EU, where the traditional nation state is being most directly challenged, we can still see its strengths, particularly on the security side and in how its citizens define their own identity. In fact, the continuation of the nation state and the slow speed, particularly of the non-economic integration process within the European Union, make it increasingly difficult for the EU to compete with the leading Great Powers of the day.

WHY BOTH GLOBALIZATION AND FRAGMENTATION?

In explaining the simultaneous globalization and fragmentation of the world, it should be noted that, to a large extent, the two processes take place in different spheres. Although examples of political globalization and technological–economic fragmentation can be found, it is still true that globalization is overwhelmingly a technological and economic process, while the fragmentation is primarily political. It is often assumed that there is a close relationship between the two spheres—and of course there often is—but sometimes this is less true than we think.

Both Marxists and economic liberalists have argued that national boundaries would break down. However, both Marx and Cobden were largely wrong. The outbreak of the First World War showed that the workers of Europe did not unite; nor did free trade necessarily lead to peace. To a large extent the industrial revolution actually coincided with the rise of the nation state. As Ernest Gellner and others have argued, in many respects the industrial revolution created nationalism (improved communications brought the country together; the creation of a national school system did the same, as did the introduction of conscription.)

In fact, in several ways technological–economic globalization probably stimulates political fragmentation. The stronger the globalization, the stronger the fragmentation. The explanations may be found at four different levels: political–psychological, ideological–cultural, technological, and economic.

The political–psychological explanation can easily be grasped by anyone who has done even the slightest traveling abroad. When we travel we find many interesting things to see, and we may even become great admirers of the country we visit. At the same time, however, we often discover that we become quite patriotic. Abroad we realize who we are and what our identity means to us. This can be seen not only among tourists travelling abroad, but also in so-called long-distance nationalism (the Irish in the United States, Third World students in the West) and in the blossoming of all kinds of local cultures in the face of increased pressure from the outside.

Globalization frequently means that white, Christian, rich, Western culture is exported to other parts of the world, the implication often being that there must be something wrong with local cultures. It should not be difficult to understand that this might cause a reaction in many circles. The entire process of decolonization can be seen from this perspective, although it certainly also involved turning Western ideals against Westerners themselves. Modernization was frequently welcomed; Westernization was more controversial. The striking rise in religious fundamentalism, which we see in virtually all religions, may in part be a response to Western culture spreading throughout the world. In Western Europe religion is declining in significance; in much of the rest of the world it is becoming increasingly important. Obviously we cannot talk about the challenge of globalization as the only explanation for fundamentalism and nationalism, but it may well be an important part of the explanation.

On the ideological–cultural level, it is true that ideologies cross borders much more easily than before. Thus, the rise of democracy in one part of the world often stimulates democracy in other parts as well. One of the ideologies that spread most easily, however, was nationalism. In the old days ethnic groups simply disappeared as separate cultures or were amalgamated into larger groups. This is what happened to Angles, Saxons, Picts, Vandals, and Visigoths. This process continues today; groups are still merged into other groups and languages disappear on a large scale. (There may still be about 6,000 languages in the world, but 2,500 of them may be in danger of disappearing.) However, for many large groups, nationalism—not assimilation— has become the preferred alternative. In modern times there have always been historians who help to create the necessary "invented traditions" or "imagined communities," that is, to inform their people and the rest of the world that the "nation" in question has had a long and distinguished history.

Technologically, to take television as an example, we can now watch all kinds of events "live" on a huge number of available channels. However, both indirectly and directly, technological advances stimulate not only globalization, but also fragmentation. Often technology becomes so simple that even small groups can exploit it for their own purposes. Thus, the Welsh language in Wales and the Sami language in Norway are now doing much better than only a few decades ago. This probably has to do with a combination of the establishment of niche television and radio stations, and educational reforms benefiting these languages. Somewhat more surprisingly there is also a clear trend that in the "global village" international news is losing out to national and local news. Many would rather learn more about "us" than about "the others." The contradictory effects of the Internet have already been mentioned.

Finally, there is the economic level. Often globalization has a negative effect; and the groups affected work to modify or reverse the globalizing policies of their respective governments. We see this almost every day in many countries of the world. There is also the effect, already referred to, whereby the economy has become so globalized that virtually any region, however small, can break out and form its own country without suffering significant negative economic consequences. Globalization has made the size of a country almost irrelevant to the success of its economy.

GREAT POWERS AND THEIR WILL TO RULE

For centuries Great Powers were local or regional at best, certainly not global, despite their own claims to the contrary. In the course of the 200s BC two Great Powers emerged on each side of the Eurasian landmass: Rome and China. The two empires controlled territories roughly similar in size and population; their capitals were the largest cities in the world. Rome was explicitly called "the capital of the world" (*urbs Roma, caput mundi*); at its largest the city may have had one million inhabitants. Yet despite its claim to rule the world, its size and its great resources (military and otherwise), the Roman world was primarily Mediterranean. The Chinese empire fluctuated a great deal in territorial size, but was unique in that it was largely able to maintain its territorial core for more than two thousand years. The Romans had only the vaguest notions about China. The Chinese may have known even less about the Romans.[4] In between these two geographical areas, so far apart, other major empires developed. For 900 years an Indo–Iranian empire existed. In India more or less imperial constructions rose and fell. The nomads from Central Asia and elsewhere—from Attila to Genghis Khan and his successors—threatened all these areas, and for briefer periods of time created their own huge structures.

With the Age of Exploration a deeper understanding of the world developed. Spain and Portugal laid claim to huge territories in the Western hemisphere. With the American and French revolutions of the eighteenth century, states with true universalist ambitions arose for the first time. In principle the political rights developed there were to apply to all the peoples of the earth. For France, the leading country in Europe, to have such ambitions was perhaps not so surprising. For the distant United States, on the other side of the Atlantic, thirteen colonies that had just successfully rebelled against Britain, and with a population of only four million, this was less expected.

The British Empire, by far the largest and most complex of the colonial structures, had only limited global aspirations. It was larger than any other

---

[4] For comparisons between China and Rome, see Walter Scheidel (ed.), *Rome and China: Comparative Perspectives on Ancient World Empires* (New York: Oxford University Press, 2009).

empire, but many different European states, large and small, claimed huge territories in Asia and Africa. Some of the largest territories, however, such as most of China and all of Japan, remained outside these imperial structures. And by the time Asia, and particularly Africa, came under colonial domination in the nineteenth century, practically all the colonies of the Western hemisphere had already become independent states. In the 1930s, when the British Empire was at its largest, London's difficulties in Ireland and India indicated what might follow. Japan's defeats of the colonial powers in East Asia during the Second World War represented a huge blow to their empires. The white man had clearly lost his magic.

In hindsight we clearly see that many imperial powers were gradually losing their will to maintain their empires. For the British, the Great Indian Uprising of 1857–58 did not lead to any serious questioning of Britain's right to rule India. On the contrary, the "Indian Mutiny," as it was called for so long, showed the treacherousness of the Indians. They first had to be taught a lesson, then civilized. The uprising showed how much they had to learn. The much more limited events in Amritsar in 1919, where general R. E. H. Dyer ordered Indian Army troops to fire into a crowd of demonstrators, leaving about 400 Indians dead, were to lead to some initial celebration of the general, but soon to his early retirement. Serious questions were raised about Britain's role in India.[5] After Britain had left India in a hurry in 1946–47, riots in Accra in 1948 were sufficient to raise the prospect that London would offer independence to Africans much more quickly than virtually anyone had assumed. This was probably more a question of will than of power, as the weakest of the European colonial powers, Portugal, hung on to its colonies until the democratic revolution there in 1974–75.

Even in the Soviet case this weakening of the will could actually be seen. The Red Army intervened without much questioning in 1953 in East Germany, and again in 1956 in Hungary. In 1968 the Kremlin felt that some justification had to be offered for its intervention in Czechoslovakia, in the form of the Brezhnev Doctrine and the participation of its Warsaw Pact allies. No country could simply abandon socialism; other socialist countries had a duty to help the Soviet Union enforce this point of view. In 1980–81 in Poland the Soviet Union did not intervene at all, but left the response to the Polish party and the army. Something had shifted dramatically in the relationship between the ruler and those ruled. When Moscow in the early years after the Second World War also exploited its new allies economically, thus paying Poland a small fraction of world prices for its coal, it was perhaps to be expected. Some

---

[5] For a short account of Amritsar and its consequences, see Denis Judd, *Empire: The British Imperial Experience from 1765 to the Present* (London: Fontana, 1996), 258–72. For the long account, see Nigel Collett, *The Butcher of Amritsar: General Reginald Dyer* (London: Hambledon, 2005).

decades later, however, the Soviet Union ended up subsidizing its allies for Moscow's deliveries of oil and gas.

The mechanisms involved in such developments were complex. In democracies, in the long run, it gradually became almost impossible to use substantial force over long periods of time to keep foreign peoples under control. This was true not only of Britain, but also of France. Although its colonies were formally incorporated into France, the wars in Indochina and Algeria ultimately had to be abandoned. The Fourth Republic collapsed under the burden of the latter. In Portugal, democracy led to decolonization. For the United States the wars in the Philippines after the Spanish–American war, in Vietnam in the 1960s and 1970s, and, most recently, even in Afghanistan and Iraq, led to crises and gradually brought dramatic withdrawals. A voting public mostly concerned with domestic matters would not, in the long run, pay the expenses in money and lives for such foreign (and to a considerable extent failing) adventures.

In the Soviet case too, similar mechanisms kicked in. As even the elites in the Soviet Union and the Eastern and Central European countries lost their enthusiasm for the Soviet–Communist system, changes had to be introduced. As contacts with the West were developed and the feud with China intensified, even the smaller allies could bargain with Moscow. The Kremlin needed their support and gradually had to offer something in return to get it.

The global ambitions of the United States and the Soviet Union after the Second World War were something new in history, if not in theory, then certainly in practice. The United States had a unique power base and possessed an ideology which meant that few questions anywhere in the world were without relevance to its various administrations. The Soviet Union had more limited power and for a long time primarily focused on its huge border regions, despite the universalist aspirations of its communist ideology. Over time, however, as its power increased and its aspirations grew, Moscow came to claim some sort of equality with Washington. Few questions were without interest even to the rulers in the Kremlin, and the Cold War spread to the most distant corners of the world.

GREAT POWERS AND EMPIRES[6]

Edward Gibbon stated that "There is nothing more contrary to nature than the attempt to hold in obedience distant provinces." Most Great Powers first consolidate their core areas and then expand by taking control of

[6] The following section is based on Geir Lundestad (ed.), *The Fall of Great Powers: Peace, Stability, and Legitimacy* (Oxford: Oxford University Press, 1994), particularly 383–402.

territories outside these areas. They become empires, and this applied to Great Britain, the Soviet Union, and the United States. These empires generally provided stability compared with the previous order, but over time the traditional legitimacy—international, national, and local—on which the empires rested was undermined. In the end they collapsed. The successor states that arose were often based on ethnic self-determination; in this respect they were more legitimate than the old empires, but the new order also tended to be less stable. So the conclusion is that there often appears to be a tension between peace and stability on the one hand and modem legitimacy on the other. And a lack of legitimacy leads to collapse and impotence.

The rise and fall of Great Powers were partly related to war. As we have seen, nothing contributed more to swift and comprehensive change in Great Power configurations in the twentieth century than the two world wars. It may be argued that most of the sweeping changes caused by the world wars would have happened sooner or later anyway, but, at the very least, the wars greatly accelerated the fall of certain states and the rise of others.

Practically all Great Powers developed empires in the sense that they came to control territories outside their core areas. The falling away of these "distant provinces" represented a crucial aspect of the decline of most Great Powers, a point largely ignored by Kennedy in *The Rise and Fall of the Great Powers*.

When we say that empires fall, we primarily mean that the "distant provinces" fall away. The outlying areas of the empires could be vast; far greater than the home countries. While the "distant provinces" fall away, the core areas usually remain intact. The larger the core area, the better a Great Power is generally able to retain its position. This is the main reason why many of the comparisons made between late nineteenth-/early twentieth-century Britain and today's United States are misleading. Britain has a rather limited geographical core; the United States a much larger one. Thus, the twentieth century was to a large extent dominated by the United States and Russia/the Soviet Union with their vast cores, as Tocqueville and others before him had predicted.[7] Germany had to give up its hopes for *Lebensraum*, but with its core largely intact, it has been able to stage two comebacks as a Great Power; Japan managed one.

In most cases the geographical line of division between the core and the more distant lands seemed obvious, although complications could certainly arise. At the turn of the century, British politicians, with Joseph Chamberlain in the lead, hoped that imperial federation and customs union could compensate for Britain's rather limited base.[8] The French, and the Portuguese as well,

---

[7] Theodore Draper, *Present History: On Nuclear War, Detente, and Other Controversies* (New York: Vintage Books, 1984), 323–51.

[8] Bernard Porter, *The Lion's Share. A Short History of British Imperialism 1850–1970* (London: Longman, 1975 and later editions), 129–39; Aaron L. Friedberg, *The Weary Titan: Britain*

tried to do away entirely with the formal separation between homeland and colonies. These efforts all failed. However, the fall of the Soviet Union illustrated better than anything the lack of absolute lines of division between the core and "distant provinces." Not only did the outer empire in Eastern Europe fall away, but the Soviet Union itself collapsed.

In this sense the United States seems rather unique. What distinguishes it from a traditional empire is the fact that the semi-distant lands, most of which were captured from Mexico in the 1830s–1840s, have been so successfully integrated into the larger unit. The same applies to the 11 states that broke away from the rest of the United States in the Civil War; after a difficult period of reconstruction they were successfully reintegrated into the Union. The more distant lands on many continents, while being strongly influenced by the US, virtually all maintained their independence. Today the United States is one of the few very large states whose territorial integrity is accepted by virtually all of its citizens.

OLD AND NEW FORMS OF LEGITIMACY

The falling away of the "distant provinces" was related to deep moral–political changes leading to a gradually disappearing legitimacy for imperial rule. In the final analysis empires rested on force, but the use of such force became increasingly difficult. Little by little imperial rule came to break with accepted norms at three basic levels: the international (the world community), the national (in the home country), and the local (in the colonies or provinces).[9] In other words, imperial rule lost its "legitimacy."

Legitimacy is here defined as a certain state of affairs being perceived as "in accordance with established rules, principles, or standards"; in other words, that this state of affairs "can be justified."[10] The traditional basis of legitimacy for imperial rule was dynastic. The ruler had the right to conquer whatever territory he or she was able to conquer; this territory could then be passed on to their heirs, more or less in the same way other forms of property were passed on to the next generation. Early on, emperors came to desire some

and the Experience of Relative Decline, 1895–1905 (Princeton: Princeton University Press, 1988), 49–51, 83–8.

[9] This section is in part inspired by William Roger Louis and Ronald Robinson, "The United States and the Liquidation of the British Empire in Tropical Africa, 1941–1951" in Prosser Gifford and William Roger Louis, *The Transfer of Power in Africa: Decolonization 1940–1960* (New Haven: Yale University Press, 1982), 31–56.

[10] Jess M. Stein, *The Random House College Dictionary* (New York: Random House, 1984), 765; *The Advanced Learner's Dictionary of Current English* (London: Oxford University Press, 1967), 558.

form of religious blessing for their rule, since this could strengthen their position. Imperial rulers could even find it opportune to mobilize popular, or national, sentiment, but this, again, was not something they had to do. This traditional world was one of subjects, not citizens.[11]

Into the twentieth century the Austro–Hungarian Empire, for instance, reflected the dynastic principle. Many pragmatic reasons, particularly of a security and economic nature, existed for the continuation of Habsburg rule, but these did not constitute the basis of imperial rule as such.[12]

Traditional forms of legitimacy have lingered to this day, but with the French Revolution the basis for legitimacy began to change. More and more, rule, including imperial rule, had to be justified with reference to what it did for the citizens. Modern, as opposed to earlier, empires, had to provide some form of popular justification for ruling over "distant provinces."

As William McNeill has argued, "the norm for civilized governance was laminated polyethnic empire".[13] But this norm gradually changed to that of the nation state. The national doctrine came in two basic versions: the French and the German. In the French version it meant popular sovereignty and constitutional rule within a more or less given territory, almost regardless of the ethnic and cultural background of the various groups living inside that territory. (In France itself, this background was relatively homogeneous anyway.) France expanded far beyond its traditional borders of the Atlantic, the Rhine, the Alps, and the Pyrenees without showing too much concern for the actual support it enjoyed in the various areas. Later on, France incorporated its colonies directly into the mother country.

The German version emphasized the connection between the right of self-determination and cultural and ethnic unity, in the sense that the various cultural and ethnic groups had this right of self-determination. The problem was that in Central and Eastern Europe the various peoples lived side by side, and not in nicely separated areas. The German version, too, was undoubtedly biased in favor of more traditional interests, as the rather

---

[11] For some interesting comments on early legitimacy, see James Mayall, *Nationalism and International Society* (Cambridge: Cambridge University Press, 1990), 26–32.

[12] Among the many histories of Austria–Hungary I have relied most upon Robert A. Kann, *A History of the Habsburg Empire 1526–1918* (Berkeley: University of California Press, 1974); Stanley R. Williamson, Jr., *Austria–Hungary and the Origins of the First World War* (London: Macmillan, 1991); F.R. Bridge, *The Habsburg Monarchy Among the Great Powers 1815–1918* (New York: Berg, 1990); Alan Sked, *The Decline and Fall of the Habsburg Empire 1815–1918* (London: Longman, 1989); Adam Wandruszka und Peter Urbanitsch (eds.), *Die Habsburgermonarchie 1848–1918. Band VI. Die Habsburgermonarchie im System der Internationalen Beziehungen* (Wien: Verlag der Osterreichischen Akademie der Wissenschaften, 1989); István Deák, *Beyond Nationalism: A Social and Political History of the Habsburg Officer Corps, 1848–1918* (New York: Oxford University Press, 1990).

[13] William McNeill, "Introductory Historical Commentary," in Lundestad, *The Fall of Great Powers*, 3–21.

comprehensive definitions of German territory from 1848 onwards showed. Some groups were quite simply seen as more equal than others. Nevertheless, nationalism—in whatever version—presented a dramatic challenge to any form of imperial rule.

From Europe, the concept of the nation state gradually spread to the rest of the world, normally in the French version, since the alternative (the German model) could easily have led to chaos in the form of many states endlessly quarreling over borders. This change of norms—from empire to nation states—this erosion of the basis of imperial legitimacy, came to mean the end of imperial rule.

IMPERIAL RULE AND INTERNATIONAL
AND NATIONAL LEGITIMACY

In Western Europe, the process of formation of nation states was largely complete with the unification of Germany in 1870–71. (Norway, Ireland, and Iceland followed later.) In the eastern part the Ottoman Empire was, at this time, continuing to disintegrate. Until the First World War Austria–Hungary held up well, although Vienna's fear of a breakup was an important part of the origins of the war itself. The nationality question only got out of control in 1917–18. As late as January 1918, in his Fourteen Points, President Wilson still favored "the freest opportunity of autonomous development" for the peoples of Austria–Hungary, only later amended to read "complete independence for the people of Austria–Hungary." Similarly, only in early 1918 did even the South Slavs and the Czechs give up reform of the empire into a multinational federation, for full independence.[14]

After the First World War, national self-determination became the norm— the legitimate standard in all of Europe. Even where this norm was violated in practice, as in the Soviet Union, it was accepted in theory. The appeasement policy of the 1930s was partly based on the difficulty of opposing the right of Germans in Austria and Czechoslovakia to join the mother country. In another way, however, Germany under Hitler presented an extreme version of imperial legitimacy in that here the *Lebensraum* ideology reflected the total victory of home country considerations over any attempt whatsoever to achieve support in "non–Aryan" areas.

Outside Europe and the Americas, despite the successes of different kinds of nationalism in Japan and in China, the system of imperial rule generally

---

[14] Kann, *A History of the Habsburg Empire 1526–1918*, 487–520. See also István Deák's contribution in Lundestad, *The Fall of Great Powers*, 81–102.

remained strong until the Second World War. In the interwar period
the primary colonial powers, Britain and France, dominated The League of
Nations, and the main revisionist states, Germany, Italy, and Japan, were
not opposed to imperial rule as such. Rather, they wanted to create empires
of their own.

Only after the Second World War, with the domination of the two anti-
colonial powers, the United States and the Soviet Union, and with the increase
in the number of new states, did imperial rule gradually lose its legitimacy at
the international level.[15] But by then imperial rule was also losing its legitimacy both at the national level in the home country and at the local level in the
colonies.

The starting point for imperial rule was for it to have legitimacy in the home
area. The basis for this legitimacy varied. The British, like other colonial
powers, were long convinced that they brought progress and civilization to
backward areas of the world. This view was summed up by one Victorian
administrator of India, Fitzjames Stephen, in the following rather comprehensive way: "The essential parts of European civilization are peace, order, the
supremacy of law, the prevention of crime, the redress of wrong, the enforce-
ment of contracts, the development and concentration of the military force of
the state, the construction of public works, the collection and expenditure of
the revenue required for these objects in such a way as to promote to the
utmost the public interest, interfering as little as possible with the comfort or
wealth of the inhabitants, and improvement of the people."[16]

This was a tall order; an order almost impossible to fulfill. In the Soviet case,
domestic, as well as foreign, legitimacy was primarily grounded in Marxist–
Leninist ideology. Through the class struggle, history marched inevitably on
from feudalism to capitalism, and on to socialism and communism. In Eastern
Europe this march of history was expressed in the form of the establishment of
the people's democracies.[17] Although communism had only minority support
in Eastern Europe, its expansion there, and later in China, made even many
non-communists around the world feel that communism might well come to
represent the wave of the future.

Since the United States did not see itself as having an empire, it did not have
to provide justifications of this sort. Most Americans agreed that the United
States had to take on the global role it did after 1945 "to protect democracy
against the totalitarian evil of communism." The underlying assumption was

[15] For a fine short analysis of this process, see Hedley Bull, "The Emergence of a Universal
International Society," in Hedley Bull and Adam Watson (eds.), *The Expansion of International
Society* (Oxford: Clarendon Press, 1984), 117–26.
[16] Quoted from J. M. Roberts, *The Triumph of the West: The Origins, Rise, and Legacy of
Western Civilization* (London: BBC, 1985), 318. See also Porter, *The Lion's Share*, 134–8.
[17] See, for instance, *Soviet Foreign Policy. Volume II: 1945–1980* (Moscow: Progress Publishers, 1981), 16–17.

that Washington did not do this primarily for its own sake, but for the sake of the many states threatened by Soviet communism. If the Americans were not wanted, they would presumably go home.

Most imperial powers lost the *will* to maintain their empires before they lost the *power* to do so, although the two were of course closely related. Much of the explanation for the loss of will was found in the erosion of old-fashioned imperial legitimacy. In Britain, many different forces undermined this kind of legitimacy: the spread of democracy, which brought new forces to power and made it increasingly difficult to deny democratic rule to the colonies; the concentration on expanding the social welfare of the home country; the many different effects of the First, and particularly the Second, World War, from the destruction of racist, social Darwinist thinking, to the emphasis on democracy in the fight against fascism; evolving concepts of interest and security that undermined the imperial rationale.

Ultimately imperial rule rested on force, but it became increasingly difficult to use this force. The tolerance level for the use of force varied from imperial capital to imperial capital. It also changed over time. The Great Indian Uprising of 1857–58 was suppressed with considerable ferocity. The ferocity did not weaken the legitimacy in Britain of imperial rule; it rather strengthened it: the "bettering" of the Indian would take even longer than had been expected. In 1945 the new viceroy, Lord Wavell, commented on "the weakness and weariness of the instrument still at our disposal in the shape of the British element in the Indian Civil Service." The massive use of force was now quite simply out of the question, even for an emotional old imperialist such as Winston Churchill.[18] France, on the other hand, even after the Second World War, accepted quite massive use of force, as evidenced by the wars in Indochina and Algeria; but in the end the moral–political crisis over Algeria led to the fall of the Fourth Republic.

In the Soviet case, at least in hindsight, we can see that Moscow's will to use force had been eroding, even before Mikhail Gorbachev took over in 1985. However, in 1988–89, Soviet physical power remained intact; but not the will to use this power. At the very moment when the Soviet Union finally became the equal of the United States in some important respects, the entire system imploded. A high degree of external legitimacy could not compensate for the slow erosion in domestic legitimacy related to faltering economic growth,

---

[18] The Wavell quote is from P. J. Cain and A. G. Hopkins, *British Imperialism: Crisis and Deconstruction 1914–1990* (London: Longman, 1993), 195. An interesting appraisal of Churchill is Robert Blake and William Roger Louis (eds.), *Churchill: A Major New Assessment of his Life in Peace and War* (Oxford: Oxford University Press, 1993). See particularly the chapters by Ronald Hyam, "Churchill and the Empire," 167–85, and by Sarvepalli Gopal, "Churchill and India," 457–71. For India in general, see for instance Percival Spear, *A History of India* (Penguin Books, 1965). Useful, as always, is also Porter, *The Lion's Share*, particularly 254, 289.

increasingly serious nationality, health, and environmental problems, and rife corruption.

Gorbachev knew the system had to be reformed, but had only the vaguest notion of what the reforms ought to lead to; he gave up the old basis of communist legitimacy, however weak, without understanding the need to establish a new one. If he were able to do away with the vast layers of bureaucracy in the Soviet Union, he assumed that the bonds between him as the leader and the people could produce remarkable results. He was convinced that if communism had solved one thing, it was the problem of nationalism.[19] On this point he was massively wrong. With glasnost, what emerged was not the creative powers of the people but the strength of nationalism—in the Caucasus, in the Baltic states, and even in Russia. However, Gorbachev was clear on one point: force would not be used on a major scale. With popular support for communist rule dwindling, both in Eastern Europe and the Soviet Union, this meant the end of Soviet rule.[20]

The growing legitimacy problems of imperial rule made the imperial power take on a substantial and, generally, an increasing share of the total expenses involved in maintaining the empire. The subsidies which imperial capitals often came to supply to the provinces represented an attempt to stop the erosion of imperial legitimacy. But, in turn, the growing costs undermined domestic support for the continuation of imperial rule. A vicious circle was created.

In the British case, the best studies available indicate that while the absolute expenses involved in running the empire were small, the British level of taxation in the late nineteenth-/early twentieth-century years was higher than in its industrial competitors. On the other hand, taxes in the dependent Empire were 20 to 40 percent lower than in other "underdeveloped" areas. In India, where the British pressed the hardest for self-financing, taxes were actually lower than in the Princely States. For the state, the trend was clear: the colonies cost more and more. The profits that British individuals and companies, as opposed to the British state, made were also generally higher before 1885 than after.[21]

[19] Mikhail Gorbachev, *Perestroika: New Thinking for Our Country and the World* (New York: Harper and Row, 1987).

[20] Gorbachev, *Perestroika*; Adam B. Ulam, *The Communists: The Story of Power and Lost Illusions 1948–1991* (New York: Scribner, 1992). John Miller, *Mikhail Gorbachev and the End of Soviet Power* (New York: St. Martin, 1993); Jeffrey Gedmin, *The Hidden Hand: Gorbachev and the Collapse of East Germany* (Washington, DC: AEI Press, 1992).

[21] Lance E. Davis and Robert A. Huttenback, *Mammon and the Pursuit of Empire: The Political Economy of British Imperialism, 1860–1912* (Cambridge: Cambridge University Press, 1986), 315–16. Patrick K. O'Brien, "The Costs and Benefits of British Imperialism 1846–1914," *Past & Present*, 120 (August 1988), 163–200 and *Past & Present*, 125 (November 1989), 192–9; D. K. Fieldhouse, *The Colonial Empires: A Comparative Survey from the Eighteenth Century* (London: Macmillan, 1982), 380–94.

In the Austro–Hungarian case, after the *Ausgleich* of 1867 the distribution of common expenses between Austria and Hungary was renegotiated every ten years. Here the Austrians were actually able to reduce their share somewhat, but after 1907 they still paid 63.6 and the Hungarians 36.4 percent of common expenses. (In 1900 the population relationship was 55.7 percent for Austria, and 41 percent for Hungary.) But in this case Vienna paid a heavy price for small economic concessions in the form of increasing Hungarian political autonomy.[22]

Even in the Soviet case, where the element of consent on the part of the governed was smaller than in the other empires we are dealing with, similar developments can be seen. In 1956 the Polish communists protested, for the first time, against deliveries of coal to the Soviet Union far below world market prices. In the 1970s the relationship was reversed. Now the Soviet Union was subsidizing oil and gas deliveries to Eastern Europe, and in return the Eastern Europeans often paid with rather shoddy industrial goods which could not be exported to Western markets. As one study of energy supplies within the Soviet bloc concludes, "The Soviet insistence, in 1968, on maintaining limits on East European autonomy also entailed accepting the responsibility for the cost of making compliance possible."[23] Within the Warsaw Pact the highest defense expenditures had to be borne by the Soviet side, despite the Soviet economy clearly being weaker than that of several of its Eastern European allies.[24]

Related mechanisms can also be detected within the loosest of all imperial structures—the American one. After 1945 the United States was clearly the world's economic leader. This status undoubtedly involved economic benefits, but it also involved great expenses—varying from the more than 100 billion dollars provided in credits and grants from 1945 to 1965, to the many economic concessions made within the General Agreement on Tariffs and Trade (GATT) in general, and vis-à-vis the Japanese in particular.[25]

In NATO the United States paid much more for defense than did its allies. And *American* troops, not the troops of the "vassals," were deployed to suffer the heaviest initial casualties in case of war, a rather special arrangement in

---

[22] Williamson, *Austria–Hungary and the Origins of the First World War*, 11–15; Kann, *A History of the Habsburg Empire 1526–1918*, 605; Sked, *The Decline and Fall of the Habsburg Empire*, 233.

[23] William M. Reisinger, *Energy and the Soviet Bloc: Alliance Politics after Stalin* (Ithaca: Cornell University Press, 1992), 112.

[24] Daniel N. Nelson and Joseph Lepgold, "Alliances and Burden-Sharing: A NATO–Warsaw Pact Comparison," *Defense Analysis*, 2:3 (1986), 205–24, particularly 220.

[25] Charles P. Kindleberger, "Hierarchy versus Inertial Cooperation," *International Organization*, 40:4 (Autumn 1986), particularly 841; Lundestad, *The American "Empire" and Other Studies of U.S. Foreign Policy in a Comparative Perspective* (Oxford–Oslo: Oxford University Press, 1990), 37–9, 63–5. See also Alfred E. Eckes, "Trading American Interests," *Foreign Affairs* (1992), 135–54.

historical terms.[26] In an effort to reduce its expenditures and bring back the troops, the United States promoted European integration. Such a structure, in which the imperial center did not even participate, was again a historical novelty. Thus, Vienna worked hard to centralize decision-making within the Habsburg Empire, London was always at the center of any Commonwealth arrangement, and Moscow came out against federative plans for Eastern Europe.[27]

Even the British and Americans set up their international orders with their own advantage in mind. But we know the outcome. Under these very orders, Britain came to be surpassed economically by several other powers, while the United States in the 1960s and 1970s entered a period of relative economic decline, vis-à-vis both Western Europe and Japan.

IMPERIAL LEGITIMACY IN THE "DISTANT PROVINCES"

The legitimacy of imperial rule was not only decided in the home country. The attitudes of the "distant provinces" were even more important, in part because they had such a decisive impact on attitudes in the home country. Independence was something the "distant provinces" seized, at least initially, until decolonization developed into a flood.

After the early period of establishing control, colonial rule generally functioned well and met little opposition. For instance, in the 1920s and 1930s the British Empire was generally quieter than it had ever been before. There was definitely a basis of white supremacist thinking behind colonial rule. As long as the "provinces" accepted the white colonialists' right to rule, few problems existed. But once black and yellow people rejected white supremacy, imperial rule rested rather directly on force. After the Second World War the days when "every white skin automatically extracted a salute" were gone. Many different factors led to such rejection: western Enlightenment values, often imbibed by the local elites in their education, first in the metropole, and later in the colonies themselves; the experiences of colonial troops in the two world wars; the rise of Marxism–Leninism and the Soviet Union; and, probably most

[26] Ernest May, "The American Commitment to Germany, 1949–1955," in Lawrence S. Kaplan (ed.), *American Historians and the Atlantic Alliance* (Kent: Kent State University Press, 1991), 76.

[27] For an interesting article on the Soviet case, see Leonid Gibianski, "The 1948 Soviet–Yugoslav Conflict and the Formation of the 'Socialist Camp' Model," in Odd Arne Westad, Sven Holtsmark, and Iver B. Neumann (eds.), *The Soviet Union in Eastern Europe, 1945–89* (Houndmills: St. Martin's, 1994), 26–46.

importantly, Japan's victories in the early phase of the Second World War. The yellow man's victories swept away the idea of white supremacy.[28]

In the interwar period, in addition to the Middle East and Ireland, there was one exception to the imperial calm: India. The Indian Congress Party changed: in the initial years (after its founding in 1885) it had been a debate forum for a narrow upper class; after 1919 it became a well-organized mass movement bent on full independence. Gandhi's leadership further transformed the policies of the Congress as well as its support in the villages. To a large extent, Gandhi was able to set the political agenda which eventually led to independence. In 1945–46, India's towns and villages had slipped beyond British control, the armed forces were on the verge of mutiny, and Wavell reported that India had become ungovernable.

Once the gates had been opened in India it proved difficult to close them elsewhere. This was certainly not realized by contemporary politicians, whose time frame for independence in Africa was much longer, if in fact a possibility at all. The demonstrations and riots in Accra on the Gold Coast (from February 28 to March 4, 1948) led to twenty-nine dead and 237 injured. Earlier, these events would hardly have qualified as a major crisis, but now they led directly to Ghana's independence nine years later.[29] As A. D. Low has argued, "It is not fanciful to assert that many of the critical battles for British colonial Africa were fought, not on the banks of the Volta, the Niger, or the Zambesi, but on the Ganges."[30] The imperial rationale had been undermined, a pattern had been set, and decolonization accelerated with incredible speed.

It is difficult to escape the conclusion that empires contain within them the seeds of their destruction. It is simply impossible to run a vast empire entirely from the imperial center, and once lower units are formed, sooner or later they will almost inevitably compete with the imperial center.[31] This proved the case with the colonies, where the units were, to a large extent, artificial creations. It was even more difficult to hold historical states with well-developed identities in place. From this perspective the surprise is not that the Austro–Hungarian Empire collapsed, but that it functioned so well for as long as it did. In part this

---

[28] For a stimulating treatment of the racial aspect, see R. J. Vincent, "Racial Equality," in Bull and Watson, *The Expansion of International Society*, 239–54. See also Cain and Hopkins, *British Imperialism*, 195–6.

[29] For the Accra riots, see Colin Cross, *The Fall of the British Empire, 1918–1968* (London: Paladin, 1970), 278–9. See also John D. Hargreaves, "Toward the Transfer of Power in British West Africa," in Prosser Gifford and William Roger Louis, *The Transfer of Power in Africa: Decolonization 1940–1960* (New Haven: Yale University Press, 1982), 135–6.

[30] D. A. Low, "The Asian Mirror to Tropical Africa's Independence" in Gifford and Louis, *The Transfer of Power in Africa*, 3.

[31] Alexander J. Motyl, "From Imperial Decay to Imperial Collapse: The Fall of the Soviet Empire in Comparative Perspective," in Richard L. Rudolph and David F. Good (eds.), *Nationalism and Empire: The Habsburg Monarchy and the Soviet Union* (New York: St. Martin, 1992), 15–43.

was the result of playing off the "historical" nationalities—Germans, Magyars, and Poles, against the "non-historical" Slovenes, Croats, Romanians, Ukrainians, etc.—with the Czechs having features of both.[32]

The fall of the Soviet Empire resulted in great part from the implosion of the imperial center. But the basis for Soviet rule was never solid in that most East Europeans were not only hostile to Moscow; they also considered themselves culturally superior to the Russians. This was not a good foundation for an empire (unless the superior subjects held a privileged position, as the Greeks did in the Roman Empire, and the British liked to think they did in the modern American one).

After the *Gleichschaltung* of the Stalin years, the history of Eastern Europe after 1953 is the history of the evolution of national forms of communism where the limits of what Moscow was obliged to permit were constantly stretched. The interventions of 1953, 1956, and 1968 only temporarily interrupted this process. Even without the imperial implosion, it seems likely that, sooner rather than later, the development of these national forms would have broken not only the Soviet mould, as Yugoslavia, Albania, and Romania had already done, but even the communist one, as Poland and Hungary were getting close to doing in the 1980s.[33]

One is tempted to draw a similar, although admittedly quite speculative, conclusion about the long-term outcome of a victory in Europe for Hitler's Germany. But it is unlikely that German supremacy over such a vast and culturally strong area would have lasted, based as it was on *Lebensraum* and racial hierarchy thinking, elements that strongly limited local support in most parts of Europe.

There may be elements which hold empires together for shorter or longer periods, such as geographic conditions, economic complementarity, or ideological bonds. Common defense needs perhaps represent the strongest of all such bonds, but these needs fluctuate with the outside threat. Practically all of Austria–Hungary could unite against the Turkish advance, and the Germans and Magyars could unite against the Russian–Slavic threat; but with millions of Slavs within the empire, even the Russian–Slavic threat divided Austria–Hungary.[34] Yet, in the long run, the unifying elements all seem to lose out to the desire for independence.

---

[32] John-Paul Himka, "Nationality Problems in the Habsburg Monarchy and the Soviet Union: The Perspective of History," in Rudolph and Good, *Nationalism and Empire*, 82 in particular.

[33] Timothy Garton Ash, *The Uses of Adversity: Essays on the Fate of Central Europe* (Cambridge: Granta Books, 1989) and Ash, *We the people: The Revolution of '89 Witnessed in Warsaw, Budapest, Berlin and Prague* (Cambridge: Granta Books, 1990). See also Richard Pipes, *Communism: The Vanished Specter*, Norwegian Nobel Institute Spring Lecture 1993 (Oxford: Oxford University Press, 1994) 52–67.

[34] Kann, *A History of the Habsburg Empire*, 25–7, 337–8, 607–8.

The post-1945 American "empire" was built very much on the Soviet–Communist threat. With the collapse of the Soviet Union, history seemed to suggest that a gradual but comprehensive redefinition of relations between the United States, Western Europe, and Japan would take place. To some extent it has. The fight against terror does not have the unifying force that Soviet Communism had. NATO certainly still exists, but it has become a looser organization than during the Cold War. Almost all the new crises take place outside the traditional NATO area; such crises had always presented problems for the alliance, as seen over Suez and Vietnam. Still, Atlantic cooperation continued. NATO was important for America's leadership functions. The new allies in Central and Eastern Europe were virtually all hoping for American security guarantees against a possibly resurgent Russia; even the old allies in Western Europe favored a continued role for the United States, in part because it was so difficult for them to maintain their own defense spending, much less to increase it.

STABILITY AND LEGITIMACY

What then of the relationship between legitimacy and stability? While rivalry between Great Powers often results in war, and disagreement over the borders of their respective spheres may be a more specific source of tension (for instance the many conflicts throughout history over Belgium, Poland, the Yugoslav area, Afghanistan, Vietnam, and Korea), it is often assumed that Great Powers promote peace, at least within their imperial borders. But when these powers collapse, it increases the local level of conflict.

This observation seems to hold true in many cases. Thus, Britain was generally able to maintain order within its huge empire. In Africa, not only imperial but also African historians argue that colonialism brought about a greater degree of peace and stability. The African-dominated *UNESCO General History of Africa* concludes that "not even the anti-colonial and Marxist schools would deny the fact that after the colonial occupation . . . most parts of Africa, especially from the end of the First World War onwards, enjoyed a great degree of continuous peace and security."[35] In India, British rule may well have prevented a "Balkanization" on the ruins of the Mogul Empire. The

---

[35] A. Adu Boahen, "Colonialism in Africa: its Impact and Significance," in A. Adu Boahen, *Africa under Colonial Domination 1880–1935*, UNESCO General History of Africa, Volume VII (London: Heineman, 1985), 785. For a somewhat different emphasis, see J. F. Ade Ajayi's contribution in Lundestad, *The Fall of Great Powers*, 215–34. This more negative view should, however, be compared with his own more standard chapters in Ajayi (ed.), *Africa in the Nineteenth Century until the 1880s*, UNESCO General History of Africa, Volume VI (London: Heineman, 1989), particularly 5, 788–9, 791.

British were able to control vast territories with few forces; 75,000 British troops, supported by 150,000 Indian troops, controlled a population of about 300 million.[36]

Austria–Hungary's stability was celebrated in the famous 1848 dictum of the Czech historian and politician František Palacký: "If Austria did not exist, it would be necessary to invent her," a dictum which found echo not only among contemporary statesmen, but also among later historians.[37] Finally, in Eastern Europe from 1945 to 1989, the Soviet Union was able to maintain an even more stable structure than had Austria–Hungary.

However, some qualifications are required. Pax Britannica, like other orders, did not mean that there was peace everywhere. In such a vast empire smaller wars were almost always taking place somewhere. In fact, "there was not a single year in Queen Victoria's long reign in which somewhere in the world her soldiers were not fighting for her and for her empire."[38]

More specifically two observations should be made. First, the initial period, when imperial control was established, was seldom peaceful, and frequently led to great losses of life among the local populations; the imperial troops suffered much smaller losses. In Africa the worst example was probably the Congo, where the population may have been halved in three to four decades (famine and disease undoubtedly contributed greatly to this tragic outcome).[39] The establishment of Habsburg control in Central Europe and Soviet control over Eastern Europe were so closely related to wars with outside powers—the Ottoman Empire and Nazi Germany respectively—that it is virtually impossible to separate the two aspects.

Second, as we have seen, empires collapsed in great part because of local resistance. The British yielded early and were therefore able to give up power largely peacefully. India had been the prime target of colonialism; in 1946–47 it took the stage again by gaining its freedom. (An earlier model was of course found in the independence of first the United States from Britain, and then of Latin America from Spain and Portugal.) The French experience in the bloody wars of Indochina and Algeria illustrated what could take place if an attempt was made to hang on to power in the face of great opposition. Thus, the peace and stability of Great Power rule were often limited to the long years in the middle of its rule, less present in its beginning and its end.

[36] Friedberg, *The Weary Titan*, 220–1; Fieldhouse, *The Colonial Empires*, 277–8.
[37] Bridge, *The Habsburg Monarchy Among the Great Powers*, 41.
[38] Byron Farwell, *Queen Victoria's Little Wars* (New York: Norton, 1972), 1.
[39] Boahen, "Colonialism in Africa," 785; John Lonsdale, "The European Scramble and Conquest in African History" in Roland Oliver and G. N. Sanderson (eds.), *The Cambridge History of Africa. Volume 6 from 1870 to 1905* (Cambridge: Cambridge University Press, 1985), 680–766, particularly 748.

Whether we are talking about the Pax Britannica, the Pax Sovietica, or other orders, compared with what preceded and what followed, the imperial orders generally represented stability. The stability of the long middle period of the Pax Britannica was replaced by local wars, for instance between India and Pakistan and in the Middle East. The Cold War sometimes enhanced the level of conflict, as in Korea and Vietnam, but often it served to contain violence. When the Cold War ended there was at first an increase in the number of local conflicts. Conflicts that had been kept under wraps exploded; the lid flew off in Yugoslavia and the Caucasus. Gradually, however, the number of conflicts appeared to diminish. Colonial and post-colonial conflicts became fewer; Cold War proxy wars more or less ended; democratic rule became stronger; many forms of international activism to contain or end such conflict increased.[40]

When the ethnic nation states were formed, the expectation had been that this would lead to a more peaceful world. As J. G. Herder expressed it in the 1780s: "Cabinets may deceive each other; political machines may exert pressure on each other until one is shattered. *Fatherlands* do not march against each other in this way; they live quietly side by side and help each other like families."[41]

Herder's conclusion was much too simplistic. The complicated, not to say tense, relationship between stability and legitimacy, and then legitimacy in the sense of ethnic–national independence, are seen in Asia and Africa, but are best illustrated in Central and Eastern Europe. The long period of European peace from 1815 to 1859 rested upon Austrian control over, or suppression of, Italy. Italy could only be united after the French had helped defeat the Austrians in 1859. German national aspirations could only be fulfilled after three wars, against Denmark, Austria, and France. From 1870 to 1914 the Austro–Hungarian order was remarkably stable and, one might add, rather flexible. But, at least in modem national(ist) terms, it was based on the suppression of the national rights of most groups other than the Hungarians and, to a lesser extent, the Germans.

The interwar order was more legitimate than the Austro–Hungarian one in the sense that many large ethnic groups finally acquired their own states, but it was also rather unstable. The new states quarreled over borders and population rights. With Eastern Europe's many different ethnic groups living so interspersed, no order could be fully legitimate, and the right of Germans to

[40] Lotta Themnér and Peter Wallensteen, "Armed Conflicts, 1946–2010," *Journal of Peace Research*, 48:4 (2011), 526–36.
[41] The Herder quotation is from M. S. Anderson, *The Rise of Modern Diplomacy 1450–1919* (London: Longman, 1993), 196. For a modern argument along similar lines, see Michael Walzer, "The Reform of the International System" in Øyvind Østerud (ed.), *Studies of War and Peace* (Oslo: Norwegian University Press, 1986), 227–50.

join the mother country proved only the most explosive of the many unresolved issues.[42]

The Soviet Empire represented the most clear-cut example of the tension
between stability and legitimacy. Despite the Red Army's interventions, on the
whole the Soviet order was remarkably stable, and "the long peace" in Europe
was based on Soviet domination of the Eastern half.[43] But this most stable of
orders was also the least legitimate. When the Pax Sovietica collapsed, a host of
ethnic–national questions sprang to the surface. The new post-Cold War
order was clearly more legitimate than the Soviet one, but it was definitely
also less stable.[44]

One should hasten to add that neither the Austro–Hungarian nor the Soviet
Empire was able to solve the ethnic–national questions which represented
such a problem from a legitimacy point of view. At best they simply postponed
them; at worst they aggravated them. The latter was almost certainly the effect
of the Soviet Empire. In reacting against oppressive uniformity and the
extreme degree of centralization, once the various ethnic–national forces
finally had a chance to express themselves, they tended to go to the extreme.[45]

Most of us probably find a positive message in the fact that the "distant
provinces" became independent states. However, this process now raises
serious questions. About 3,500 groups define themselves as "nations." This
means that so far only a good 5 percent of them have achieved statehood.[46]
How many states will there "eventually" be, and how will the creation of the
new states affect peace and stability?

It may well be true that democracies are more peaceful, certainly toward
each other, than other forms of government. Yet the transition from one form
to another often appears to lead to more conflict, as we have seen in the former
Yugoslavia and in the Caucasus. After the Cold War these regions became
more democratic, or certainly less undemocratic, but also less stable than they
had been under the autocratic rule of, respectively, Tito and the Kremlin.

In this overall perspective, the attempt to form new and larger units out of
smaller ones is dramatic. The history of the United States is interesting, but so
special that few conclusions can probably be drawn on the basis of the
American experience. The European Community has been able to combine

[42] My thinking on this point has been influenced by Michael Howard, "The Causes of War" in
Østerud, Studies of War and Peace, particularly 26–7.
[43] John Gaddis, The Long Peace: Inquiries into the History of the Cold War (Oxford: Oxford
University Press, 1987), 215–45.
[44] The most pessimistic analysis of the new situation was found in John Mearsheimer, "Back
to the Future: Instability in Europe after the Cold War," International Security, 15:1 (Summer
1990), 5–56.
[45] For an interesting statement on this point, see Václav Havel, "The Post-Communist
Nightmare," tr. Paul Wilson, New York Review of Books (May 27, 1993), 8–10.
[46] Eugene Robinson, "Experts Fear Rise in Bosnia-Type Ethnic Conflicts as Peoples Fight for
Identity," International Herald Tribune (August 20, 1992), 5.

geographic widening—from six, to twelve, to twenty-seven members—with a deepening of the content from a common market to a fully integrated market with a common currency for most of its members, and even (at least formally) a common security and defense policy. In view of three major wars between France and Germany in seventy-five years, this level of integration is remarkable; but outside "the four freedoms" the emphasis is still more on the national than the joint Europeanboth level. The EU's regulations are many and quite important, but the EU budget still makes up only around 1 percent of the total EU gross domestic product, compared to about 25 percent for the federal budget in the US. The nation states of the EU spend an average of 45 percent of their GDPs.[47]

[47] Amélie Barbier-Gauchard, "Thinking the EU budget and public spending in Europe: the need to use an aggressive approach," *Policy Brief Notre Europe*, 29 (2011).

7

Visions and Defeats

America's vision was of one world, inspired by American ideals. These ideals were presumably relevant for all countries and all peoples. The United States also became by far the strongest country in the world. After 1945, despite the power and the will to influence the entire globe, the United States suffered many defeats. The Soviet Union came to control Central and Eastern Europe. Communism took charge in China. Although the United States was able to fulfill almost all its most important objectives in key areas Western Europe and Japan, it also met with half-successes and even defeats in relations with its allies. "Empire" was combined with many different local forces. That had almost always been the case with empires. In the end they were all defeated. It turned out that even small states could successfully challenge the United States. The new decentralized technology made it possible even for single individuals, in the form of terrorists, to challenge the US. Why was even the mighty United States so impotent?

AMERICA'S VISIONS AND AMERICA'S FEARS

America was constantly tempted to create a world in its image. It was "the city upon the hill"; it stood for "life, liberty and the pursuit of happiness." So many of its presidents saw themselves on a mission. The mandate to change the world came not only from the American people: sometimes it came from the foreign inhabitants themselves; often it was implied, or even directly stated, that God had a hand in America's actions.

In the twentieth century Woodrow Wilson was the first clear-cut representative of this faith. In January 1918 he set out his Fourteen Points to change the world. The most important of these points was the creation of The League of Nations. In Europe after the First World War he was seen as the great savior, the spokesman for millions. Frustration followed for Wilson, the League, and millions of Europeans. During the Second World War Franklin D. Roosevelt was to present a similar vision through the Atlantic Charter and other key documents, in part inspired by Wilson, but also haunted by his failure. It turned out that FDR was much more successful than Wilson had been, although he was not yet convinced of his success when he died on April 12, 1945. Washington was to create so many of the institutions that lasted for so many decades; many of them, from the United Nations, the World Bank and the International Monetary Fund, to NATO, are of great importance even today.

Again and again, America's presidents saw themselves not only as the most powerful individual in the world, but as the designated leader of the world. They virtually all expected success, whether we are talking about John F. Kennedy's "best and the brightest," Ronald Reagan's optimism that allegedly liberated not only Eastern and Central Europe but also the Soviet Union itself, and George W. Bush's mission to set Iraq and the Middle East free. Or, in Bill Clinton's seemingly more moderate version: "We cannot, indeed we should not, do everything or be everywhere. But where our values and our interests are at stake, and where we can make a difference, we must be prepared to do so."

Hubris was never far away.[1] Yet there was also the fear of failure. And even the smallest of failures could lead to the unraveling of great structures. This was the point of the domino theories proclaimed in different versions by so many administrations. The original version came from President Eisenhower when he stated at a press conference on April 7, 1954, that "Finally, you have broader considerations that might follow what you would call the "falling domino" principle. You have a row of dominoes set up, you knock over the first one, and what will happen to the last one is the certainty that it will go over very quickly."[2]

Most Americans had probably always seen even international relations as a struggle between good and evil. But the collapse of isolationism during the Second World War showed that there was no way in which America could isolate itself from the corrupt Old World. The devil was always there, ready to do his work. Hitler was the modern version of the devil. America had failed to stop him. It therefore had a guilty conscience. The lesson learned from the Second World War was that the West had done something terribly wrong when it had not tried to stop Hitler early, when he could be stopped. This lesson was then applied to the Cold War. There were many reasons why the United States could not just grant the Soviet Union a sphere of influence in Eastern Europe. One was that establishing such a glacis would presumably only encourage Stalin to press for more in the next layer of states.

---

[1] This is the theme of Peter Beinart, *The Icarus Syndrome: A History of American Hubris* (London: HarperCollins, 2010).

[2] Stephen E. Ambrose, *Eisenhower: The President* (Simon & Schuster, 1984), 180, 197, 236–7. The quotation is from 180.

Compromise was often bad. Soviet threats were almost always seen in the most comprehensive light. The Korean War was really a diversion for the big attack that would follow in crucial Europe. The Vietnam War was a battle for the hearts and minds of Southeast Asia, and then Japan. Or it was a worldwide test of the Chinese model of wars of national liberation. The Soviet invasion of Afghanistan was aimed at the Persian Gulf and the oil resources of the Middle East. In almost every case Washington's analyses were wrong, or at least quite seriously overstated.

In almost every administration there is a constant debate between the globalizers, who see things in a global perspective, and the regional and local specialists who want to emphasize the peculiarities of each and every crisis. In most cases the globalizers win. The highest positions are generally held by those who are able to see the connections between the various crises. Area specialists rarely become presidents or secretaries of state. The public are also generally more persuaded by an analysis that simplifies matters, instead of one based on local complexities that makes generalizations difficult. However, time and again it is ultimately discovered that the local factors have not received their due attention. And if the analysis is incorrect or misleading, the chances of failure increase dramatically. This is one basic reason why power sometimes leads to impotence.

Hitler appeared to illustrate the validity of the domino theory. Developments in one country often influenced events in another, particularly if they were neighbors. It was a fact that Soviet expansion in some countries had also led to control in other countries, although in Eastern Europe this had primarily been determined by the positions of the Red Army when the Second World War ended. In 1989 the collapse of Soviet–Communist rule in one Central and Eastern European country led to the collapse of such rule in all the countries. This was logical in the sense that Soviet rule was crucial in all, with the exception of Romania.

It could often be difficult to predict the nature or even the direction of the change, if and when developments in one country influenced those in another. A country could try to balance negative development in one way or another; or it could bandwagon, and move with the change. The domino theory assumed the latter and underestimated chances of the former. Yet, what policymakers believed was crucial. Thus, in February 1965, President Johnson explained to Senator Everett Dirksen that "We know from Munich that when you give, the dictators feed on raw meat. If they take South Vietnam, they take Thailand, they take Indonesia, they take Burma, they come right back to the Philippines." In fact, policymakers of many different stripes believed in their own versions of the domino theory—that events in one area clearly influenced developments elsewhere. Thus, in April 1965, Zhou Enlai told the Pakistani president that if the United States thwarted the Vietnamese communists, anti-American forces in the rest of the world "will suffer heavy losses." Leading politicians in many smaller countries expressed similar views. The war in Vietnam would have consequences not only in Southeast Asia, but also in parts of the world far from the region.[3]

In Vietnam it was true that what happened in that country would influence its neighbors. The Vietnamese communists had made no secret of their Indochinese perspective. They also wanted to determine developments in Cambodia and Laos. In the end, however, Thailand and Indonesia followed their own paths. It may well be that the fighting of the Americans and the South Vietnamese gave these countries extra time to organize their societies so as to counteract Vietnam's enhanced position. Of course Indonesians and Thais had their own interests and agendas; they were not simply dominoes ready to fall. The situation in 1975, when South Vietnam fell, was very different from what it had been ten years earlier. And it was never clear in the first place whether the Vietnamese communists had any plans to take control in these countries. One thing soon became obvious, however, if it had not been clear all along: the Vietnamese were achieving their own goals, not those of the Soviet Union or China.

Domino effects could also be seen outside the East–West framework. In late 2010 to early 2011, demonstrations against authoritarian rule in Tunisia stimulated similar demonstrations in many other Arab countries. The governments in Tunisia and Egypt collapsed. In Libya, civil war raged until Gaddafi finally fell. Most other regimes were forced to make serious concessions to the demonstrators. Here the common factor was the long-time domination of an authoritarian ruler combined with high population growth and highly unsatisfactory economic and social conditions. Yet the outcomes varied depending on local circumstances in the countries concerned. Most of the regimes did after all survive, at least in the short run.

AMERICA'S DEFEATS AND AMERICA'S SUCCESSES

With its vast objectives, it was to be expected that even the most powerful country in the world, the United States, like all previous Great Powers, would face defeats. After all, although clearly the leading country, the US was far from omnipotent. During the Second World War Washington thus dreamed of One World; but there would soon be two—East and West. In the East the United States exercised very little influence indeed.

In the first five years after 1945 the US met with two major defeats, in Eastern Europe and in China. Eastern Europe was the Soviet Union's priority

[3] Mark Moyar, *Triumph Forsaken: The Vietnam War, 1954–1965* (Cambridge: Cambridge University Press, 2006), 375–91.

area; it was already controlled by the Red Army as a result of the war against Germany. Only a new major war could possibly end Soviet control there. After four years of fighting together against Nazi Germany, a new war was entirely out of the question. China was the world's most populous country. The United States largely chose to stay out of the civil war there: the country was simply too large for any outside power to control; America's resources, however vast, were limited; the Soviet Union basically stayed out; Chiang Kai-shek was far from the ideal ally. Still, "the fall" of Eastern Europe and of China brought serious Republican charges against the Roosevelt and Truman administrations. How could America, so strong and so pure, be defeated? Was not America omnipotent? The Republicans found their explanation in domestic treason. Presumably no outside power could defeat the US.

Later there were to be other setbacks. The Korean War ended in a draw, which could in some ways be seen as an American achievement considering Korea's distance from the US and the opposition it faced there. The Vietnam War ended in defeat, although only after the United States had pulled out most of its troops. Some of America's most useful allies fell from power without the United States being able to protect them. New enemies emerged, whether these be Fidel Castro in Havana, or Muslim clerics in Teheran. But America also fought successful wars far from home. Saddam Hussein was thrown out of Kuwait and out of power in Iraq, and Slobodan Milošović out of Kosovo and even Belgrade, although in the latter case the direct US role was quite limited. Later events in Iraq and Afghanistan showed that it was one thing to win the initial war, quite something else to run a distant country after that early phase of the war was over, although the signs in Iraq are now slightly optimistic.

It is little surprise then that many American presidents at the end of their terms expressed a sense of frustration. The powers of the president might be considerable, but in the end they were much more limited than the presidents themselves or their advisers had imagined beforehand. When National Security Adviser McGeorge Bundy was later asked what most surprised him about the Vietnam War, he replied it was "the endurance of the enemy." Washington's assumption was that the enemy almost always had a breaking point. Once you reached that, America was bound to triumph.[4]

American politicians were not the only ones to feel this. When asked what drove his policies, British Prime Minister Harold Macmillan answered, "events, my boy, events." In the Middle East, the Arab tail often wagged the Soviet dog. In 1967, Soviet Prime Minister Andrej Kosygin was furious: "Whatever I do, things will be either bad, or really bad. . . . If we publicly state the whole truth—that our Syrian allies did not consult us—then firstly, no one will believe us, and secondly, they'll ask: 'Who's supposed to be the lead

[4] Gordon M. Goldstein, *Lessons In Disaster: McGeorge Bundy and the Path to War in Vietnam* (New York: Times Books, 2008), 225–6.

partner in this alliance—the Soviet Union or Syria?'" In 1967 the Soviet Union did not want a war in the Middle East, but it certainly did not want to lose its influence in Syria or elsewhere. This limited Moscow's ability to influence events and stop the drift toward war.[5]

Even an offensive step, such as the Soviet invasion of Afghanistan in December 1979, can be seen in a similar light. It was far from an effort to realize an age-old Russian dream to gain direct access to the Persian Gulf. Instead, as Odd Arne Westad has argued, the aging Soviet leadership had initially been opposed to such an invasion, but in the end it "saw no other way to respond than through a military intervention" if it were to maintain the investment it had already made in the country. And then Moscow actually intervened against a regime that the Soviet leaders had spent so much effort and money to protect.[6] In North Korea only the Chinese had any leverage. But even they did not have much of it. Beijing's fear of the regime in Pyongyang simply imploding, weakening China's position and leading to thousands and thousands of refugees, severely limited what could be achieved. This was the communist version of the "tyranny of the weak."

Compared to that other superpower, the Soviet Union, the United States was actually doing remarkably well. In the long run it was impossible for Moscow to claim military equality with Washington when the Soviet economy was so much smaller than the American one. And in the end, the Soviet Union collapsed.

Yet there was a discrepancy between America's vast strength and the more limited influence it frequently came to exert even over its allies and friends, not to mention its enemies.

THE UNITED STATES AND WESTERN EUROPE: IF SO STRONG, WHY SO MANY CONCESSIONS?[7]

America was the undisputed leader of the "free world." It exerted great power over the military, political, and economic structure within which all America's allies had to operate. As we have already seen, Washington's basic objectives

---

[5] Guy Laron, "The Cold War and the Middle East. Playing with Fire: The Soviet–Syrian–Israeli Triangle, 1965–1967," *Cold War History*, 10:2 (May 2010), 163–84.

[6] Odd Arne Westad, *The Global Cold War* (Cambridge: Cambridge University Press, 2007), 316–30. The quotation is from 325.

[7] With some revisions, this section largely follows my *The American "Empire" and Other Studies of U.S. Foreign Policy in a Comparative Perspective* (Oxford–Oslo: Oxford University Press, 1990), 70–81.

were all largely fulfilled, although most countries went rather less far on the road to economic multilateralism than Washington desired. Much of the rest could be seen as details. The United States had tremendous influence in the occupied countries, and this influence continued in somewhat modified form even after West Germany became formally independent. Washington also frequently had a very significant impact on matters in non-occupied countries. This was particularly true when Washington had considerable local support for its position, as was almost always the case.

Despite its tremendous strength, the United States frequently compromised. There were American half-successes such as the increasing cooperation and integration of the Western European countries, the introduction of full currency convertibility in 1958, the imposition of restrictions on trade with Eastern Europe, and the increased defense expenditures in Western Europe. These were only half-successes in that Britain, and the smaller countries that still followed Britain in such matters, refused to join any supranational European grouping, be this the European Coal and Steel Community, the European Atomic Energy Community (Euratom), or the European Common Market; full currency convertibility came at least ten years later than the Americans had hoped; and as soon as the Cold War subsided somewhat, particularly after Stalin's death and the end of the Korean War, European trade restrictions and defense increases were modified more than Washington would have liked. The different countries simply followed different policies, although some deference was naturally shown to what the Americans wanted.

Then there were the outright refusals to heed America's advice. With exceptions such as Suez in 1956, and the German treatment of the Franco–German treaty in 1963, the United States rarely dictated even to its allies in Western Europe what they were to do. The rejection of the European Defense Community (EDC) by the French National Assembly in 1954 was the most striking example. Washington's threats of an "agonizing reappraisal" of its role in Europe if the plan was defeated did not help. France did reject the EDC, although Paris could not stop the rearmament of West Germany, which now took place through NATO and the Western European Union (WEU). More American defeats were to follow after the coming to power of General de Gaulle in 1958. De Gaulle refused to let Britain into the EEC, tried to make West Germany follow France's security lead, and ultimately took France out of NATO's military organization. Britain never played the kind of constructive role in European integration many administrations in Washington hoped for. The Europeans consistently did less for NATO's defense than Washington desired. Once President Eisenhower even blurted out in frustration: "I get weary of the European habit of taking our money, resenting any slight hint as to what *they* should do, and then assuming, in addition, full right to criticize us as bitterly as they may desire. In fact, it sometimes appears that their indulgence in this kind of criticism varies in direct ratio to the amount of help we give them."[8]

The troop issue was quite problematic. Eisenhower insisted that the American troops were in Europe only as a temporary measure. The Europeans ought to handle the long-term problem by themselves. As early as at the end of his first year, the president was nevertheless forced to conclude that "Unhappily, however, the European nations have been slow in building up their military forces and have now come to expect our forces to remain in Europe indefinitely."[9] Many later American presidents came to a similar conclusion. In the nuclear field, first the British, and then the French, built their own forces, generally to Washington's dislike, particularly under Kennedy.

America's defeats were not as dramatic as they sounded. The EDC lost out, but West Germany was brought into NATO; the Europeans did increase the number of troops, and their failure to do even more had the somewhat redeeming effect of further strengthening America's domination of NATO; the British did not join Europe, but worked closely with Washington and integrated their deterrent with America's; de Gaulle's first years in power were actually seen by Washington as relatively positive. When America felt its overall position was threatened, it could act swiftly and directly. Suez in 1956 and the Franco–German treaty in 1963 were to provide the clearest evidence of Washington's ability to put even the largest allies in their place.

However, there *was* a discrepancy between America's vast strength and the more limited influence it frequently exerted over its allies and friends. Many reasons can be found for this. One set of reasons had to do with the ways in which Washington more or less directly weakened its own leverage.

First, sometimes the United States consciously promoted arrangements that reduced its role because it recognized its own strength as excessive. As William Borden has argued, "the sheer economic supremacy of the United States . . . caused a tremendous imbalance in the world economy that threatened both the prosperity of the United States and its foreign policy objectives."[10] Western Europe (and Japan) had to be rebuilt and integrated; within limits, discrimination against US goods was even encouraged. Yet, there was nothing automatic here. In the interwar period the United States had shown that it was quite possible to pursue policies far less enlightened than it did after the Second World War.

Second, American leverage was limited by its official ideology; any country had the right to choose its own government and policies. (This applied

    [8] Ambrose, *Eisenhower: The President*, 143–4.
    [9] Ambrose, *Eisenhower: The President*, 143–5. The quotation is from Zbigniew Brzezinski, *Game Plan: How to Conduct the U.S.–Soviet Contest* (New York: Atlantic Monthly Press, 1986), 176.
    [10] William S. Borden, *The Pacific Alliance: United States Foreign Economic Policy and Japanese Trade Recovery, 1947–1955* (Madison: University of Wisconsin Press, 1984), 5.

especially in Western Europe vis-à-vis the democratic governments there.)
Cold War revisionists are fond of quoting William Clayton, the negotiator of
the 1945 loan to Britain, when in response to criticism that he had not done
enough to stop socialism, he stated that "We loaded the British loan negotiations with all the conditions that the traffic would bear." He went on to say,
however, and this part is less frequently quoted: "I don't know of anything that
we could or should do to prevent England or other countries from socializing
certain of their industries if that is the policy they wish to follow. The attempt
to force such countries to adopt policies with respect to their domestic
economies contrary to their wishes would, in my opinion, be an unwarranted
interference in their domestic affairs."[11] Similarly, in France, Washington
certainly came to regret de Gaulle's anti-NATO and anti-US policies, but
there was very little it could do as long as the French people had expressed
their preference for the general as clearly as they had.

On some occasions Washington actually circumscribed its own influence
quite directly. Thus, the European Recovery Program, which undoubtedly
represented the single strongest American lever, was to be worked out primarily by the Europeans themselves. Although the American role clearly
exceeded the "friendly advice" foreseen, much was indeed left to the Europeans. For instance, to a large extent they decided themselves how the
American aid was to be divided up among the participating countries. In a
rather paradoxical twist, Belgian leader Paul-Henri Spaak in 1954 blamed the
United States for the lack of unification in Western Europe. The alleged reason
was Washington's "over-generous policy": the Americans "had missed a
golden opportunity when at the outset of the Marshall Plan they did not
make all Marshall aid contingent upon the creation of a unified political
community in Europe."[12]

Third, occasionally the American political system was an obstacle to strong
and concerted action. America *was* strong, but in many ways it was weakly
organized. The system's many checks and balances frequently made decision-
making a rather cumbersome process. The divided nature of the American
political system, in addition to its openness, also gave foreigners rather
unique access to it, and a chance to influence the outcome. Within the
executive branch there would almost always be some who defended the
position others wanted to modify. For instance, the Treasury Department on
the whole favored a relatively pure multilateral world open to American
business, while the State Department showed much greater sympathy for
political considerations, including the views of foreigners. The State

[11] Geir Lundestad, *America, Scandinavia, and the Cold War 1945–1949* (New York: Columbia
University Press, 1980), 114.
[12] *Foreign Relations of the United States* (hereafter *FRUS*), *1952–54, VI*: 1, Ambassador Dillon
to the Department of State, April 26, 1954, 385.

Department tended to receive the support of both Presidents Truman and Eisenhower. "Localitis," in the form of strong sympathy for a foreign country, was widespread within the geographical offices of the State Department and most local US embassies.

Then there was another related set of reasons that served to weaken the bargaining power of the US and strengthen that of the allies. These reasons were not, as the first set, primarily products of America's political system or own decisions. Instead, they either flowed from more indirect circumstances, or had to do with the nature of America's partners.

First, since the Europeans realized perfectly well that Washington had essential reasons of its own for pursuing the policies it did, American threats to back out of Europe tended to lack credibility. This is another way of saying that before the United States was really committed to Europe, it had great leverage. Once the commitment had been made, the leverage lessened. Whatever leverage remained after the formation of NATO and the build-up of American strength in 1950–51 was significantly reduced with Eisenhower's election in 1952, and the gradual disappearance of the unilateralist–isolationist alternative.

This point was well illustrated in the French EDC debate. Dulles's threat of an "agonizing reappraisal" of the American role in Europe was quite simply not credible. Even before the negative vote in the French National Assembly, the key American ambassadors in Europe reported that "the agonizing reappraisal had not in general been taken seriously."[13] The Americans would not withdraw. At the time, the alternative of bringing West Germany directly into NATO was well known in advance, and was seen by quite a few on both sides of the Atlantic as at least as satisfactory as the EDC solution itself. However, this was rarely explicitly stated because so much prestige had been committed to the EDC, and because it was feared that to suggest alternatives would only prolong the French process further.

More generally, whenever Washington reflected on the possibility of threatening to "bring the boys home," four main reasons strongly discouraged this course. First, such threats could, even if they were not actually carried out, strengthen the Soviet Union in its competition with the West. This was definitely not the image of allied relations that Washington wanted to project. If carried out, Moscow would achieve one of its main objectives and the risk of war might presumably even increase. Second, the threats would also stimulate Adenauer and West Germany's "neurotic fears regarding US disengagement from Europe." At worst they might even encourage West Germany to develop its own nuclear weapons to compensate for the American withdrawals. Third, after de Gaulle had come to power, the threats to withdraw would play directly

---

[13] *FRUS, 1952–54, VI:* 1, Memorandum by Assistant Secretary Merchant to the Secretary of State, June 11, 1954, 691.

into the general's hands in that they seemed to confirm his warnings about the unreliability of the United States. Finally, as just mentioned, threats lacked credibility because the US had its own reasons for staying in Europe.[14]

With the US in, Washington was bound to dominate NATO. Political economists have made us realize that public or collective goods theory applies to alliances as well as to national and local matters. One aspect of the domination was that since the hegemon—the United States—would provide most of the goods in question—for instance security—largely on its own, there was less of an incentive for the allies to come up with substantial contributions of their own, particularly if these were as small in real size and as controversial domestically as they often were. The great temptation for the allies was then to take America's role for granted, and to pursue policies that demanded less of themselves.

Second, some countries were so strong and so insistent on certain points that if the United States were to get its way, this would at best be only after a bitter struggle. Britain was America's closest ally, but on some questions also its main challenge. It was financially weak, but it still carried considerable political weight. When, in 1947, the British were forced to make sterling convertible, leading to the collapse of Britain's foreign exchange position, Washington could not very well drive Britain into bankruptcy. Britain also simply refused to join continental schemes that would dilute its sovereignty. Here too Washington eventually adjusted. Finally, the Attlee government had established a comprehensive system of social welfare and economic regulations. Many US policymakers thought this system went too far. They could do little to change it, however, and once it was "permitted" in Britain, it had to be accepted in the smaller Western European countries as well. In this respect the protection offered by the British was a prominent element in the policies of, especially, the Scandinavians.

There is also the phenomenon already referred to earlier as "the tyranny of the weak." Attempts to apply pressure on the Europeans might, as one official put it, be a "successful operation, but the patient would be dead." This was the primary reason why, for instance, the many ways of using Marshall Plan counterpart funds to pressure various centrist governments in France so often failed. The alternatives—the communists on the left and the Gaullists on the right—were simply unpalatable to Washington. In the EDC debate both Eisenhower and Churchill thus referred to what they called "the tyrannical weakness of the French Chamber."

Even occupied West Germany had considerable leverage in its dealings with the United States. Adenauer was dependent on the United States, but the United States also became dependent on Adenauer and the Christian

---

[14] National Archives, Record Group 59, The Papers of Charles E. Bohlen, Box 26, Memorandum for the President: Answers to Eight Questions, June 17, 1962.

Democratic Union (CDU). If the "Allied" Chancellor did not do well, Kurt Schumacher and the Social Democratic Party (SPD) would probably take over. Initially Washington had preferred a CDU–SPD coalition government, but with the SPD coming out so strongly against NATO, support for Adenauer's party was stepped up. In a longer perspective, holding Germany down could lead to resurgence of nationalism, possibly even to a new Hitler, or, more likely, bring about its increased cooperation with the Soviet Union—another Rapallo, like the original one from 1922. Thus, one State Department memorandum concluded that Adenauer was "bargaining with us from what is essentially a position of strength."[15]

---

[15] *FRUS, 1951, III*, Hillenbrand to the Director of the Office of German Political Affairs, October 1, 1951, 1,539.

Conclusion

POWERS MOVING UP AND POWERS MOVING DOWN

The world is a complex place. Obviously no single power can dictate solutions for all of the world's almost 200 countries. Some of them are just too strong and too proud to be told what to do. Others are, in a sense, too weak to be dictated to. If Washington simply dictated a solution, a government could fall; then more extreme parties would gain influence. Washington's choices were always limited. Realities on the ground consistently limited Washington's leverage. This was the meaning of President Kennedy's famous statement in May 1961 in the context of the Dominican Republic. There were three choices in descending order of preference: "a decent democratic regime, a continuation of the Trujillo regime, or a Castro regime. We ought to aim at the first, but we really can't renounce the second until we are sure that we can avoid the third."[1]

Global norms and standards may be spreading, whether they be political, economic, or cultural. In this sense globalization is making more and more of us more and more alike—in what we desire materially, in the technology we use, the food we eat, the music we listen to, and the way we dress. At the same time, however, ever new groups of people insist on their own nation states, various forms of religious fundamentalism are proliferating, and individuals insist on developing their own norms, sometimes totally at odds with their own wider communities. As we have seen, globalization and fragmentation work in conjunction; they are even, to some extent, dependent on each other.

The international political and economic systems certainly produced structures and policies that had an impact on virtually all the countries of the world. The leading powers of the world definitely influenced the policy choices of others, particularly the smaller states. Yet there was no shortage of evidence that the world was constantly changing and that states and individuals could respond to these changes in many different ways.

---

[1] Arthur M. Schlesinger, Jr., *A Thousand Days: John F. Kennedy in the White House* (Boston: Houghton Mifflin, 1965), 769.

Although the United States remained the leading power throughout the years analyzed in this book, the balance between its strengths and weaknesses changed. Other powers moved up and down in the hierarchy. In 1945, when the United Nations was established, the United States, the Soviet Union, and Great Britain were the obvious leading powers. They were the three "superpowers" when the term was first used toward the very end of the Second World War. China was included on the Security Council because the United States insisted, and France primarily because Britain pressed for its inclusion.

The Great Powers of today are different. Britain and France have much weaker claims to such status than they did in 1945. Germany is now the leading economic power in Europe. The European Union has become increasingly important, but is far from unified in its security and defense policy, or even in its economic and financial policy. The Soviet Union has been replaced by Russia. China has solidified its claim to Great Power status. The obvious omissions on the Security Council are Japan (now with the world's third largest economy), India (with its rising economy and status), and possible regional Great Powers, such as Brazil and South Africa.

Japan, China, South Korea, and several other countries in East Asia provide dramatic evidence of how quickly states can move up economically. The Soviet Union provides the grand example of how quickly powers can collapse; Zimbabwe and even Argentina show how a state can rapidly slide down the economic ladder. In 1960, South Korea and Ghana were at the same economic level; so were Indonesia and Nigeria. In 2010, on a per capita basis, South Korea was at least at the level of Spain, Greece, and Portugal, and almost 20 times richer than Ghana; Indonesia was two times richer than Nigeria.[2]

Most countries behaved fairly predictably in relation to the rest of the world, but those that absolutely insisted on going their own separate way certainly had the opportunity to do so. The weakest of the colonial powers, Portugal, kept its colonies longer than virtually anyone else; Cuba, although the neighbor of the world's most powerful country, could challenge the United States decade after decade; North Korea, bordering on China and Russia, pursued its own fiercely nationalistic course, more or less immune to advice from any outsider; South Africa long defied the world's basic norms, until in 1989–90 it decided to change its course; Burma and Zimbabwe moved their own very separate ways; and Rwanda and Cambodia killed off large parts of their populations without the world doing anything of significance to stop the parties involved. In Somalia, nothing seemed to work; neither outside efforts nor domestic reconciliation. War continued year after year, despite the country's 7–8 million inhabitants speaking the same language (Somali) and practicing the same religion (Sunni Islam). No basic cultural or ethnic

---

[2] See Tables 4 and 5 in the present volume.

differences existed. Society seemed to be ruled by clans, sub-clans, and sub-sub-clans. This was indeed "the narcissism of minor difference" that Sigmund Freud had discussed.

If we look at Washington's lists of rogue states we find they have been remarkably similar for more than three decades. The list reached its climax in George W. Bush's condemnation of the Axis of Evil in January 2002, and the ensuing invasion of Iraq in March 2003. But Iraq, Iran, and North Korea had been broadly condemned for many years. So also had Libya, Syria, Burma, Zimbabwe, and Cuba. The sad outcome of the invasion of Iraq discouraged a repeat of any similar action in these other countries.

Negotiation ended Libya's nuclear program and its support of terrorism; in 2011 the regime itself collapsed, in part due to foreign intervention, although primarily by Britain and France. Nevertheless, if the dictators of the world refused to listen, there was normally little the outside world could do to change the outcome. Sanctions rarely overthrew governments. At any one time the United States applied an almost endless list of different kinds of sanctions against a great number of governments. Only when such sanctions worked in concert with strong local factors of opposition, such as in South Africa, might they change the situation dramatically.

Indeed, big powers do not always secure big outcomes; they often get only small outcomes. Due to the divisions of the international community, rogue states almost always had alternative powers they could work with. South Africa was more important to Zimbabwe than the US and the EU; in Burma's case, China, India, and countries of the Association of Southeast Asian Nations (ASEAN) were more significant than the West; and for North Korea, China was clearly the crucial power.

Even intelligence organizations, such as the CIA, were unable to produce the striking results of the past, partly because some of their previous actions were no longer acceptable at home, and partly because the local scene was even more complicated than before. And actions—such as in Iran in 1953, Guatemala in 1954, and Chile in 1973—had only succeeded because they had crucial backing from important groups in the country itself, although probably not from the majority of the people in any of the three countries. Darioush Bayandor has suggested that the fall of Mosaddeq in August 1953 flowed largely from domestic factors, and that the role of the CIA and MI6 is vastly overstated.[3] In Guatemala the army played a crucial role. Allende in Chile never had the support of the majority of the people.

Successes of the past, real or mythical, had a tendency to become the failures of the future, as the knowledge about the transgressions of the past strengthened the groups that were critical of the United States. This has certainly been

---

[3] Darioush Bayandor, *Iran and the CIA: The Fall of Mosaddeq Revisited* (Basingstoke and New York: Palgrave Macmillan, 2010).

the effect in all three countries mentioned. The same happened in the Soviet case. In the long run, Moscow's interventions in Eastern Europe in 1953, 1956, and 1968 undermined the Soviet role and ultimately helped prepare the ground for the momentous changes in 1989.

Many different elements tended to weaken the impact of even the world's superpowers, particularly when they were in decline. In the Third World the number of independent countries had dramatically increased; they now held a majority in most international forums. Flagrant interference in their affairs was becoming less acceptable and more difficult. Democratic rule might be spreading in the world, but so was nationalism. It strengthened resistance to most forms of foreign rule, and often made it difficult even for superpowers to acquire, and certainly to manipulate, clients. Local regimes were generally better organized and could mobilize larger parts of the population than before, some on the basis of political, others religious, doctrines.

Technology was being diffused, particularly modern weapons. Whereas in 1950 only five Third World countries (Argentina, Brazil, Colombia, India, and China) could build anything more than small arms, by 1980 that number had increased to twenty-six, and the range of products had grown to include much heavier weapons in 2011, even in some cases nuclear ones (India, Pakistan, North Korea, potentially even Iran). What they did not produce themselves, they could purchase, if necessarily, covertly. Not only countries, but even small groups could now, through modern weapons technology, cause terrible losses, even to a superpower. Asymmetrical warfare was taking its toll almost everywhere a superpower intervened. Terrorist actions could lead to quick exits, as shown by the Reagan administration's withdrawal from Lebanon in 1983, and the Clinton administration's departure from Somalia ten years later. The days of small Western colonial groups with machine guns defeating thousands of "natives" were definitely gone. Now it was the other way around; a few terrorists could defeat thousands of Western troops.

In the light of the Jasmine Revolutions in the Arab world in 2011 there has been much focus on the effects of the Internet and social media. These were allegedly a major explanation for the collapse of regimes that had been in power for decades. People could connect independently of the government in ways that were impossible until the new media developed. The opposition could swiftly assemble and work out positions as developments quickly unfolded.

There would seem to be much to this argument. Compared to the days of radio and television that could relatively easily be controlled by the government, control was much more difficult with social media. As has been said, the traditional one-to-many geometry of communication was replaced by the many-to-many model. This left much more scope for independent action.

A few argued, however, that social media represented a means of transmission that could be used by many different forces. Governments have always tried to push back and shape developments in their own mold, as was the case with radio and television. This has happened with social media too. For instance, the government in Egypt shut the Internet down for five days. The Syrian government cut power entirely in parts of the country. The Chinese government pushed Google out, shut off the entire Internet in Xinjiang for a period in 2009, and worked hard every day to prevent the spread of materials that undermined its cause. In many respects it was successful, although there would frequently be ways around the barriers thrown up. The authorities would use the new media for their own purposes; they would often get the necessary passwords from members of the opposition and could thus hack, infiltrate, and create chaos. These actions undoubtedly had their effects. If really desperate, governments could of course still put demonstrators in prison, or even shoot them.

Many revolutions failed, even with the help of the Internet and social media. In the Arab world, some governments collapsed; others survived. The efforts to overthrow the government in Iran after the falsified presidential elections in 2009 failed; even in Europe the authoritarian regime in Belarus survived. Many factors always have to be taken into account in explaining such changes. Yet the conclusion is probably that the new media strengthened bottom-up political activity at the expense of centralized government.[4]

And, most significant for the relationship between small powers and big powers, the locals were frequently much more committed to their cause than was the outside power. Kissinger stated that "I can't believe a fourth-rate country like North Vietnam doesn't have a breaking point." But, as Ho Chi Minh told a French diplomat in 1945, "You will kill ten of our men, but we will kill one of yours, and it is you who will finish by wearing yourself out." General Vo Nguyen Giap made the same point after the Vietnam War was over: "Despite its military power, America misgauged the limits of its power. In war there are two factors—human beings and weapons. Ultimately, though, human beings are the decisive factor. Human beings! Human beings!"[5] Admittedly Vietnam was an extreme case, but the basic point applied to other areas as well. Most American presidents after the Second World War had in fact withdrawn from one or more exposed areas—Truman from China, Johnson and Nixon from Vietnam, Reagan from Lebanon, George H. W. Bush

---

[4] The various positions are spelled out in Joseph Nye, *The Future of Power* (New York: Public Affairs, 2011), 113–51; Tim Wu, *The Master Switch: The Rise and Fall of Information Empires* (New York: Knopf, 2011); Evgeny Morozov, *The Net Delusion: The Dark Side of Internet Freedom* (New York: Public Affairs, 2011).

[5] Thomas A. Schwartz, "Henry Kissinger: Realism, Domestic Politics, and the Struggle Against Exceptionalism in American Foreign Policy," *Diplomacy & Statecraft*, 22:1 (2011), 121–41, (the quotation is from 129); Stanley Karnow, *Vietnam: A History* (New York: Penguin, 1997), 20–1.

and Bill Clinton from Somalia, Obama from Iraq. When their presidencies were threatened, they withdrew, whatever promises they had made earlier.

Countries are indeed moving up and down. So are companies. The list of the world's leading companies fifty years ago looks remarkably different from an equivalent list today. Companies from many different countries, certainly including China (Sinopec, State Grid, China National Petroleum) are now on the list; so are American companies that did not even exist only a few decades ago (Microsoft, Google, Facebook).[6] Even single individuals can do large-scale damage, as many a lone terrorist shows. Individuals can also face up to the world's greatest powers, as when dissidents in Eastern and Central Europe played such an important role in ending Soviet domination. Now the same battle is being waged in China. Could individuals such as the Nobel Peace Prize laureate for 2010, Liu Xiaobo, possibly influence the future of the rapidly growing China?

FINAL WORDS

Superpowers are still super, in the sense that they can accomplish things that nobody else can. If they are really super, they create their own spheres of influence, even their own empires. In many ways the United States played an imperial role in the world after the Second World War. It was able to set up a liberal political and economic order based on the UN, the World Bank, the International Monetary Fund, the General Agreement on Tariffs and Trade and the World Trade Organization, NATO, and a host of other regional organizations. Washington was able to incorporate its Second World War enemies, West Germany and Japan, firmly into this new order and, decades later, so many of the allies of the former Soviet Union. The US even kept its biggest allies in their place when this was needed, as Suez in 1956 made so explicit vis-à-vis Britain and France; and it kept communists and communist sympathizers out of the governments of virtually all the alliance countries. American investment and culture spread to the most distant corners of the world. When needed, the United States reserved the right both to intervene more or less unilaterally almost anywhere around the globe to maintain this order, and to make its own exceptions to the general principles of democracy and free trade it normally promoted. So strong and self-confident was the United States in fact that it tried to promote regional centers which, at least in the long run, could limit America's own power—successfully so in Europe, less so in East Asia. In historical terms these were impressive achievements. And

---

[6] Global 500, 2010, CNN Money, *Fortune* (February 10, 2011).

much of this order is still with us today. The question now is whether the order will be extended to include even China.

America's general position, certainly including its vast military might, often made the US preferable as the ultimate military guarantor in case everything should go wrong, whether this be in Europe against an unpredictable Russia, or in Asia against a surging China. Washington's political weight showed in most negotiations. Only the United States was involved in the solution of all the most difficult issues, whether these be North Korea, Israel/Palestine, Iran, Afghanistan, Pakistan, or even the Balkans, the Caucasus, Sudan, or Congo.

In today's world the United States is the only truly global power; others, such as China and the EU, are still primarily regional powers, although with certain global aspirations. With the limits of America's military and economic power so clearly demonstrated in recent years, it is, however, questionable to refer to an American "empire." The US has suffered major military defeats; its debt is piling up; not only China but other powers are clearly rising; and the process of globalization is, in several ways, making the world playing field more level. In the economic sphere the focus is broadening, from the traditional Western powers and Japan, to include China, India, Indonesia, Brazil, South Africa, and others. The G-7 and G-8 (with Russia) are being replaced by the G-20. Negotiations about world trade and climate change are now being determined more and more by the United States, China, and even India. It is symptomatic of the lack of unified leadership that many of these negotiations no longer produce as significant results as in the past.

The questions are many. Why did the Soviet Union collapse? Why did the countries of East Asia enjoy more rapid growth than most other countries? And, when we reach the individual level where the various decisions are made that together constitute "development," what makes one person change, whereas another sticks to a traditional pattern?

With regard to Great Power politics, development and poverty, as in most North–South and East–West issues, comprehensive explanations must always be supplemented with a knowledge of local conditions. Such conditions tend to modify nearly any generalization. Local diversity is difficult to grasp, and virtually impossible to cover in any book surveying the world situation after 1945; it is easily downplayed, or even entirely forgotten, in the stream of top-level international events. Yet, despite the growing significance of political, economic, and cultural globalization, many different local factors still remain crucial.

Index

Bull, Hedley and Watson,
    Adam 163n.15,168n.28
Bundy, McGeorge 179
Burbank, Jane and Cooper, Frederick 96
Burma, *see* Myanmar
Burns, John F. 55n.22
Bush, George W. 23–6, 29, 34, 37, 64, 93, 98,
    145, 189, 191
  Bush administration 23, 25, 29, 32, 49,
    97–8, 126
Byrnes, James 16, 103, 107
Byzantine Empire 1

Cabot Lodge, Henry 106
Cain, P. J. and Hopkins, A. G. 164n.18,
    168n.28
Calleo, David 4
Cambodia 178, 188
Canada 50, 105–7, 111–12, 116, 125, 153
  GDP 26, 43, 58–9
Canary Islands, the 106
  see also Spain
capitalism:
  communism and 22
  from feudalism to 163
  Japan and 44
  in the USA 143
Caribbean, the 97, 102
Carolingian Empire 1
Carrere d'Encausse, Hélène 132, 133n.2,
    134n.9
Carter, Jimmy 3
Caryl, Christian 81n.79
Casablanca 111
Castañeda, Jorge G. 39n.1, 51n.16
Castle, Stephen 56n.25
Castro, Fidel 179, 187
Caucasus region 42, 44, 88, 165, 172–3, 193
Ceaușescu, Nicolae 147
Central Treaty Organization (CENTO) 124
Chamberlain, Joseph 159
Chang, Gordon 75
Chechnya 44
Chen Jian 56n.26
Cheney, Dick 97
Chernyaev, Anatoly 140
Chile 63, 103, 189
China:
  Africa and 63
  anti-democratic vein 64
  Asia and 63, 78, 91, 128, 193
  Beijing 61, 63–4, 66, 68–9, 73, 77–81,
    100, 180
  Beijing Olympics 61
  Brunei and 65
  Burma and 65

China National Petroleum 192
Civil war 121
the Cold War and 131
Communist Party 61, 63, 67, 73–4
Communist Revolution 67, 175
Cultural Revolution 70
culture ('soft power') 63–4, 100
currency power 75
defence 49, 61
East China Sea 65
economy 70
education and 71
environmental issues in 68n.49, 71
the European Union and 55–6
fertility rate in 35
Five-Year Plan 56
GDP 5, 57–8, 74, 89
GNP 62, 63, 76
Google and 67
Great Leap Forward 70
as a 'great power' 67, 79, 83, 85
Han Chinese 61, 69–70, 153
homosexuality in 67
Hukou system 73
immigration policy in 35
India and 42, 65
inequality in 36, 73
Japan and 65, 46
life expectancy in 42, 59
Malaysia and 65
Manchu dynasty 61
media, the, in 63
Ming dynasty 61
Mongolia and 65
navy, Chinese 42, 61
neo-Confucianism 64, 70
Nepal and 65
nuclear power 61
one-child policy 35, 69
one-party rule 41
Pakistan and 62, 65
People's Liberation Army (PLA) 88
Philippines, the, and 65, 104
population of 58–60
Qing dynasty 61
as a quasi-superpower 79
retirement age 60
Russia and 65
South China Sea 65–6, 81, 88
Three Gorges Dam Project 71
Tiananmen Square 21
United Nations and 61
US relations with 60
women, position of 64
World War I and 79n.74
see also Asia; BASIC